THE U.S. AIRLINE INDUSTRY

End of an Era

Paul Biederman

PRAEGER

PRAEGER SPECIAL STUDIES • PRAEGER SCIENTIFIC

Library of Congress Cataloging in Publication Data

Biederman, Paul.
  The US airline industry.

  (Praeger studies in select basic industries)
  Bibliography: p.
  Includes index.
  1. Aeronautics, Commercial—United States.
I. Title. II. Series.
HE9803.A35B5 387.7′065′73   81-17845
ISBN 0-03-060324-2   AACR2

HE
9803
.A35
B5

Published in 1982 by Praeger Publishers
CBS Educational and Professional Publishing
a Division of CBS Inc.
521 Fifth Avenue, New York, New York 10175 U.S.A.

23456789   145   987654321

Printed in the United States of America

for Nota

PREFACE

While the theory of markets can predict various modes of economic conduct and performance, it is left to empirical analysis to verify such prophecies in the real world. Microeconomic theory may postulate precise behavioral patterns for monopolistic or competitive firms, for instance, but the realities may not always conform to the forecasts. The industry study technique provides for an in-depth examination of the mode and efficiency of operation and the degree to which the ideal, as laid down by theory, is accommodated. In the field of industrial organization, the generally accepted format for the investigation of a single industry stems from the pioneering work of Bain who stressed the importance of structure in the determination of behavior and performance. Typically, industry studies are broken down into those three components.

For an industry directly contributing only 0.7 percent of the gross national product,[1] domestic air transport seems to have attracted a disproportionate amount of attention. The industry does transcend its small size in that it is the principal carrier of domestic intercity passengers and a major transporter of goods. As a high-technology industry, the airlines also have been subject to controversial government regulation and, in general, have been a favorite of the media.

Although written 20 years ago, the standard industry monograph of the domestic airline industry has been Richard Caves' Air Transport and Its Regulators. Considering that the study was completed on practically an infant industry only at the start of the jet age, it is noteworthy that a considerable portion of the author's insights and predictions have stood the test of time. During the deregulation debates of 1975-78, for instance, critics of the status quo basically argued along lines espoused by Caves in offering suggestions to improve industry performance and economic welfare. Caves' study also bears testimony to a methodology emphasizing the importance of structure which, for the airlines, has only recently started to undergo significant change.

Perhaps in acknowledgement of Caves' achievement, the multitude of subsequent volumes on the airlines have been inclined to focus on important but narrower subjects such as strategy, pricing, regulations, etc. This book, however, attempts the ambitious mission of updating Caves' study chronologically and corroborating his observations and predictions from a current perspective. The approach and framework will be essentially the same as those of the earlier work, but a new set of hypotheses on observed and future behavior will be offered. The point of departure that differentiates most industry studies from one on the airlines is the notice that must be paid to the regulatory aspect. Although the Civil Aeronautics Board (CAB) may expire as early as 1982 if sunset* provisions currently under debate become law, the overwhelming regulatory presence during the years has surely altered the industry structure and deflected conduct and performance away from a path that an unregulated climate would have produced.

Following a brief historical sketch, the domestic industry structure is explored in the context of its degree of concentration, patterns of air transport demand, cost aspects, natural barriers to entry, and input markets. The next section deals with the impact of over 40 years of government intervention in the areas of pricing, product competition, and entry and exit. Actual market conduct is then detailed, followed by a review of airline performance on welfare issues and in comparison to other sectors of the economy. Finally, future prospects are assessed.

NOTE

1. Calculated from U.S. Department of Commerce, Bureau of Economic Analysis, Survey of Current Business, July 1979.

---

*Refers to the elimination of the Agency as a regulatory body.

INTRODUCTION

BACKGROUND

The domestic air transportation industry had its origins in the delivery of mail. Airmail service was launched by the Post Office Department on a limited basis in 1918 and was operated by the Army Air Corps using training airplanes. With the passage in 1925 of the Kelly Act, which authorized airmail contracts to private companies, private carriers were allowed to carry mail. An important feature of the act restricted the government contract to 80 percent of the revenue derived from the sale of the postage to the carrier. This was designed to guarantee that the Post Office could not lose money. However, to enforce the provision, each letter had to be individually tallied to compute the payment, which proved cumbersome. A 1928 amendment reduced airmail postage to 5¢ per ounce and established fixed rates depending on weight and distance carried; the cheaper postage rate greatly increased business.[1]

In 1930 another comprehensive piece of airline legislation was passed to deal with passengers as well as mail transportation. Until then mail dominated the industry to such an extent that airplanes were referred to as mailplanes. The 1930 Act made the postmaster general the czar of the industry with power to grant contracts without competitive bidding. The new law also enabled payment for mail to be computed on the basis of space instead of poundage, which encouraged the purchase of larger aircraft and, in turn, helped promote passenger travel.[2] The postmaster general, Walter Brown, who opposed industry fragmentation, awarded contracts to mostly large airlines so that by 1932, 90 percent of the mail business was carried by three companies, which were the predecessors of United Airlines, Trans World Airlines, and American Airlines.[3] Many carriers were forced out of business amidst charges of scandal and, with the election of Roosevelt, contract awards were suspended and an investigation ordered. A Senate subcommittee determined that Brown had illegally colluded with the larger carriers in a series of secret meetings held in May and June of 1930. Brown was later exonerated in 1941 by a U.S. Court that held that he was innocent of the collusion charges, but delinquent in good judgment.[4]

Nevertheless, the new postmaster general, James Farley, ordered the Army to start carrying mail again. However, tragedy stalked the effort. Before the service even got underway, 3 pilots were killed flying to their assignments. Then, in the first week of operation, 5 more were killed and 6 seriously injured in crashes involving eight aircraft. In a span of three months, 66 accidents occurred and 12 pilots lost their lives before the program was halted. This led to a restoration of the private contract awards.[5]

In June 1934 Congress passed still another Airmail Act opening up competitive bidding from which the carriers involved in the 1930-32 problems were to be excluded. In response the rejected companies simply reorganized, changed their names and rejoined the bidding. Three government agencies were given jurisdiction over the airlines—Post Office, Interstate Commerce Commission (ICC), and Department of Commerce—while another commission was set up to hammer out future policy proposals. The 1934 Act allowed the Post Office to award mail contracts to the lowest bidder and later the ICC granted a "fair-return" subsidy to the carrier if the performance was satisfactory within a certain time frame. This resulted in the airlines submitting fantastically low bids, expecting to absorb a short-term loss in return for the ICC subsidy, which would guarantee future profits. On the Houston-San Antonio route, for instance, Braniff submitted a bid of .00002¢ per pound mile, while Eastern tendered a flat zero for the same contract. This prompted a new investigation.[6]

Throughout the post-1934 period, passenger traffic enjoyed strong growth, and by 1936 airline income from passengers surpassed that from airmail.[7] The industry was also one with great ease of entry since anyone with a plane could operate almost anywhere that person chose. It was in this environment that the larger carriers started to seek protection. They formed the Air Transport Association of America (ATA) to lobby Congress with this aim. In testimony before hearings on proposed legislation, the head of ATA provided the gist of the complaint by saying, "It is literally possible to institute a common-carrier service by renting a second-hand plane, many of which are available, and calling up an airport to make arrangements for landing and departure. It is not necessary to accumulate the millions requisite to the construction of a vessel or a line of railroad. A line which has precariously developed traffic between two cities is always faced with the real possibility that another operator may institute service on comparatively short notice."[8] The latter was referred to as "cut-throat" competition and the ATA asked Congress to guarantee route security to the existing carrier. This refrain was echoed 40 years later when the established airlines attempted to forestall deregulation.

Since the New Deal never held competition in high esteem, the ATA arguments generally struck a responsive chord. In the middle of 1938, Congress passed the McCarren-Lea Act, which superseded all previous legislation having to do with civil aviation. Better known as the Civil Aeronautics Act, it was signed into law by President Roosevelt on June 23, 1938, culminating a period (1918-37) that had 15 congressional investigations and, in its later stages, had almost continuous debate over the kind of regulation needed for the industry. [9]

Prior to 1978, the basic enabling legislation underwent relatively few changes, so that the original provisions and purposes remained essentially intact for 40 years. The model for the legislation was the Interstate Commerce Act of 1887 and the Motor Carrier Act of 1935. The Civil Aeronautics Act and subsequent legislation in 1940 set up a Civil Aeronautics Board consisting of five members appointed by the president, one of whom was designated chairman, to govern the industry. Not more than three Board members could come from one political party, and each served a six-year term. Title I of the Act set forth the general policy:

> In the exercise and performance of its power and duties under this Act, the Board shall consider the following, among other things, as being in the public interest, and in accordance with the public convenience and necessity:
>
> (a) The encouragement and development of an air-transportation system properly adapted to the present and future needs of the foreign and domestic commerce of the United States, of the Postal Service, and the national defense;
>
> (b) The regulation of air transportation in such manner as to recognize and preserve the inherent advantages of, assure the highest degree of safety in, and foster sound economic conditions in, such transportation, and to improve the relations between, and coordinate transportation by, air carriers;
>
> (c) The promotion of adequate, economical, and efficient service by air carriers at reasonable charges, without unjust discriminations, undue preferences or advantages, or unfair or destructive competitive practices;
>
> (d) Competition to the extent necessary to assure the sound development of an air-transportation system properly adapted to the needs of the foreign and domestic commerce of the United States, of the Postal Service, and of the national defense;

(e) The promotion of safety in air commerce;

(f) The promotion, encouragement, and development of Civil Aeronautics.[10]

The articles were replete with contradictions. The fostering of "sound economic conditions," for instance, could involve price discrimination or national defense considerations that might detract from domestic service requirements. However, it was the task of the Board to reconcile such conflicts and pursue policies based on this general framework.

The detailed regulatory provisions of the Act were contained in Titles IV and X. The provision most desired by the airlines appeared in Section 401, which forbade any airline from operating without a certificate of "public convenience and necessity" issued by the Board. All carriers operating continuously on routes from May 14 to August 28, 1938 were entitled to keep those segments for themselves.[11] This statute became known as the "Grandfather clause" since the 18 carriers operating steady routes in that three-month period "begot" the family of Trunk* carriers. In order to obtain route authority, petitioners had to prove that the market was big enough and that added competition would not financially endanger the incumbent carrier or the petitioner.

Other important clauses were contained in Sections 403 and 404, which gave the Board price-setting responsibility and forced airline compliance.[12] These provisions had the effect of establishing uniformity among the carriers. Section 407 forced the airlines to provide detailed data and information on request to the Board, and Section 408 gave the Board power to approve or disapprove mergers as well as route and equipment exchanges.[13] In short the Civil Aeronautics Act enabled the Board to set fares, decide what routes airlines should fly and which airlines should fly them, and pass on all merger proposals. In addition CAB took it upon itself, sometimes with and sometimes without legal backing, to grant immunity from antitrust laws, determine subsidy levels, write consumer regulations covering overbooking, flight delays, lost baggage, etc., and also negotiate overseas route awards with foreign governments.

The Civil Aeronautics Act was superseded in 1958 by the Federal Aviation Act, which established the Federal Aviation Agency (FAA) to replace the CAB in the regulation of air safety but essential-

---

*Refers to a group of airlines which primarily operate routes connecting the larger communities within the 50 states.

ly left intact the original pricing and route articles and the responsibility for administering them with the CAB. The ambiguous Declaration of Policy from Title I of the Civil Aeronautics Act was reiterated verbatim in the 1958 Act. This legislation thus represented a continuation of federal intent and guided the CAB policy until the Airline Deregulation Act of 1978 considerably altered the ground rules.

The essential discontinuity in the 1978 Act was the planned cessation of economic regulation and a termination date (1985) for the CAB.[14] However, given the equivocal guidelines of the earlier legislation, the Board was able to turn 180 degrees from a stance that staunchly protected the industry during the early 1970s to one favoring competitive forces before the 1978 Act formalized the latter approach. Under the chairmanship of Alfred Kahn during 1977 and 1978, the CAB certified charter and intrastate carriers for scheduled interstate service and awarded routes to virtually all applicants. In the area of price, resistance to rate increases stiffened somewhat while discounting was encouraged.[15] Earlier in the decade, the CAB refused even to hear new route requests and set up a liberal cost pass-through formula to facilitate fare increases.

Aside from regulatory matters, air transport was among the more spectacular growth industries of the postwar period. While the real gross national product grew by 3.6 percent a year between 1949 and 1980,[16] constant dollar domestic airline passenger revenues increased by 9.0 percent per annum.[17] In terms of volume, domestic air passenger miles rose by 11.4 percent annually from 1949 to 1980.[18] During the same period, intercity rail and bus passengers were declining by 1.8 percent a year.[19] Air transport volume exceeded the rail and bus total in 1964[20] and by 1981, 65 percent of the U.S. adult population had flown at least once.[21]

Technological progress was particularly rapid in air transport as new aircraft development gained favor under the competitive environment that evolved. Since price rivalry was rendered quiescent by both the concentrated industry structure and advance filing requirements, product competition emerged as the lone instrument by which management could alter its market share. Amenity innovations such as more elaborate meals or better movies, while possible important in the short run, could be matched relatively quickly. However, given the long lead time required for the delivery of aircraft, an airline operating a faster, quieter plane carried the potential for an enormous competitive advantage. The fact that industry management was more dominated by technical or pilot types during the earlier period also promoted a higher degree of aircraft turnover. Between 1936 and 1959, a total of 37 new aircraft was introduced compared to only 8 during the 1970-80 period.[22] Caves observed that technological progress was perhaps inefficiently rapid,[23] meaning that some new aircraft development may have been unnecessary from a financial standpoint.

Unpressurized, two-engine propeller aircraft dominated the skies in the immediate postwar period, eventually giving way to larger pressurized equipment; Boeing and Douglas jet aircraft were introduced in 1958. Capable of 600-mile-per-hour speed, the typical jet halved the time required to make most domestic trips. The other aspect of jet aircraft, an outgrowth of the higher utilization capability, was productivity improvement, which permitted fares to decline without a diminution in profitability. Attractive fare levels, in turn, popularized air travel for vacations, and business traffic became less dominant. During the 1960s, for instance, domestic revenue passenger miles (passengers times miles flown) increased by an average 13 percent a year[24] and the business/pleasure ratio moved from about 60/40 to 50/50.[25] Concurrent with the advent of the jet aircraft were technological advances in reservations systems and ground service, which facilitated the handling of the rapidly growing volume of traffic.

The delivery of a new generation of aircraft known as "jumbo" jet with approximately 350 seats ushered in the 1970s. This wide-bodied equipment was favorably received by the public because of its comfort but did not offer the productivity improvements of the initial jet phase, which was partially due to the need it created for new ground equipment. Moreover, as a consequence of two recessions during a five-year period, the 1970s were initially marked by frequent periods of excess capacity made worse by stupendous price increases in fuel, which triggered high inflation rates in the economy at large. Without significant offsetting productivity gains, airline profits came under pressure and requests for rate hikes became increasingly frequent. However, this, in turn, reinforced arguments of critics of the industry who believed that protective regulation had made the industry inefficient and kept fare levels too high. Whatever the true merits of the situation, the end result was the passage of the Airline Deregulation Act of 1978, which encouraged new entry and other competitive forces from which the industry had largely been insulated for 40 years.

NOTES

1. Robert Kane and Allan Vose, Air Transportation (Dubuque, Iowa): Kendall/Hunt, 1971), p. 25.
2. Ibid., p. 27.
3. Horace Gray, "Air Transportation," in The Structure of American Industry, ed. Walter Adams (New York: Macmillan, 1954), p. 467.

4. Kane and Vose, Air Transportation, p. 29.

5. Ibid.

6. Peter Passell and Leonard Ross, "The CAB Pilots the Planes," New York Times Magazine, August 12, 1973, p. 34.

7. Kane and Vose, Air Transportation, p. 31.

8. Passell and Ross, "CAB Pilots," p. 34.

9. Richard E. Caves, Air Transport and Its Regulators (Cambridge, Mass.: Harvard University Press, 1962), p. 123.

10. Civil Aeronautics Act, Section 102, 72 Stat. 740, 49 USCA 1303.

11. Civil Aeronautics Act, Section 401 (a)-(e), 72 Stat. 754, 49 USCA 1371.

12. Civil Aeronautics Act, Section 403 (a)-(c), 758, 49 USCA 1973; Section 404 (a)-(b), 72 Stat. 760, 49 USCA 1374.

13. Civil Aeronautics Act, Section 407, 72 Stat. 766, 49 USCA 1377; Section 408, 72 Stat. 768, 49 USCA 1379.

14. Rush Loving, Jr., "How the Airlines Will Cope with Deregulation," Fortune, November 20, 1978, p. 38.

15. Ibid.

16. Computed from U.S. Executive Branch, Economic Report of the President 1981, p. 184.

17. Computed from U.S. Civil Aeronautics Board, Handbook of Airline Statistics 1973; and Airline Financial Statistics, December 1980. Personal consumption expenditure deflator from Economic Report of the President 1981, p. 186.

18. Computed from Handbook of Airline Statistics 1973; and U.S. Civil Aeronautics Board, Airline Traffic Statistics, December 1980.

19. Calculated from Handbook of Airline Statistics 1973, p. 539; and Air Transport Association, Air Transport 1980, p. 25.

20. Handbook of Airline Statistics 1973, p. 605.

21. Gallup Organization, The Frequency of Flying Among the General Public 1981, p. 7.

22. Handbook of Airline Statistics 1973, pp. 546-54; and Air Transport Association, Air Transport 1981, pp. 8-9.

23. Caves, Air Transport, p. 359.

24. Handbook of Airline Statistics 1973, p. 546.

25. Trans World Airlines, Continuous On-Board Surveys, various issues.

CONTENTS

Put books in Briefcase for Debra

LIST OF TABLES AND FIGURE

1

CONCENTRATION OF
THE FIRMS

Economic theory holds that industries containing many firms behave more competitively with regard to price and product than those dominated by a few companies. Such a generalization is based on the way the industry is structured. In practice, the bulk of U.S. industry could be described as oligopolistic, but the degree of rivalry among firms within the sectors may vary considerably. Although price competition is rarely active, product and service rivalry in the major industries can be passive or fierce, depending on the size and number of firms involved or special characteristics prevailing in a sector.

Government regulation is a unique factor that, in many instances, has deflected managerial conduct from a path that an unregulated structure might have dictated. These regulated sectors together have accounted for roughly 13 percent of the gross national product in recent years.[1] Although the nation's airlines are scheduled for complete deregulation by no later than 1985, their market behavior has been conditioned by structure and government regulation for almost their entire history.

This chapter delineates the domestic airline industry organization by major segments based on size, then industry and market concentration levels are outlined before mention is made of the changing intensity of airline rivalry over time.

INDUSTRY ORGANIZATION

Airlines come in many forms ranging from the large, longer-range, mostly scheduled passenger carriers known as "Trunks," to small commuter lines and firms only handling cargo. Although the Airline Deregulation Act of 1978, through its eased entry provisions, in fact eliminated prior definitional distinctions,

1

statistical reporting by the Civil Aeronautics Board continued to group carriers into traditional categories until the end of 1980.

The largest group of carriers are the Trunks, whose route systems generally extended across regions. The second in importance were called the Local Service carriers, whose operations tend to be more regional in scope than the Trunks. The Intra-Alaskan and Hawaiian carriers have much in common with the Locals, since they operated in a specified region but were administratively separated from the Locals by CAB-reporting requirements.

The Supplemental, or "Charter" carriers, provided only unscheduled service before the 1978 legislation unshackled this group. The newest major segment of carriers comes under the classification of "Commuters" whose activities had always been largely unregulated because of their size, but which still were required to report their operating statistics to the CAB. These carriers provided service between sparsely populated towns and cities, as well as connections from major hubs to small outlying points.

Another type of carrier, which was outside CAB supervision, was the Intrastate airline, whose operations were concentrated between major points within state boundaries before 1978. Other operations include Helicopter and Commuter-type companies, which usually function as airport connectors in large metropolitan areas. There are also company-owned services and travel club operators, but passenger volume on both are small and data are hard to find.

Table 1.1 offers an idea of the relative sizes of the groups comprising the domestic airline industry in terms of the number of passengers carried. Other criteria, such as revenue passenger miles or operating revenue are also commonly used. Both would show the Trunks to have an even greater share of the total by virtue of their more extensive route mileage and higher revenue per passenger. On a revenue-passenger-mile basis, the Trunk share in 1980 approached 83 percent[2] while their portion of industry revenue was 80 percent compared to the current 67 percent passenger share.[3] The latter figure is about one percentage point higher than it might have been under the pre-1969 48-state domestic definition because the Trunks control the mainland-Hawaii market.

The Trunk carriers currently active are the survivors from the 19 companies originally operating following certification by the Civil Aeronautics Board in 1938. Numbering 10 at the end of 1980, they included American, Braniff, Continental, Delta, Eastern, Northwest, Pan American, Trans World, United, and Western. Of the 19 originally active carriers, only 1 disbanded operations. The others that are no longer operating independently were all consolidated into the present 10 Trunks.[4] The last merger of Trunks took

TABLE 1.1

U.S. Domestic Air Passengers by Major Carrier Group, 1960 and 1980

Carrier Group	1960[a] Firms	1960[a] Enplanements Number (thousands)	1960[a] Enplanements Percent	1980[b] Firms	1980[b] Enplanements Number (thousands)	1980[b] Enplanements Percent
Trunks	12	48,888	83.8	10	191,524	67.0
Locals	13	6,054	10.4	6	51,914	18.2
Intra-Hawaiian/Alaskan	10	1,202	2.1	7	7,893	2.8
Supplementals	30[c]	950[c]	1.6	6[e]	1,522[e]	0.5
Helicopters	3	527	0.9	n.r.	n.r.	n.r.[e]
Commuters	n.a.[d]	n.a.[d]	n.a.[d]	300[c]	14,500[c]	5.1
Intrastate	1	675[c]	1.1	4	17,712	6.2
Other	1	64	0.1	4	863	0.3
Total	70	58,360	100.0	240	285,928	100.0

a48-state basis.
b50-state basis.
cEstimated.
dNot available.
eNot reporting.

Sources: U.S. Civil Aeronautics Board, Handbook of Airline Statistics, 1961; William Jordan, Airline Regulation in America, pp. 308-16; U.S. Civil Aeronautics Board, Air Carrier Traffic Statistics, December 1980; Airline Executive, April 1981, p. 121.

place at the start of 1980 when Pam Am bought out National. Before that, ailing Northeast was absorbed by Delta in 1972, while three Locals—North Central, Southern, and Hughes Airwest—were joined in 1979 and 1980 as Republic Airlines. Numerous other merger attempts have been rejected by the CAB or the Justice Department on anticompetitive grounds, while individual carriers have resisted takeovers from time to time. Until 1978 no new carriers had been permitted entry to Trunk-like status. However, two Local airlines—U.S. Air and Republic—actually carried more domestic passengers than the five smaller Trunks in 1980 and Southwest, a former Intrastate airline, outcarried the remaining four Locals. As deregulation proceeds, distinctions between these groups is bound to become more and more blurred.

The relative position of the Locals improved markedly since 1960, rising from a 10 percent share to 18 percent, though the Trunk proportion, while still formidable, decreased by 17 percentage points. These movements were largely the result of Trunks leaving unprofitable markets to Locals, all but one of which still receive federal subsidies, as well as new CAB route awards to Locals in Trunk markets granted in an effort to financially strengthen these carriers and at the same time to reduce the cost of subsidies. The gain in the Locals' share might have been even greater had they not themselves abandoned many marginal routes to the Commuters. The process of shedding unprofitable routes and adding Trunk-like markets led one observer to assert that the Locals, especially after 1966, were no longer "feeders," which was their original purpose, but instead had become "junior" Trunks.[5]

Though the Commuter carriers have existed since the CAB exempted them in 1952 from the strict supervision it exercises over the Trunks and Locals, their number was small and data on them were unreliable until the late 1960s. Now over 300 commuter firms regularly report data, but some operate outside of the 50-state domestic definition. (After 1980 the domestic definition encompassed Puerto Rico and the Virgin Islands.) Prinair, the largest outsider before 1981, flies only in the Caribbean and, therefore, is not counted in the 1980 figures. Ransome Airlines, the biggest wholly domestic carrier, operates in Washington, Philadelphia, New York, Boston, and other New England points, and carried over 805,000 passengers in 1980. Other Commuters whose passenger volumes exceeded 300,000 in 1980 included Golden West, Air Wisconsin, Penn Commuter, Henson, Golden Gate, Aspen, and Provincetown Boston. Between 1975 and 1980, Commuter enplanements grew by 16 percent per year compared to 5 percent for the Trunks and 9 percent for the Locals.[6] In total the Commuter group accounted for about 5 percent of all domestic air passengers in 1980.

The intra-Hawaiian and intra-Alaskan carriers have also raised their share since 1960. The average annual percentage increase in traffic of this group came to about 12 percent over the 20-year period. Growth of the larger Hawaiian portion has been at a relatively stable rate of 9.5 percent a year, while that on the Alaskan routes showed only moderate growth until 1972 when the oil boom generated a tremendous increase in the level of air service. Between 1960 and 1971, passenger growth averaged 5 percent annually but surged to 38 percent per year through 1975 and has since settled back to an 8 percent annual rate.

As their modest share of total traffic might suggest, the Supplementals have usually had to struggle for existence, and only recently, with entry to scheduled service eased, has this group been given a chance to attract a wider market. Prior to deregulation, the Supplementals had confined their activities mostly to the Hawaii and Las Vegas vacation markets, while entry into the scheduled transcontinental markets, in particular, remained a long-run objective. However, the CAB and Congress were generally unresponsive, preferring instead to protect the scheduled carriers from this potential source of new competition. Over the years, the ranks of the Supplementals decreased from about 30 firms in the late 1950s to six passenger carriers by 1980.

The former Intrastate airlines, with a 6 percent share of domestic passengers, attracted wide attention during the 1975-78 period on the part of critics of federal regulation, who claimed that fares were higher and service poorer in the CAB-controlled interstate air network than in places outside of its jurisdiction. In city pairs such as Dallas-Houston and Los Angeles-San Francisco, Southwest Airlines and Pacific Southwest, respectively, reduced prices and earned profits while their CAB-certified rivals generally found these routes unprofitable at the prevailing fares. State regulation tended to be less restrictive with regard to pricing and entry. Southwest was the largest of the group, carrying 6.8 million passengers in 1980,[7] but California-based Pacific Southwest was the oldest and most consistently profitable of the Intrastate airlines. In addition to those two, Air California and Air Florida rounded out the remaining members of the Intrastate group. All of these carriers have inaugurated interstate services and some have obtained dominant shares in many regional markets.

SIZE DISTRIBUTION OF THE TRUNKS

As noted earlier, by virtue of their size and influence the Trunks long overshadowed the rest of the industry. One of the ways in which these carriers could formerly be differentiated was along

east-west and north-south directional lines, which also largely iden-
tified each carrier's competitors. In the former category were
American, Continental, Northwest, Trans World, United, and
Western, while Braniff, Delta, Eastern, and Pan American (National) basically fell into the latter grouping. After 1978 such divisions were less significant, since carriers entered markets that the
CAB had denied them in the past. The size distribution of the
Trunks for 1959 and 1980 is illustrated in Table 1.2. The year
1959 is used as a benchmark rather than 1960 because of the large
amount of strike activity in 1960, which resulted in traffic shifting
among the carriers. Six shutdowns of various lengths affected the
Trunks in 1960 compared to only one in 1959.[8] Data for 1980 are
shown as reported since strike activity was minimal in that year.
To bridge the changeover from the 48-state definition of the earlier
period to the current 50-state framework, Hawaiian traffic for
United and estimates of Pan American's Hawaiian and Alaskan totals
were included in the 1959 data.

TABLE 1.2

Domestic Trunk Carriers by Scheduled Revenue
Passenger Miles, 1959 and 1980
(RPMs in millions)

Airline	1959		1980	
	Number	Percent	Number	Percent
American	5,614	19.6	24,264	14.4
Braniff	935	3.3	7,336	4.4
Continental	672	2.3	7,305	4.3
Delta[a]	2,075	7.2	24,209	14.4
Eastern	4,432	15.5	23,586	14.0
Northwest	1,384	4.8	8,443	5.0
Pan American	1,350[b]	4.7	8,916	5.3
Trans World	4,579	16.0	18,418	10.9
United[c]	6,720	23.5	37,893	22.5
Western	896	3.1	7,853	4.7
Total	28,657	100.0	168,224	100.0

[a]Includes Northeast for 1959.
[b]Estimated.
[c]Includes Capital Airlines and Hawaiian traffic for 1959.
Sources: U.S. Civil Aeronautics Board, Handbook of Airline
Statistics, 1961 edition; U.S. Civil Aeronautics Board, Air Carrier
Traffic Statistics, December 1980.

Prior to 1972, the CAB reported operating statistics for the Trunks individually and also lumped by "Big Four" and "All Other" categories. The Big Four referred to American, Eastern, Trans World, and United, while the remaining carriers were aggregated into the All Other group. The reasoning behind the carrier group differentiation was clear in 1959, since each of the Big Four accounted for at least 15 percent of Trunk traffic and collectively totaled nearly 75 percent. The fifth largest airline, Delta (including Northeast) carried just over 7 percent of the total revenue passenger miles.[9] Writing in 1961, Caves was uneasy with the apparently overbearing position of the large carriers and fretted about the future financial viability of smaller airlines.[10] Since then, a conscious CAB policy of awarding new route authority on financial-strengthening criteria as well as some aggressive marketing and cost control by individual carriers succeeded in essentially erasing the Big Four/Others disparity. In point of fact, these efforts have apparently tipped the balance in the other direction. Industry financial analysts in recent years have listed carriers such as Delta, Northwest, and Continental as preferred companies, suggesting that presumed size advantages may have been overrated in the past.

By 1980 the original Big Four carriers accounted for 62 percent, with American, Eastern, and Trans World losing the most ground. Moreover, the Big Four designation was not even appropriate by then, since Delta (including Northeast) had already moved ahead of Eastern in 1971 and passed Trans World during 1973. Delta had merged with Northeast in 1972 and aggressively expanded the absorbed carrier's presence in the Florida markets in competition against Eastern and National. The bulk of Delta's gain overall apparently came at the expense of Eastern as both were predominately north-south carriers. It would also appear that Delta's gains were not aided by increases in north-south traffic larger than east-west volume, since a representative sampling of market growth between 1959 and 1980 showed the reverse to be the case.[11]

In addition to Delta, Continental also greatly improved its relative size during the period shown, having benefited enormously after 1969 when it was among six carriers receiving new mainland-Hawaii route authority. Mainland-Hawaii traffic raised Continental's traffic volumes by at least 20 percent. Previously, United and Pan American alone had dominated this market. Another of the six, Western, also owed a good part of its higher industry share to the Hawaiian decision.

MARKET CONCENTRATION

Relative company size, while useful in describing the broad outlines of any industry structure, in reality still tells us very little about the degree of competition among the firms. This is especially true among the Trunk airlines, some of whose members have only indirect contact with one another. In the well-structured climate prior to deregulation, a carrier such as Braniff, for instance, had little or no direct competition with Eastern, National, Northwest, United, or Western.

The basic airline product, which is an available seat between two points at a given time, is essentially homogeneous in any one city pair. However, the markets assigned to each carrier by the CAB were very specific. Airlines competed only where they held a certificate of "public convenience and necessity" granted by the CAB. Frequently, carriers elected not to develop a particular route authority out of financial considerations or equipment constraints. Prior to deregulation, if service between authorized points were deemed sufficient by the CAB, the carrier with the unused certificate was allowed to keep the authorization dormant. If not, the Board revoked the authority and awarded it to another airline. During 1976 approximately 70 percent of domestic nonstop certifications went unused, either being replaced by multiple-stop service or by not at all. [12] One of the early colorful events of the deregulation era was the giving away of dormant authorizations to the first bidder. Carrier representatives had camped outside CAB offices for days in advance in order to bid for them.

Table 1.3 indicates the degree of competition among the 100 largest city pairs in 1959, 1978, and 1980. In addition to the Trunks, some of the markets include Local Service Airlines and Intrastate carriers where such penetration has occurred. Only active competitors, which accounted for at least 10 percent of the departing passengers in a market, were included. A basic discontinuity exists between 1980 and the earlier years in that the 1980 data include many new city pairs that have entered the top hundred list strictly by virtue of the inclusion of traffic from Intrastate and other new carriers previously excluded from the CAB origin-destination survey. For instance, while Los Angeles-San Francisco and Dallas-Houston were large enough to make the 1978 list despite the exclusion of passengers carried by Pacific Southwest and Southwest from the data base, others such as Ontario-San Francisco and Dallas-Lubbock were not. In addition to the latter two markets, the 1980 roster included eight other markets of this type, five of which were monopolies. [13]

TABLE 1.3

100 Largest City Pairs in Passenger Size by Number
of Active Carriers, 1959, 1978, and 1980

Number of Carriers	Number of Markets		
	1959	1978	1980
1	23	0	8
2	49	65	47
3	21	26	31
4	5	7	12
5	1	1	2
6	1	1	0
Number per market	2.15	2.47	2.53

Sources: U.S. Civil Aeronautics Board, Origin-Destination
Survey, fourth quarter 1978 and third quarter 1980, Tables 6 and
10; U.S. Civil Aeronautics Board, Competition Among the Domestic
Carriers, 1959, Tables 1 and 2.

The change over time toward more carriers per market is the
most obvious feature of Table 1.3. Where 72 percent of the largest
domestic city pairs were either one- or two-carrier dominated in
1959, 65 percent fell into that category by 1978 and only 55 percent
were included by 1980. Moreover, while the shift exceeded that of
the much longer 1959-78 span, had it not been for the definitional
qualifications noted above, the change during the latest period
might have been even more pronounced, since five newly included
intrastate markets inflated the one-carrier total.[14] In the three
remaining single-carrier situations—New York-Washington, New
York-Boston, Boston-Fort Lauderdale—the first two dominated by
Eastern and the latter by Delta, the Eastern monopolies were terminated in 1981 upon the entry of New York Air, a new airline,
which purportedly obtained 25 percent shares in quick order.[15]
Before 1978 the major force in the broadening of competition
was the route award system under which the CAB added new carriers
to markets when conditions seemed propitious. This process is detailed in a later chapter. During the second half of the 1970s, in a
climate set in motion by the deregulation debates and formalized by
the 1978 Airline Deregulation Act, the carriers began to rationalize

their route structures wherein unprofitable markets were shed in favor of those more promising. Between November 1978 and June 1981, for example, Republic, the most active practitioner, added 114 markets and deleted 110 while United entered 91 new segments and dropped 132.[16] Nevertheless a substantial number of monopoly markets continued to exist.

In 1980 four airlines—Braniff, Delta, Eastern, and United—received 15-25 percent of their traffic this way. The remaining Trunk carriers averaged 8 percent from monopolies with Pan Am at the lower end and Northwest at the higher limit of the range. The less-developed Locals derived a much higher proportion of traffic from monopoly segments (38 percent). Texas International with 16 percent had least, while Piedmont had most with 44 percent.[17]

During 1959 large monopolies included Chicago-Minneapolis, Dallas-Houston, Dallas-Los Angeles, Chicago-Milwaukee, and Dallas-New Orleans.[18] By 1978 Chicago-Minneapolis and Dallas-Houston had become three-carrier markets, and Dallas-Los Angeles and Dallas-New Orleans two-carrier markets; Chicago-Milwaukee was still a monopoly, but not among the top hundred any longer because of surface transit competition.[19] The six-carrier market noted in 1959 was Baltimore-Washington in which over 80 percent of the passengers were not local in nature, but were connecting to flights going to other points. This market has since been virtually eliminated by surface transit. The five-carrier city pair of the earlier period was New York-Philadelphia, whose air traffic also has since been sharply reduced by surface modes. The prospective six- and five-carrier markets of 1978 were Los Angeles-San Diego and Miami-Tampa, both of which contained active intrastate operators but whose traffice was not needed to place those markets in the top 100. The four-carrier markets of 1978 included Los Angeles-San Francisco, Chicago-Los Angeles, Honolulu-Los Angeles, Los Angeles-Phoenix, Honolulu-San Francisco, Houston-New Orleans, and Portland-Seattle, while the 1959 group also counted Los-Angeles-San Francisco and Chicago-Los Angeles, but included Chicago-New York, Los Angeles-San Diego, and Philadelphia-Washington as well.

Some of the 1980 monopoly segments have already been mentioned, but additionally included Burbank-San Francisco, Los Angeles-San Jose, Los Angeles-Oakland, Orange County-Oakland, and Orange County-San Jose, all of which were dominated by Pacific Southwest or Air California. The 1980 five-carrier markets were Portland-Seattle and Denver-Salt Lake City. The former actually had seven airlines with at least five percentage point shares and New York-Los Angeles, the second largest city pair, contained six participants under the expanded criterion.[20]

As has been hypothesized, the degree of competition among the airlines, as in other industries, should be positively correlated with the number of rival firms. However, this relationship is by no means fixed in real practice. Moreover, the whole question of what constitutes real competition is a very subjective matter. What industry sources consider competition may be in sharp contrast to what some groups might think. In any case, Caves wisely observed that, for the airlines, the issue of whether competition was active or passive could be decidedly influenced by the presence in any market of at least one carrier that was either a new entrant, was small, or otherwise felt insecure.[21] If a market contained such a carrier, rivalry would probably be active until some equilibrium could be established, while the lack of an airline of that type would probably promote passivity in a city pair regardless of the number of participants. From another standpoint, rivalry may also be intensified when a strong carrier, sensing weakness in its competitors, attempts to render their position untenable through capacity overloading or other "cut-throat" means.

Within the top hundred markets, there has been a decided movement toward a greater number of firms per market between 1959 and 1978, but the impact in terms of affecting relative traffic shares appeared to have been small. As indicated by Table 1.4, the traffic share shifts associated with competitive activity mostly involving product seems to have moderated considerably during the 1959-78 period. Where swings in share greater than ten percentage points seemed commonplace between 1955 and 1958, movements of such magnitude were rare during the later three-year span. Less than 20 percent of the share changes in either direction exceeded ten percentage points during 1975-78 as against some 54 percent between 1955 and 1958. The city pairs chosen for the later period were all within the largest 100 in terms of passengers and included only those carriers that accounted for at least 10 percent of the traffic in both years. Markets in which different airlines were active at the beginning or end were excluded, a condition that sharply limits application of this type of analysis for the 1978-80 period. Moreover, the great bulk of relative market share movements in the later span stemmed from wholesale new entry as opposed to product rivalry among existing firms.

The evidence of the traffic share changes presented in Table 1.4 does not guarantee that rivalry was more intense in the earlier period. The example of competition in the three-carrier New York-South Florida market during 1975-78 seems appropriate here since the firms concerned have had a reputation for relatively active rivalry. First Delta, having acquired weak Northeast in 1972, sought to create a larger market share through aggressive scheduling, and later National, having suffered two long strikes in 1974 and 1975, sought to restore its higher prestrike market position through price ("no-frills" fares) and marketing (controversial advertising and free movies) initiatives. By 1978, however, the main change was that Delta relinquished 3 points in the New York-Miami market and 13 points in the New York-Fort Lauderdale market that it had apparently gained from National during the strikes. In the more relaxed entry/exit climate following 1978, Delta subsequently abandoned New York-Miami altogether but increased service in New York-Fort Lauderdale, where between 1978 and 1980 its traffic share rose by 3 points. Meanwhile, the total traffic accounted for by the incumbent carriers in the two markets dropped by 10 points as Air Florida and Trans World entered the marketplace.[22]

TABLE 1.4

Airline Share Changes in Major City-Pair Markets,
March 1955-March 1958 and Second Quarter
1975-First Quarter 1978

Number of Percentage Point Changes	1955–58	1975–78
+41 to +50	4	0
+31 to +40	4	0
+21 to +30	5	0
+16 to +20	6	1
+11 to +15	15	8
+6 to +10	11	12
+1 to +5	14	33
0	8	13
−1 to −5	17	27
−6 to −10	9	12
−11 to −15	15	11
−16 to −20	3	1
−21 to −30	11	0
−31 to −40	6	0
	128	120

Sources: Data for 1955–58 from Richard E. Caves, Air Transport and Its Regulators, p. 26; Data for 1975–78 calculated from U.S. Civil Aeronautics Board, Origin-Destination Survey, Table 10 for second quarter 1975 and first quarter 1978.

The five major transcontinental segments in the sample also experienced relatively little market share movement in the 1975-78 period except for the New York-San Francisco and San Francisco-Washington markets, where United gained 9 and 11 points, respectively, at the expense of Trans World. In the aftermath of the transcontinental capacity agreement period, which had lasted from October 1971 to April 1975, United had launched a program of seat expansion, emphasizing all wide-body service in certain key markets. TWA was particularly vulnerable to such an incursion since it had been forced to sell one-third of its B-747s in 1975 to stave off bankruptcy.

By and large, however, the three carriers that long dominated these markets—American, Trans World, and United—have recognized their interdependence and, when market shares have fluctuated, the causes have been mainly external to the markets themselves. System-wide factors, such as labor problems or poor performance in basic service areas, have generally been responsible for such shifts. Prior to the commotion caused by new carrier entry in 1979, only a short movie monopoly by Trans World in the early 1960s, the 1970-73 "lounge war," occasional scheduling initiatives by United, and American's 1974 night coach program marred what had become a relatively passive set of markets. The interdependence was actually formalized for a time by the capacity-limiting agreements which, exempted by CAB from the antitrust laws, enabled the participating airlines to jointly trim flights and seats offered in four markets. This eliminated what was probably the most potent competitive weapon available to the carriers. This agreement was voided by the Federal Court of Appeals in April 1975. As in the New York-South Florida case, the post-1978 environment caused share shifting in several transcontinental markets as well but to an even greater extent. In New York-Los Angeles, where the new entrants Eastern, Pan American, and Capitol competed for traffic, the incumbents' share declined by almost 20 points while in New York-San Francisco, the loss slightly exceeded 20 points between 1978 and 1980.[23]

One element that might explain the results given in Table 1.4 is the difference in the type of competitive tools emphasized during the two preregulation periods. Apart from new entry, the capacity offered on a segment appears to have had the largest effect on market share, while in-flight amenities probably have had a more peripheral impact. However, both of these devices may be matched within a reasonably short time, if a rival so chooses. In contrast, during the 1955-58 period, the capacity and "frills" weapons were also available, but technological changes in aircraft were far more important in airline rivalry. Carriers flying more advanced equip-

ment were preferred, and this type of competitive advantage tended
to last longer because of the lead time needed for the procurement
of new aircraft. Financial constraints, brought on by two recessions within a relatively short time span, have been the primary
factor in the slowdown of the aircraft reequipment process during
the 1975-78 period.

The heavy indebtedness of the airline industry introduces another element that may have a bearing on the intensity of competition, since a few financial institutions appear to hold the bulk of
this debt. For example, at the end of 1977, Prudential Insurance
was the major creditor of Braniff, United, and Western; Lazard
Freres of Delta and Eastern; and Chase Manhattan of Continental,
Allegheny, Frontier, and Ozark; while all three banks were involved
to a lesser extent with other carriers either directly or through a
special holding company called Cede. Metropolitan Life, Chemical
Bank, Bankers Trust, and Irving Trust were also among the largest
creditors. In certain cases, overt interlocking directorates resulted from these financial connections. [24]

The obvious question about these relationships is whether institutions holding the debt of active competitors have sought to
restrain management prerogatives in price and product rivalry that
might jeopardize joint profitability. Moreover, there is the issue
over whether the airlines have been free to obtain the least costly
borrowing terms given the presence of the large banking institutions
in the existing arrangements. The fundamental point here involves
freedom of action whether in the purchase of equipment or resource
deployment in the marketplace. Unearthing evidence of covert influence, if it exists, however, is a very difficult enterprise.

CONCLUSION

Summing up, it would appear that the industry structure two
years into the deregulation period was still very much the one
Caves described in 1961. The aggregate national market remained
heavily dominated by the Trunks even though their share of passengers had fallen by 17 percentage points. In the current environment, further erosion seems assured as the smaller groups formerly known as the Locals, Intrastaters, Commuters, and Supplementals not only appear to have better growth possibilities but have
been more aggressive than the Trunks. With regard to the individual markets, we have seen a reduction in the number of one- and
two-carrier segments, but market concentration remains high by
any standard. At the same time, the carrier composition in a
market will probably be the leading determinant of the degree of

competiton. It must be recognized, of course, that the greater the number of firms, the greater will be the chance for carrier imbalances and heightened rivalry. In the absence of a new entry, the rivalry itself, however intense it appears on the surface, may not be as effective in altering market shares as in earlier periods, since the competitive devices currently emphasized in the product appear easier to emulate. This may have resulted from a slowdown in the pace of new aircraft introduction; new aircraft afford carriers a relatively long technological edge on their competition as opposed to the only briefly effective supply, price, and "frills" devices.

NOTES

1. Estimated for 1976-80 from national account data based on definitions given in F. M. Scherer, Industrial Market Structure and Economic Performance (Chicago: Rand McNally, 1970), p. 519.

2. U.S. Civil Aeronautics Board, Air Carrier Traffic Statistics, December 1980, pp. 5, 7.

3. U.S. Civil Aeronautics Board, Air Carrier Financial Statistics, December 1980, pp. 2-3.

4. Richard E. Caves, Air Transport and Its Regulators (Cambridge, Mass.: Harvard University Press, 1962), p. 13.

5. George Eads, The Local Service Airline Experiment (Washington, D.C.: Brookings Institution, 1972), p. vii.

6. Airline Executive, April 1981, pp. 121-23.

7. Air Carrier Traffic Statistics, December 1980, p. 100; PSA, Inc., Annual Report 1978.

8. U.S. Civil Aeronautics Board, Handbook of Airline Statistics, 1961 edition, pp. VII-27, 28.

9. Ibid., p. V-21.

10. Caves, Air Transport, p. 118.

11. Calculated from U.S. Civil Aeronautics Board, Origin-Destination Survey, 1959 and third quarter 1980.

12. Ibid.

13. Calculated from U.S. Civil Aeronautics Board, Origin-Destination Survey, 1959 and third quarter 1980.

14. Ibid.

15. Ibid.; Business Week, June 15, 1981, p. 78.

16. Aviation Week and Space Technology, June 29, 1981, p. 33.

17. Origin-Destination Surveys, third quarter 1980, Table 10.

18. U.S. Civil Aeronautics Board, Competition Among Domestic Air Carriers, 1959, Tables 1 and 2.

19. U.S. Civil Aeronautics Board, Origin-Destination Survey, fourth quarter 1978, Table 10.

20. Ibid., third quarter 1980, Table 10.

21. Caves, Air Transport, p. 346.

22. Origin-Destination Survey, third quarter 1980, Table 10.

23. Ibid.

24. U.S. Civil Aeronautics Board, Reports to Congress, Fiscal year 1978, p. 149.

2

DEMAND QUESTIONS

Oligopolists may select alternative strategies in their pursuit of profits. For instance, they may choose to cooperate with the other firms in the industry, in which case active competition is discouraged or, alternatively, they may engage in activities designed to increase market share at the expense of their rivals. Although conflicting, both tactics may be accepted and implemented at different levels of firms' interaction. That is to say that rivalry may simultaneously be intense in some markets and quiescent in others, or active in product areas but passive with regard to pricing.

One of the more important structural elements affecting airline corporate decision making involves the composition of the demand facing the industry, the price and income elasticities of demand, cross-elasticities between competing types of service and transportation modes, and characteristics of passengers. This chapter examines these topics and their connection to airline management strategies. In addition, a new hypothesis is presented on the subject of the cyclical nature of traffic demand, and the question of industry maturity is also addressed.

ELASTICITY ISSUES

In the airline industry, the extent of price elasticity has special relevance with regard to the type of fares offered and changes contemplated in the prevailing price level. If the aggregate elasticity happens to be unitary, for instance, firms will gain nothing in revenue from increases or decreases in fare levels, since changes will be exactly offset by counter movements in traffic volumes. However, less than unitary price elasticity will bring about revenue increases if fares are raised, since traffic declines will be proportionately less than the price rise that induced the traffic reduction. Conversely, fare advances under conditions in which the elasticity coefficient exceeds -1.0 mean that total revenue will decrease, since traffic erosion will more than offset the increase in price.

The degree of income elasticity measures the changes in traffic volumes associated with the increases or decreases in personal income. The important issue here, however, is not the elasticity measure itself, but the strength or weakness of industry's demand. What the income elasticity coefficient signifies is the relative dependence of demand on economic conditions. When aggregate demand is strong, strategies aimed at unilateral market share aggrandizement are not urgent since profit pressures diminish. Stagnant or declining industry traffic volumes, on the other hand, should push firms in the direction of individual market share building in order to secure profit improvement or protection. The evidence on the question of price elasticity appears to be inconclusive despite the numerous attempts at its definition. The main problem lies in an inability to isolate and separately measure the impact of the important variables under different conditions.

The earliest studies of price elasticity in the airline industry appeared during the 1940s but concentrated on cross-elasticity issues involving air transport and rail service. These surveys were highly subjective and failed to develop either short- or long-range elasticity coefficients.[1] Two studies in 1950 and 1951 by Wolfe and Nicholson,[2] respectively, advanced the notion of price-inelastic business travel and price-elastic pleasure travel demand, again without providing quantitative evidence or estimating coefficients.

The first comprehensive review of airline pricing was carried out by Cherington whose 1958 work subjectively reviewed policies followed by the Trunk carriers. He concluded that price changes of less than 10 percent produced an inelastic response, but that fare differentials for dissimilar classes of service caused irregular traffic growth rates.[3] A 1958 study prepared by United Research, Inc. for the Federal Aviation Agency derived the earliest price elasticity coefficient. Among other things, the report estimated a demand function for Trunk traffic, using quarterly data from 1947 to 1957, and established an elastic -1.23 coefficient for its price variable.[4] A year later, the CAB produced a coefficient of -2.46 in attempting to forecast traffic for the 1959-65 period. However, its multiple regression model, incorporating fares, income, and time, was criticized because the accompanying income elasticity coefficient of 0.49 was thought to be unrealistically low.[5]

Cross-sectional quantitative analysis was first performed by Taffe in 1959. He studied traffic growth between Chicago and 91 cities between 1949 and 1955. His conclusion was that price elasticity was apparent in medium- and long-haul markets but not in short-haul markets. [6] In 1961 another FAA-sponsored study disaggregated business and pleasure traffic by trip distance and suggested that long-haul pleasure demand was particularly price elastic. [7]

The General Passenger Fare Investigation (GPFI) started by the CAB in 1960 created a forum in which the airlines could express themselves on the elasticity question. The gist of the carrier responses was that demand was price inelastic, perhaps as low as -0.2. [8] The key variables in the determination of airline traffic changes were thought to be income, the quality of service, and the value of time savings rather than price. The fact that aggregate traffic growth had proceeded in the face of fairly substantial rate increases during the 1948-56 period was the principal evidence, while favorable survey material provided additional support. During the Domestic Passenger Fare Investigation (DPFI) ten years later, the airlines maintained this stance on the elasticity question. A study by United Airlines placed the price elasticity coefficient at -0.58 for the 1965-70 period, while a Trans World analysis indicated a coefficient of -0.57 for the 1954-69 span. [9] The CAB Bureau of Economics also produced elasticity analyses during the DPFI and reached conclusions opposite to those presented by the carriers. [10] In addition to the analyses mentioned above, numerous independent studies have continued to pour forth on the same subject in the form of journal articles and doctoral dissertations. But anything approaching a consensus on the true price elasticity coefficient has remained elusive.

Among 24 studies, catalogued by Oswald, [11] that offered definitive results, 17 concluded that prices were elastic. The sources of the divergent conclusions involve the explanatory variables and data selected, and specification of the equation. Investigators who found that prices were inelastic considered that those who held them to be elastic had simply presented output in lieu of subjecting the data to interpretive analysis. With regard to the time-series studies, criticism focused on the point that certain factors were ignored, such as the effect of quality of service and the increasing length of trips. In a regression equation in which average fares, income, and time are the sole explanatory variables, the three might be improperly credited with explaining all of the traffic growth when other forces may also have been important. The improvement in quality of service in terms of speed, comfort, and more flights to a greater number of destinations was apparently a key factor in growth, and its omission would have pushed up the coefficients of the other variables. It was felt that since real average fares declined throughout most of modern airline history while traffic growth proceeded, albeit not as smoothly, the elasticity results were biased because depressants such as higher coach usage and an increasing average trip length, which were not directly related to traffic generation, also occurred throughout the period. Failure to adjust for these movements would result in a higher elasticity coefficient than was justified. Critics also pointed out that the use of heterogeneous periods had been a source of confusion in several studies. They claimed that elasticity varied from period to period; thus a single coefficient covering a long time span would be meaningless.

Regarding cross-sectional studies, the principal criticism concerned the methodology itself. It was contended that estimating the coefficients that caused disparate growth patterns between markets did not address the problem of traffic response to a price change but simply the levels of demand. If a measurable price differential exists between two alternative destinations from the same city, for instance, it will not matter to businessmen, who account for roughly half of the air travel market, that a given destination might carry a higher price than a comparable city. That is to say, businessmen do not alter their plans simply because they could save money by going to the city with the lower fare. Alternatively, vacationers confront a host of preference variables when selecting a holiday destination of which the airline fare is only one. Climate, popularity, and other costs may even outweigh fare in importance. The CAB, despite its own evidence to the contrary, apparently acquiesced to industry criticism and generally applied a coefficient of -0.7 where such a measure had been needed during cases heard in the 1970s.[12] Cross-sectional analysis, however, has at least pointed out the traffic growth potential of markets where airlines compete directly with surface modes for intercity transportation. The post-1971 experience of the Dallas-Houston segment, where prices were reduced when Southwest Airlines entered the market and higher traffic volumes were generated and not duplicated in other markets of similar length and density, clearly illustrates the popularity of air transport when it becomes price competitive with automobiles, buses, and railroads.

On the subject of cross-sectional analysis, Verleger raised serious objections to studies that failed to take special market characteristics into account or that ignored changes in income distribution among the city pairs.[13] These two factors were thought to be more strongly correlated with relative traffic levels than price differentials.

Objections to the point of view that stresses inelasticity were primarily directed against the unverifiable, subjective nature of the supporting arguments. However, criticism of what quantifiable evidence was put forth was somewhat less sweeping than that leveled against studies stressing elasticity. For instance, the CAB Bureau of Economics review of TWA's submission to the DPFI centered on the choice of its fare and income variables, while it questioned United's use of quarterly instead of annual data.

It has already been said that the airlines rationalize their belief in a low price elasticity coefficient mainly on subjective grounds, but empirical evidence also can be cited. For instance, while average domestic industry prices rose by 29 percent from 1979 to 1980, under sluggish economic conditions, total passengers enplaned declined by only 8 percent. In addition to the objections noted above to the studies that stress elasticity, there exists the feeling that since business travel, which is the mainstay of the industry in terms of size, year-round consistency, and revenue per passenger mile, entails a cost that is rarely fully borne by its user, and this cost should be inelastic.[14] Vacationers are undoubtedly more price conscious, but it is felt that holidays have become necessities for the U.S. population in the same way that the automobile, television, and air conditioners have changed from discretionary to necessary items.[15] The question of vacation travel thus is seen more within the context of which transportation mode is selected, rather than whether or not a trip is taken. There also exists a feeling that airline prices would have to take a decisive leap beyond some threshold point in order to have any clearly negative effect on air travel because of an inflationary psychology that has reputedly overtaken consumers. This reasoning holds that perhaps 1-5 percent increases might be tolerated, while increases of 6 percent or more might not.[16] Supporters of the "threshold" theory could point to the traffic recovery of 1975-76 for confirming evidence. Traffic growth in this period was strongest in the fall and winter when three fare increases, averaging 2 percent each, were levied within the space of three and a half months during the heart of the period.

What does seem apparent from the work in the price elasticity area is that the various types of traffic have different coefficients that probably change over time. Moreover, since the mix of traffic is never fixed for a long period, the search for one aggregate industry coefficient appears to have little relevance. Nevertheless, prior to the deregulation era, the belief by the industry in a relatively inelastic coefficient, particularly when the movement was up, led to a mode of conduct in pricing that stressed joint profit maximization.

The belief in relatively inelastic demand has been widely shared and cost pressures provided the main rationale in justifying applications filed with the CAB. (Requests for fare discounts to bolster slumping load factors by catering to infrequent, price-conscious traffic, traditionally have been structured carefully to minimize downgrading by full-fare passengers.) The rate-making machinery of the CAB, promulgated during the early phase of the 1970-74 Domestic Passenger Fare Investigation, encouraged joint action by applying industry-wide standards known to all carriers. Fares were permitted to rise to the point where, after discount traffic and nonstandard seating configurations were disallowed, the average annual industry return on investment equaled 12 percent at a 55 percent industry load factor. Thus, even if several carriers might be earning profits at an adjusted rate exceeding 12 percent, that group along with the others that might be under the standard, could still raise fares further as a reward for presumably efficient operation under the DPFI formula. A total of 15 general fare increases were awarded from 1971 through 1978, compared to only 2 during the preceding ten-year period. Operating expenses per seat mile did hold relatively steady in the earlier period but rose particularly sharply between 1973 and 1974 due primarily to escalating fuel costs.[17]

The same problem that makes price elasticity so hard to gauge accurately, namely the difficulty in separating the impact of each causal element, renders the measurement of income elasticity equally difficult. The pure statistical relationship, of course, is simple enough. The percentage change in real domestic airline passenger revenue associated with a 1 percent change in real disposable income averaged +2.1 between 1970 and 1980, compared to the +3.5 during the last half of the 1950s.[18] The decline in the coefficient may have been due to a leveling off in the rate at which nonincome factors, such as reduced fear of flying and poor rail service, spurred the popularity of air travel. The positive income elasticity coefficient indicates that when an economic expansion is in progress, airline business should grow at an even greater pace and should decline more steeply than income during a cyclical downturn. Thus, theoretically at least, traffic should be extremely sensitive to economic fluctuations, and recent evidence does indicate a good correlation between almost any coincident national income variable and industry revenue passenger miles. This appears to contradict the contention of Caves who found in air traffic patterns, "no marked sensitivity to business fluctuations"[19] despite the statistically high-income coefficient prevailing at the time of his writing. At least part of the explanation for Caves' observation could be attributed to the fact that business travel, which is appreciably less volatile than vacation travel, accounted for proportionately more traffic at that time than it did subsequently.

By itself, however, income elasticity provides little in the way of behavioral insights about how airline managers respond to changes in the level of demand. Nevertheless, the evidence seems clear that sluggish demand frequently prompts individual carriers to pursue market share improvement at the expense of mutual interdependence. Most often, these marketing efforts have been confined to the "frills" area, involving in-flight amenities where the carriers try to achieve a monopoly, however short-lived, on some passenger service. Perhaps the best recent illustration of this marketing "one-upmanship" occurred during the 1969-70 recession when United installed more comfortable five-across instead of six-across seating on many of its narrow-bodied planes. United's main competitors, American and Trans World, in retaliation pulled seats out of their newly delivered and rarely filled 747s, replacing them with a stand-up bar lounge in the coach compartment. Not to be outdone, United then removed even more seats and installed two coach lounges on its 747s. A fourth carrier, Continental, eventually was drawn into the lounge fray by virtue of its certification in the Chicago-Los Angeles market where the other three carriers were operating. [20] Before the "war" ended in 1973, Trans World had placed lounges on its long-range, narrow-bodied 707s and American had introduced live entertainment. By 1973 demand expanded markedly and the carriers needed the seats that had been removed from the original configurations. Ironically, the "lounge war" conducted by American, Continental, Trans World, and United happened to coincide for over two years with the Transcontinental Capacity-Limiting Agreement, which perhaps constituted the most ambitious joint venture toward profit maximization ever conducted in the industry. Contradictory behavior has not been uncommon among the Trunk carriers, but the "lounge war" no doubt lasted longer than the participants wished. Actually, traffic growth had resumed by late 1970, but each carrier appeared reluctant to play the "guinea pig" in fear of even a temporary competitive disadvantage. At this time, a slippage of just one percentage point in market share on a segment such as New York-Los Angeles could have meant an annual revenue loss of $2 million. The "war" only ended when CAB approved a Trans World petition to allow a $10 reduction in coach fares for flights on planes without lounges. Not willing to risk a price disadvantage, the carriers subsequently eliminated the lounges. [21]

Prior to the deregulation period, pricing initiatives were usually just as prominent as those involving product marketing during periods of slack demand. Invariably, discount fares, designed especially for discretionary travelers and out of the reach of the businessman, were filed in an attempt to bolster sagging load factors. While price cutting almost always was matched, the initiating carrier still hoped to gain a public relations advantage that would help in terms of market share. On some occasions, a carrier chose not to match the discount, reasoning that its probable loss of volume to the discounting carrier would be smaller than the cost of the potential yield dilution. A rash of discounts appeared in late 1974 and early 1975 just before the end of the 1973-75 recession and must have been at least partially responsible for the rise in demand that slightly preceded the recession trough.

PASSENGER CHARACTERISTICS

Airline managers also base their strategies on passenger characteristics. The sex, age, income, and purpose of trip, etc. of air travelers all have ramifications with regard to the kind of product offered as well as the type of advertising strategy chosen. What had once been of prime concern to the airlines, namely the competition between the common carriers—air, rail, and motor buses—no longer seems as important. By 1980 the airlines accounted for 86 percent of intercity revenue passenger miles[22] compared to only 43 percent in 1960.[23] Domestic rail passenger volume had actually exceeded air traffic as recently as 1956.[24] In 1980, however, railroads handled less than 3 percent of all intercity common carrier revenue-passenger miles.[25] The changing qualities of the typical air passenger are illustrated in Table 2.1, which compares changes over a 14-year period.

TABLE 2.1

Selected Passenger Characteristics, 1964 and 1980
(percent distribution)

	1964	1980
Sex		
Male	71	59
Female	29	41
Age		
0-21	7	8
22-39	43	39
40-59	41	38
60+	9	15
Purpose of trip		
Business	56	42
Pleasure and other	44	58
Where ticket was purchased		
Travel agency	28	54
Airline and other	72	46

Source: Trans World Airlines, Continuous On-Board Surveys, second quarters 1964 and 1980.

Male travelers accounted for just under three-fifths of all air passengers, having slipped slightly from an earlier even more dominant position. The only notable variation in the age mix occurred at the upper extreme, essentially reflecting the changes in the proportions of each group within the total population. In 1964 those under 21 comprised 42 percent and the over-65 group 9 percent of the total population, while in 1980 the respective percentages amounted to 34 and 11 percent.[26] The business traffic portion of the total decreased during the period covered, but not as steeply as it had prior to 1963. Nonbusiness travel had been virtually nil in the early years of the industry. The most dramatic change among the passenger traits shown in Table 2.1 involved the place of ticket purchases; travel agencies accounted for well over half of total sales in the latest period compared to slightly over a quarter during 1964. Because of this shift, airlines have not only had to pay out more in commissions, but also have had to direct a major account of marketing time and energy toward the agencies.

PRODUCT DIFFERENTIATION

The ultimate goal of the airlines' marketing efforts is the achievement of product differentiation, and it is this drive that shapes the degree of rivalry in the industry. If a product can be considered truly unique, the owner will be insulated from competition, whereas the proprietor of an undifferentiated article may be subject to great competitive pressure. Since the carriers currently fly similar equipment and service standards are comparable, the airline product, in theory at least, should be undifferentiated among the firms. Nevertheless, we know that traffic shares within many markets still fluctuate over time. This may be the case even in city pairs where competitive equipment and schedules are virtually identical. As an example, American Airlines has been known to have a strong following among business travelers wherever they fly, and as a result, tends to outperform rivals in short-haul markets.

Most carriers do work at achieving the perception of product differentiation or at least try to defend themselves competitively through innovative marketing and pricing. Pricing activities had probably been influenced by the likelihood that, prior to deregulation, a small portion of the flying population mistakingly thought that active price competition existed within the industry. Thus, discount fare initiators stood to gain favor with this group, estimated to be about 6 percent of total air travelers.[27] After 1978 price disparities within major markets were increasingly prevalent as new entrants tended to offer an inferior service at a discounted fare.

During the immediate postwar period, real product differentiation existed while rapid technological advances occurred. Carriers flying faster, pressurized, and otherwise more attractive aircraft maintained a distinct advantage, and this spurred almost continual reequipment until the early 1960s when most carriers had acquired a sufficient number of standard, modern jet aircraft. In demonstrating the possibilities of an equipment advantage, Caves mentioned the breakthrough that Capital Airlines achieved in several major markets between 1955 and 1958 by flying Vickers Viscount turboprop aircraft, while Capital's competitors could not obtain comparably attractive equipment until the end of that period. Over the three years, Capital's market share increased by 21 percentage points in New York-Chicago, 34 percentage points in Chicago-Pittsburgh, 44 percentage points in New York-Detroit, and 45 percentage points in Chicago-Washington traffic.[28] The main technological advance since then has involved the introduction of wide-bodied aircraft, capable of seating about 350 passengers. When delivered, these planes were rushed into the most important markets in order to secure an advantage or make up for a deficiency. The largest Boeing 747s were introduced in 1969 by Pan American, closely followed by Trans World early in 1970, while the smaller-version McDonnell Douglas DC-10 and Lockheed L-1011 flew commercially for the first time in 1971 and 1972, respectively.[29] The wide-bodied equipment has tended to be more popular than the narrow-bodied jets on grounds of passenger comfort alone, since speed and range differences are narrow. Carriers with few or no wide-bodied aircraft often try to counter direct wide-body competition with more flights, reasoning that offering more departure times will diminish the relative attractiveness of the wide-bodied plane.

The percentage of capacity offered in a market clearly remains the key determinant of market share as numerous analyses of the two variables have attested. All other things being equal, this means that a carrier supplying 50 percent of the seats in a city pair should retain half of the passenger traffic. Moreover, once the capacity share increases beyond some threshold point, the traffic share associated with it may grow even larger, giving rise to an S-curve relationship. The logic here stems from the widely accepted hypothesis, which has been confirmed from surveys, that consumers choose an airline mainly on the basis of scheduling convenience. When one carrier can offer more flights in a market than its competitors, it can cover more departure time slots and thus provide travelers with a better chance at obtaining a seat at the

time desired. Therefore, the dominant capacity ca̶ ̶ ̶will probably be the first called for a reservation. Naturally, ̶ ̶ ̶
ferential will be more easily noticeable where the ma̶ ̶pacity dif-
fewer competitors and the total number of flights is als̶ ̶ontains

Less basic marketing initiatives in the pursuit of p̶ ̶ited.
ferentiation usually involve the promotion of in-flight am̶e̶ct dif-
such as wider seats, more leg room, gourmet meals, frie̶n̶es
hostesses, first-run movies, free liquor, etc. If a carrier ̶ ̶er
surprise a competitor with a popular innovation, it may ̶achieve
success in terms of market share by virtue of its temporar̶y̶ ̶mono-
oly. Other airlines almost always match a promising promotion but
sometimes cannot move quickly enough. Alterations to an aircraft's
interior, for instance, take more time to implement than changes in
cabin service.

Despite claims from marketing professionals, probably the
key determinant of competitive success is the degree to which a
carrier actually performs satisfactorily. Any marketing scheme,
no matter how brilliant, ultimately succeeds or fails on the ability
of a carrier to operate efficiently. Thus, assuming that schedules
are competitive, on-time performance, courteous personnel, speedy
baggage delivery, and prompt reservations service are of paramount
importance in determining market share. Without proper attention
to these basic factors, given the essentially undifferentiated airline
product, marketing efforts at establishing a special appeal may
achieve at best some short-lived advantages for a carrier.

THE BUSINESS CYCLE AND
DOMESTIC AIRLINE DEMAND

The fact that airline traffic moves in concert with economic
conditions is clearly demonstrable with respect to annual aggregates,
where recessions are seen to dampen traffic, while periods of economic expansion generate large rates of increase. However, more
discrete measurement involving monthly or quarterly correlations
are less obvious, since traffic developments in the airline industry
are commonly reported and analyzed in terms of year-over-year
growth rates. These tend to be unreliable because accelerating or
decelerating rates of change may be a function of events in the prior
year or special seasonal factors. While monthly industry statistics
are available within a fortnight, it is up to the users to develop a
time series comparable to the main macroeconomic coincident
variables typically used to track the business cycle. This may be
accomplished through a variety of smoothing techniques but, before
that, refinements are recommended with regard to strike adjust-

ments, disruptions, and the need to confine important holiday-
related ic to the same month.

economic turning points are determined by the National
Bureau Economic Research after an examination of the direction
of sev coincident indicators. The airline series employed in
this e cise was based on Trunk carrier traffic smoothed by a 12-
mont centered moving average method after adjustment as noted
abov Table 2.2 compares the estimated turning points of domestic
Trunk traffic with those of the economy at large.

TABLE 2.2

Estimated Airline Traffic Cycle and the
General Business Cycle

Economy	Airline	Airline Later/(Earlier)
Peaks		
April 1960	May 1960	1 month
December 1969	March 1970	3 months
November 1973	February 1974	3 months
January 1980	July 1979	(6) months
Troughs		
February 1961	November 1960	(3) months
November 1970	March 1971	4 months
March 1975	November 1974	(4) months

Source: Compiled by the author.

Ignoring, for the moment, the 1980 episode which was probably unique, the evidence suggests a shorter cycle for the airline
industry than for the overall economy, since the average length of
the latter was 12 months compared to 9 for the industry. The peak-
ing lag on the part of airline traffic may be partially explained by a
belated response in cutting back travel by business. Even though
the profits series generally declines or at best flattens out before
the peak, corporations may need to see several unsatisfactory
quarters before decisively trimming the travel budget. With regard
to pleasure traffic, the airline market is dominated by above-average

income earners whose jobs tend to be more secure than those of blue-collar workers at the outset of a recession.

In the 1980 case, when the airline traffic series peaked six months before the economy did, two factors stand out. In the first place, the economy, early in 1979, was very sluggish and in fact turned negative during the second quarter. Secondly, airline prices were escalating rapidly in response to a fuel price explosion. Despite downward price pressure from deregulation, average fares in the third quarter had increased by 1 percent over the level of the preceding quarter where, due to seasonal factors, a decline of 4 percent had been the norm for the prior four years.

The results at the trough were somewhat mixed. On the one hand, if vacation travel can be regarded as discretionary consumption, it is a postponable expenditure item, and so air travel would remain depressed until the employment outlook and personal incomes improved. Conversely, corporate profits generally lead the economic recovery and thus provide a basis for an early revival in business travel. It is noteworthy that when the airline series "troughed" earlier than the economy (1960 and 1974), both occurrences were in November, a month heavily weighted toward business travel. The 1970-71 experience case may have been special because the airline series hit bottom in September 1970, which would have conformed to the 1960 and 1974 patterns, but then rose in October and November only to decline again until March 1971. It is conceivable that the auto strike during the fourth quarter distorted the economic impact, since two key variables affecting air travel, corporate profits and personal disposable income, both declined in real terms during the fourth quarter after turning up in the prior period.

The airline series trough in the 1980-81 example was still not yet in evidence by the time of the Professional Air Traffic Controllers (PATCO) disruption even though the economic bottom had been officially designated more than a year earlier. While the 1980 recession of seven months was the shortest on record, the later half of 1980 was less than robust. Real gross national product growth averaged only 3.1 percent and, although first quarter 1981 results were more favorable, the economy later lapsed back into recession. Prices also must have played a role. Between the second quarters of 1980 and 1981, for example, the average industry price rose by 16 percent which, after a 29 percent increase over the preceding four quarters, must surely have placed a damper on air travel despite the bargains available in selected markets. Over a two-year period, average airline fares grew at a compounded rate of nearly 50 percent, while the prices of all goods and services (as measured by the personal consumption expenditures deflator) were increasing by only 19 percent.

Another factor in the failure of Trunk traffic to bounce back following the 1980 recession involved the inroads made by the non-Trunk segment of the industry. For instance, where the established carriers had accounted for 87.0 percent of industry revenue passenger miles during the first half of 1980, this percentage had slipped to 83.6 percent a year later. Trunk traffic declined by 9 percent over this period, while that of the other carriers grew by 19 percent largely due to new carrier formation and vigorous expansion on the part of many existing smaller airlines. The net result was still an industry decline of 6 percent, but the Trunk slide was exaggerated because of its lost share.

The 1980-81 experience notwithstanding, the evidence points to a shorter cycle for the airlines than for the economy at large. Those who watch airline traffic results, but are not privy to a seasonally adjusted series, would question this view especially in the recovery phase, since significant year-over-year traffic increases only materialize in the unadjusted series after two to four quarters have elapsed following the recession trough. Table 2.3 shows movements in the annual changes that probably have a more consistent rhythm than the adjusted monthly data. The objection noted earlier with respect to the problems of the base in the monthly series are alleviated somewhat by consolidating the data into quarters.

TABLE 2.3

Trunk Revenue Passenger-Mile Change from
Prior Year during Four Recessions
(percentage)

Quarters from Recession Trough	1960-61 (Feb. 1961)	1969-70 (Nov. 1970)	1973-75 (March 1975)	1980 (July 1980)
-1	(1)	0	(2)	(2)
0	(4)	(3)	(3)	(11)
+1	(4)	(3)	(3)	(10)
+2	0	2	5	(13)
+3	8	0	7	(6)
+4	16	8	12	

Source: Compiled from U.S. Civil Aeronautics Board, Air Carrier Traffic Statistics, various issues; and Air Transport Association.

Again withholding comment on the 1980-81 experience for the moment, Table 2.3 reveals that traffic growth returned fastest during 1973-75 and slowest after the 1969-70 slump. The delays in the rebound apparently stem from the points noted before that the monthly traffic series tended to peak later than the economy and hence maintained the traffic base at a relatively high level into the recession. Also traffic improvements tended to be modest immediately after the cyclical trough probably because, despite the usual fare discount availability, a large portion of discretionary travelers remained on the sidelines until the threat of unemployment abated. The jobless total typically rises for a short interval beyond the recession trough as firms find that they can increase output without commensurate new hiring. Six months after the 1970 and 1975 troughs, for instance, industrial production was up by 4.1 and 9.3 percent with nonagricultural employment up by only 1.2 and 1.0 percent, while seasonally adjusted traffic volumes had only grown by 3.7 and 2.4 percent, respectively.

The post-1980 traffic changes were far more severe than the earlier periods but with good reason given the unprecedented price increases and eroded Trunk traffic share. Even so, the direction of the quarterly variances during the latest experience still reflected the pattern set in the prior three recoveries as the deceleration abated by the third post-trough period.

In summary, the evidence supports the notion that while the airline cycle appears to be of shorter duration than that of the economy, the impact of a recession may be at least as severe due to the relatively sluggish recovery phase.

INDUSTRY MATURITY

Concern has arisen in some quarters over the idea that the airline industry has matured and, therefore, will no longer be able to expand strongly enough to restrain more unilateral attempts at increasing market shares at the expense of joint profit maximizing ventures. It has been apparent that growth in pure percentage terms slowed considerably. During the 1950s, for instance, Trunk revenue passenger miles grew at an average rate of 15.4 percent per annum and still maintained a 13.2 percent annual rate throughout the 1960s.[30] From 1970 to 1980, however, traffic growth has proceeded at a far more modest 5.8 percent annual pace,[31] a rate that has undoubtedly been retarded by two full recessions and one of short duration within the period. Nevertheless, growth during the best years has failed to match even the averages of the earlier decades. The 1950s had been marked by the newly gained acceptance of air travel over surface transportation, while the 1960s, being largely unhampered by cyclical economic downturns, saw a continuation of the growing preference for air travel, as well as the introduction of traffic-generating discount fares, especially on long-haul routes.

The problem of decelerating growth rates is at least partly due to simple arithmetic, in that the amounts necessary to maintain a double-digit rate of increase become progressively more difficult to generate as the base grows larger. As an example, the difference in Trunk revenue passenger miles between 1978 and 1979 exceeded the whole Trunk volume of 1955. Thus, the industry has probably matured in the sense that high percentage increases can no longer be sustained, given the magnitudes required. Nonetheless, ample growth opportunities continue to exist. According to a Gallup survey taken in 1981, 35 percent of all U.S. adults still had never flown,[32] indicating a pool of 55 million potential new air travelers over 20 years of age.[33] Moreover, demographic trends appear favorable since the 30-49 age group, which currently accounts for the largest bloc of air passengers, should be the fastest growing segment of the population through the year 2000.[34] Projections of real income suggest a rising proportion of the relatively affluent, and trends in paid vacation time also appear promising.[35] These factors indicate that pessimistic assessments of the industry's growth outlook may be premature.

NOTES

1. Claude Puffer, Air Transportation (Philadelphia: Blakeston, 1941); Lewis Sorrell, "Growth of Air Transport," in Prospects and Problems in Aviation, ed. Leverett S. Lyon (Chicago: Lincoln Printing, 1945).

2. Thomas Wolfe, Air Transportation (New York: McGraw-Hill, 1950); Joseph Nicholson, Air Transportation Management (New York: Wiley, 1951).

3. Paul Cherington, Airline Price Policy (Boston: Harvard Business School, 1958).

4. United Research, Inc., Federal Regulation of the Domestic Air Transport Industry, Cambridge, Mass., 1958.

5. U.S. Civil Aeronautics Board, Forecast of Airline Passenger Traffic in the United States: 1959-1965, Washington, D.C., December 1959.

6. Edward Taffe, "Trends in Airline Passenger Traffic: A Graphic Case Study," Annals of the Association of American Geographers 49 (December 1959):395-408.

7. Hale Bartlett, "The Demand for Passenger Air Transportation 1947-1962," Ph.D. dissertation, University of Chicago, 1962, pp. 113-15.

8. Richard E. Caves, Air Transport and Its Regulators (Cambridge, Mass.: Harvard University Press, 1962), p. 34.

9. United Air Lines, Rebuttal Testimony, Domestic Passenger-Fare Investigation, CAB Docket 21866-7, Exhibit no. U-RT-1, pp. 8-10; Trans World Airlines, Inc., Domestic Passenger Fare Investigation, CAB Docket 21866-7, Exhibit no. TW-R-7142, pp. 1-2.

10. U.S. Civil Aeronautics Board, Bureau of Economics, Domestic Passenger Fare Investigation, CAB Docket 21866-7, Exhibit nos. BC-7058 and BC-R-8001.

11. Donald Oswald, "Pricing for Reduction of Domestic Airline Excess Capacity," Ph.D. dissertation, Washington State University, 1977, pp. 253-54.

12. U.S. Department of Transportation, Air Transportation Policy Staff, An Analysis of the Intrastate Air Carrier Regulation Form, January 1976, vol. I, p. 27.

13. Philip Verleger, Jr., "Models of the Demand for Air Transportation, The Bell Journal of Economics and Management Science 3 (Autumn 1972):437-57.

14. Conversations with TWA Pricing Department Staff.

15. Ibid.

16. Ibid.

17. U.S. Civil Aeronautics Board, Handbook of Airline Statistics 1973; and various issues of Air Carrier Traffic Statistics and Air Carrier Financial Statistics.

18. Calculated from U.S. Executive Branch, Economic Report of the President 1981; U.S. Department of Commerce, The National Income and Product Accounts of the U.S., 1929-1965; Air Transport Association, Air Transport 1981, p. 21.

19. Caves, Air Transport, p. 36.

20. "Airlines: The Lounge War," Newsweek, July 2, 1973, p. 61.

21. Ibid.

22. Air Transport Association, Air Transport 1981, p. 10.

23. Handbook of Airline Statistics 1973, p. 605.

24. Ibid.

25. Air Transport 1981, p. 10.

26. Calculated from U.S. Bureau of Census, Current Population Reports, series P-25, no. 805, May 1979.

27. Opinion Research Corporation, Determinants of Airline Selection, Princeton, 1969, p. A-13.

28. Caves, Air Transport, pp. 26-27.

29. Handbook of Airline Statistics 1973, p. 553.

30. Ibid., p. 23.

31. Ibid.; and Air Carrier Traffic Statistics, December 1970 and December 1980.

32. Gallup Organization, The Frequency of Flying Among the General Public 1981, p. 7.

33. U.S. Department of Commerce, Bureau of the Census, Current Population Reports, series P-25, no. 796, September 1979, pp. 26-128.

34. The Conference Board Record, May 1976, pp. 26-27.

35. U.S. Department of Labor, Handbook of Labor Statistics 1977, pp. 301-2.

3

COST ASPECTS

Market conduct among the airlines frequently hinges on the relative financial health of the competing carriers. In a competitive situation, strong carriers have the obvious advantage of staying power over those that are weaker; cost schedule disparities have much to do with the causation of whatever intercarrier differences appear. For most of the industry's history, the regulatory agency, through its control of market entry and thus such variables as route structure and size, **assisted in the creation of cost inequalities.** However, as initially advanced by Gordon,[1] a broad range of policy alternatives is available to airline managers and average cost divergencies have evolved from the selection of any number of courses of action. Also important in the area of costs and their ramifications is the differentiation between fixed and variable costs, since the relative weighting of each will influence market conduct through its impact on profit levels, especially during periods of weak demand.

This chapter first defines the various types of airline costs and reviews the question of airline size and economies of scale. Next, expense determinants other than size are investigated, and a new hypothesis is proposed about the causes of intercarrier unit cost disparities. An outgrowth of the latter is an original formula detailing an industry cost function. Finally, issues affecting fixed and variable costs are examined in light of their impact on market conduct.

Since the reporting requirements of the CAB are at least as exhaustive for financial data as they are for operating statistics and are open to public scrutiny, there exists no lack of information essential for conducting cost analysis of airlines. There are certain difficulties attached to some expense categories such as depreciation, where accounting policies may differ, but the uniform rules set down by the CAB have most probably rendered airline

costs less subject to distortion or qualification than the comparable
data of most other industries, whether regulated or not. When the
CAB "sunsets" sometime before 1985, financial-reporting requirements will be greatly reduced and what remains will be collected
by the Department of Transportation.

Airline costs, as defined by the CAB, may be placed under eight
broad headings. In terms of size, the largest of these encompasses
the flying operations of the aircraft, including those resulting from
maintaining the aircraft and crew in readiness for a flight. The
next largest involves aircraft and traffic servicing, which includes
ground personnel expenses and the outlays arising from passenger
handling on the ground and the planning and monitoring of flights.
Maintenance expenses include direct charges, such as the cost of
labor and material used in the repair and upkeep of aircraft and
ground equipment, and the indirect costs stemming from the general overhead of the maintenance and overhaul facilities, periodic
inspection of aircraft and ground equipment to comply with official
standards, and the administration of the operation itself. Passenger
service expenses include cabin attendant salaries and the cost of
food, beverages, and in-flight entertainment. Promotion and sales
costs cover those outlays made for advertising, agency commissions, computer reservations, schedule printing, etc. General
and administrative expenses in large part cover those activities
carried out at the corporate headquarters and the various city sta-
tions that plan and direct the company operation. Transport-
related costs include tour operation expenses and the outlays that
result from providing services to other airlines. Finally, depreciation and amortization expenses relate primarily to the charges
associated with the aging of a carrier's tangible and intangible
assets.[2]

ECONOMIES OF SCALE

Probably the greatest amount of academic interest in the
area of airline costs has centered on the question of economies of
scale. The presence or absence of such economies carries wide
implications with regard to concentration and barriers to entry in
almost all industries, but these particular issues were somewhat
muted in the airline industry by the fact that government regulation
largely took over from market forces the determination of firm
size and the number of operating carriers. It accomplished this
through the system of route certification and its long-standing policy, prior to 1978, of prohibition of the entry of new firms to
scheduled service. Nevertheless, from the standpoint of efficiency

of operation and profitability and now deregulation, the issue of
economies of scale is of great interest. Clearly, firms with lower
average costs have large competitive advantages over those less
efficient. Moreover, the discovery of the optimum scale of operation could shed much light on the efficacy of merger proposals within
the industry.

The earliest investigations into the relationship of average
costs to the size of the firms were carried out by Crane,[3] whose
frame of reference was pre-World War II data, and Koontz,[4] who
drew on the immediate postwar period. A myriad of later studies[5]
have more or less confirmed the initial findings that only slightly
increasing or constant returns to scale, beyond some minimum
size, seem to have marked the industry and that diseconomies were
evident only among the smallest firms. Much of the apparent inefficiency attached to the smaller carriers is, of course, merely a
reflection of their flying shorter distances and thus producing fewer
available ton miles* than a longer-haul carrier. The latter can
provide more ton miles for only the relatively minor incremental
costs associated with the greater distance, which mainly involve
fuel, crew, and other in-flight expenses.

A more current cost/size relationship is shown in Figure 3.1,
where average unit costs for the Trunk and Local and Regional
carriers are plotted according to size as expressed by the available
ton miles supplied by individual carriers for the year ended September 1980. Although Trunk unit costs appeared to vary considerably regardless of size, those of the Locals tended to cluster
around 70¢ but wide size disparities were apparent. No pattern
was discernible with regard to the Regionals either. Northwest,
the lowest unit cost carrier among the Trunks, operated at roughly
two-thirds of the rate at which Eastern, the highest cost Trunk,
functioned. Meanwhile, the difference in the cost extremes among
the Locals came to nearly 30 percent. What seems particularly
significant in the Trunk distribution is the fact that Northwest was
in the middle range on the basis of size and that the unit costs of
the remaining carriers were within reasonable proximity of one
another despite the wide size differentials. Thus, even the smallest of the Trunks does not appear to be experiencing any cost disadvantages related to size. The lack of a pattern similarly affected
the other carriers. U.S. Air (Allegheny) and Republic, the two
highest cost local operators (excluding Ozark, which experienced
strike difficulties during the period) were also the largest, while

---

*Available ton times mileage flown.

FIGURE 3.1

Average Unit Costs by Airline Size, Domestic Airlines—1980

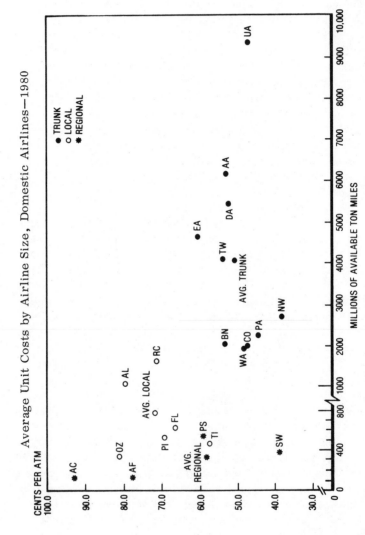

Source: Computed from U.S. Civil Aeronautics Board, "Air Carrier Financial Statistics" and "Air Carrier Traffic Statistics," both September 1980.

among the regionals, the smallest carriers, Air Florida and Air California, showed the highest unit costs. Meanwhile, Southwest vied with Northwest for low-cost honors among all airlines despite the fact that the former was 85 percent smaller.

The 1980 expense distribution suggests that the minimum scale of operation needed for a Trunk-type operation at present rests in the area of 1.9 billion available ton miles, which is the equivalent of 4 percent of the industry's capacity. This figure also amounts to roughly 12 times the level cited by Caves, who worked with a 1958 data base covering 48 states.

The figures shown in Table 3.1 reveal the changes that have taken place in the indexes of costs of the smaller carriers relative to those of the largest Trunks between 1958 and 1980. The data are not strictly comparable in that the carrier composition of the three Trunk groups are not identical for both periods. However, the size criteria remain valid.

TABLE 3.1

Total Operating Cost Indexes of the Domestic Carriers
by Size, 1958 and Year Ending September 1980

	1958	1980
Largest Trunks[a]	100.0	100.0
Middle-sized Trunks[b]	97.4	102.0
Smallest Trunks[c]	101.6	98.9
Locals	187.9	141.3

[a]1958—American, Eastern, TWA, United; 1980—American, Delta, United.

[b]1958—Braniff, **Capital**, Delta, National, Northwest; 1980—Eastern, Northwest, Pan American, Trans World.

[c]1958—Continental, Northeast; 1980—Braniff, Continental, Western.

Sources: 1958 data from Richard E. Caves, Air Transport and Its Regulators, p. 58; 1980 data calculated from U.S. Civil Aeronautics Board, Air Carrier Financial Statistics and Air Carrier Traffic Statistics, both September 1980.

If there exists some optimum size in the airline industry,
the data in Table 3.1 indicate a shift downward over time since the
smallest Trunks achieved the lowest unit costs while the middle-
sized Trunks had done so back in 1958. Moreover, the Locals'
apparent disadvantage decreased markedly between the two periods.
This movement undoubtedly owed much to the long-established
policy by the CAB of awarding route authority to new carriers while
reducing government subsidies; this tactic expanded the route net-
works of the smaller carriers much more rapidly than that of the
larger firms.[6] Actually, this phenomenon was already under way
in 1958, as Caves noted that the disadvantages of small carriers
appeared to be shrinking steadily.[7]

Among the Trunks, the greatest advantage of small size
appeared in the area of maintenance charges,[8] resulting most
probably from having to manage fewer aircraft and hence, a
smaller, less elaborate facility. Smaller carriers also tended to
operate fewer different types of aircraft than the larger ones.
This standardization has limited inventory charges and the time
needed to train the technical personnel involved in maintenance
work.

Differences in flying operation expenses, which comprise
over 40 percent of all operating costs among the three Trunk-size
classes, were relatively narrow.[9] Without doubt, this reflected
uniformities imposed by the airline unions on in-flight personnel
salaries and work rules, as well as the basic consistency of industry fuel contracts. Aircraft and traffic servicing expenses
showed the same slight variability between the largest and smallest group, while the middle-sized carriers absorbed the highest
unit costs.[10] Here union-induced wage standardization also played
a key role, in addition to the more or less uniform intercarrier
ground procedures involved in handling passengers.

The relatively higher costs recorded by the medium-sized
airlines resulted from the inclusion in this group of Eastern and
Trans World, which were the least efficient operators. The relatively higher costs of this group would have been even more pronounced had Northwest, the industry's most efficient firm, not
been a member. In point of fact, if the Trunks in 1980 had been
divided evenly between the largest five and the smallest five,
Northwest would have belonged to the latter category. The advantage of the smaller carriers would have been evident in every expense segment, amounting to 13 percent in the aggregate.[11]

Nevertheless, the evidence clearly fails to substantiate any
systematic relationship between average costs and airline size
among the Trunk carriers. This is apparent from the distributions
shown in Figure 3.1 and the insignificant correlation coefficients

derived from tests of certain variables shown in Table 3.2. Moreover, mergers between large and small carriers have yielded
contrasting results with regard to cost before and after merger.
When United absorbed the financially exhausted Capital in June 1961,
the enlarged carrier was better off in terms of unit costs relative
to the rest of the industry than were the two independent carriers
prior to the merger. Where the two together registered unit costs
11 percent higher than the total of the other airline in the 1959-60
period, the disparity had narrowed to 8 percent by 1963-64.[12]
Conversely, the Delta-Northeast merger of 1972 showed the newly
formed carrier worse off, allowing for the same 2-3 year gesta-
tion period, than before the union.[13] Apparently, factors other
than sheer size, such as the integration of route structure and
equipment and management practices, have had much more of an
impact on the degree of success of such ventures. It is too early
to assess the Pan American-National, North Central-Southern-
Hughes Airwest, or Texas International-Continental consolidations
under the criteria cited above, although initial impressions were
that the former example had been disastrous.

TABLE 3.2

Simple Correlations (r) between Unit Airline Costs
and Selected Explanatory Variables in 1980

Independent Variables	Dependent Variables	
	Unit Costs	Adjusted Unit Costs*
Relative cargo weighting	-.854	-.846
Wide-body aircraft as percentage of total	-.682	-.702
Employees per aircraft	.618	.610
Flight stage length	-.352	-.346
Aircraft utilization	.222	.233
Age of aircraft	.183	.187
Size	.157	.139
Monopoly markets	.058	.054
Route density	.023	.010

*Excludes depreciation and amortization charges.
Source: Computed from U.S. Civil Aeronautics Board, Form
41 statistics; Air Carrier Financial Statistics and Air Carrier
Traffic Statistics, various issues.

OTHER COST DETERMINANTS

Obviously, the explanations for intercarrier cost differences are clearly not simplistic, and a search for determinants other than size is clearly necessary. At this point, it might help to concentrate on the cost characteristics of one carrier in illustrating how disparities arise. Much has been written on the seemingly relentless drive for efficiency and the supposedly superior work ethic of the managers and line personnel of Northwest, the long-time leader in industry cost effectiveness. In terms of productivity, for instance, Northwest's revenue ton miles per employee were nearly twice those of Eastern, the airline at the lowest end of the productivity scale for the year ended September 1980.[14] One key item in Northwest's favor involved more efficient work rules covering its operating personnel, for which the carrier has paid heavily in strike time. Over the 1970-80 period, Northwest has been on strike 10 percent of the time and, among the other carriers, only National, before its merger with Pan American, has come close to that figure. As a result, however, Northwest has been able to obtain more hours of work per employee than other airlines while paying the going industry salary scale. Further, a greater proportion of Northwest's aircraft were of the newer, more efficient wide-bodied type than that of any other domestic carrier. These factors contributed to Northwest's 25 percent lower-than-average unit flying operation costs in the year ended September 1980.[15] Another area in which Northwest's efficiencies were obvious was in maintenance, where a management decision to buy the same engine for its two types of wide-bodied aircraft resulted in lower costs of spare parts and maintenance personnel. Here Northwest was under the industry average by 35 percent.[16] In terms of general and administrative expenses, Northwest again emerged as the efficiency leader as it maintained relatively Spartan-like facilities at Minneapolis-St. Paul International Airport, reportedly paying $1.75 per square foot in 1976 for office space compared to much higher rates charged some other carriers.[17] Northwest also habitually recorded proportionately lower advertising expenditures than its Trunk competitors.[18] The only major cost area in which Northwest was close to the industry average in 1980 was in depreciation charges, but here the airline's financial success may have been mainly responsible. During the year, only Northwest and Continental owned all of its jet aircraft. Thus, Northwest had all of its principal airline asset eligible for depreciation charges.

In most, if not all, of the activities outlined above, managerial choice, rather than structure, played the pivotal role in the establishment of the various cost efficiencies. However, while the

Northwest example demonstrates some of the flexibility of action
available to airline managers, those mentioned may not have been
the major factors shaping Northwest's or other carriers' cost
schedules. To explore some other possibilities, simple cross-
sectional regression analysis was utilized for the ten Trunk carriers, with two cost variables and nine explanatory variables.
Table 3.2 indicates the outcome of this survey, which was based
on data for the year ending September 1980.

The results suggest little difference based on the dependent
variable chosen and only three independent variables—relative
cargo weighting, wide-bodied aircraft percentage, and employees
per aircraft—with a clearly determinant role. Since wide-bodied
aircraft has decided advantages over narrow-bodied equipment in
the carriage of cargo, a high degree of collinearity (.712) existed
between the two variables. However, an extensive fleet of larger
planes did not guarantee a heavy airfreight business. While Northwest led in cargo weighting and wide-bodied aircraft percentage,
carriers such as American, Pan American, and United had wide-
bodied fleets that were larger in proportion to that of Continental,
which nonetheless was in second place to Northwest in relative
cargo volume. This suggests that the pursuit of cargo business is
primarily one of management choice.

The relative cargo weight within the total revenue ton miles
carried by each airline indicates the portion of non-passenger traffic
volume transported. Its expense ramifications are apparently great
because it costs much less to handle cargo than passengers. Thus,
the more cargo carried in relation to passenger traffic, the more
diluted becomes the unit cost of operation, since the great bulk of
airline cargo is moved in the "belly" of the passenger aircraft,
which would otherwise be carrying only nonrevenue-generating
passenger baggage. Cargo transport requires no in-flight service,
and on the ground, basically the same ramp personnel, who must
be on hand to unload passenger baggage and service the aircraft in
any case, will also process the cargo shipment. Moreover, freight-
forwarding companies generally assume the cost of delivery to and
from the shipper. Sales costs of cargo are also limited by the fact
that the computerized passenger reservations service in most
cases also serves cargo and, since scheduling convenience is of
paramount concern to shippers, high-cost, image-creating advertising has no place in cargo sales promotion. Carriers with a high
proportion of wide-bodied aircraft in their fleet are particularly
well situated to take advantage of their ability to offer greater
"belly" capacity. Continental, for instance, concentrated its wide-
bodies in highly competitive routes where it actively pursued cargo
business. This enabled that carrier to remain viable even in

markets where its passenger load factor trailed far behind those of its competitors. Not surprisingly, Northwest and Continental, who were the first and third lowest unit cost operators, carried the highest proportion of cargo in relation to total revenue ton miles among the Trunks examined, while Trans World and Eastern, the highest cost airlines, ranked eighth and tenth respectively on the cargo variable. However, the cargo insufficiency of Eastern, at least, was apparently beyond its control since its relatively short average stage length (528 miles) placed that carrier in greater competition with surface modes for freight and mail business.

The number of employees in relation to aircraft operated ranked third among the explanatory variables and provides evidence of a lean or bloated work force. This measure had Northwest and Pan American, the cost leaders, showing the lowest ratio but, at the other end, no such tight relationship existed.

Among the less meaningful variables, the average flight stage length was thought to be important because of the relatively low incremental expenses associated with flying longer distances. Aircraft utilization, which reflects flight hours, theoretically should show a positive correlation with operating efficiencies, which it did, but it also indicated very little causality to unit costs. The obvious implication of an aircraft's age involves the relatively greater technical efficiency of the newer flight equipment and size, which was fully discussed in the section on economies of scale. The portion of carrier traffic generated on monopoly segments, which purportedly affects efficiency through the absence of competitive pressure and route density which relates carrier output to the number of cities served, were only peripherally correlated with unit costs.

One application of isolating the important cost determinants is in the construction of a cross-sectional econometric model capable of projecting airline unit operating expenses, given knowledge of the values of the explanatory variables. The industry cost function, specified below, was based on the inputs of the ten carriers used in calculating the simple correlation coefficients of Table 3.2 and was chosen after considerable experimentation, both with regard to the mathematical form of the equation and the variables finally selected. The obvious shortcoming of the logarithmic multiple regression model shown below is its relative paucity of observations, but aside from this problem, it generally fulfilled the standard statistical acceptance criteria.

Log TOE/ATM = -2.7742 - 0.2184 Log CRG
(-3.67)

+ 0.2257 Log EMP + 0.2105 Log AGE
(3.08)   (2.17)

- 0.0455 Log WB
(-1.90)

S.E. = 1.49; R^{-2} = .932; D.W. = 2.41; t = statistics in
parentheses.

where TOE/ATM = Total Operating Expenses per
Available Ton Mile
CRG   = Cargo Revenue Ton Miles as a
Percentage of Total Revenue Ton
Miles
EMP   = Total Employees per Aircraft
AGE   = Average Age of Aircraft Fleet
WB   = Wide-body Aircraft as a Percentage
of Total

The independent variables selected were those whose simple correlation coefficients in the main had ranked highest in relation to unit cost. The exception involved the substitution of Age—whose correlation with unit cost appeared to be statistically nil—for Flight stage length, which had ranked comparatively high. The inclusion of the latter variable with the other three had yielded unacceptable results. Not only was R^{-2} lower, but **Flight stage length generated** an insignificant t-statistic, and the Durbin-Watson measure for autocorrelation exceeded the conventionally acceptable range. As noted earlier, inclusion of the relative cargo weighting and the wide-body aircraft proportion among the explanatory variables produces a multicollinearity problem that can only be rationalized through the superior results derived from using both. Without one or the other, all of the significant diagnostic measures would have suffered.

FIXED AND VARIABLE COSTS

Obviously, firms whose costs tend to be rigid will experience greater profit erosion under conditions of soft demand than companies having a more flexible cost structure. In an industry with many firms, the problem of a high fixed cost burden is compounded, since weak demand often generates an increase in competitive pressure. Companies operating under the same cost conditions, but in a more monopolistic environment, may be sheltered somewhat if mutual interdependence is recognized and competitive activity can be reduced. While claiming a high fixed cost burden, the airlines seem to more closely follow a competitive model during times of stress. This mode of conduct implies that the airline industry cost structure may be less inelastic than claimed. It was Caves' contention that the airlines did not bear a heavy fixed cost burden even though he thought they gave the appearance of doing so.[19]

One clue to the real relationship between fixed and variable costs may be provided by the amount of capital invested per worker. An industry whose capital-labor ratio is above average may be regarded as having relatively high fixed costs, since physical capital is thought to be less flexible than manpower as a production input. The Conference Board has compiled interindustry measures for 1975 by totaling the gross value of land, inventory, and plant and equipment, converting the sum into constant dollars, and dividing it by the number of employees.[20] Within this context, the airline industry ratio of capital per worker nevertheless exceeded those of 17 of the 20 manufacturing groups and 3 of the 6 broad nonmanufacturing categories. Among the nonmanufacturing industries, transportation and public utilities in combination totaled over $105,000 per worker in constant 1958 dollars.[21] Of the transportation components in this broad group, the railroads averaged nearly $250,000 per worker, largely on the basis of their enormous assets in the form of land, but the nonrail elements, including trucking, buses, and the airlines, invested $31,000 per employee.[22] The airlines alone invested an amount equal to the average for all industries, which makes it unlikely that the other components were much different. Thus, within their class, the airlines were not unique in terms of cost structure.

An extreme example of the extent to which airline costs may demonstrate short-run cost flexibility can be seen from the impact of a strike. From July to mid-October 1972 Northwest was shut down by labor difficulties, thus halting operations for the entire third quarter of that year. Since it had no similar problems in the comparable period of the prior year, an easy year-to-year comparison of operating costs was possible. It showed total operating expenses for the third quarter down by 61 percent during the period of the strike, whereas costs during the quarter before the strike had grown by 21 percent.[23] Thus an overall decline greater than that reported during the strike quarter was a virtual certainty. The cost categories that resisted the cutbacks, of course, involved those items whose operation did not necessarily cease, such as maintenance, which nonetheless fell by 44 percent, and general and administrative costs, which declined by 36 percent, [24] mostly owing to salary reductions and temporary furloughs of corporate employees. Depreciation charges, which were unrelated to operations, rose slightly. [25] By virtue of mutual aid payments made to Northwest during the strike by other Trunk and Local carriers, in addition to its own unilateral actions on cost reduction, the carrier actually reported a net operating income of nearly $4 million for the quarter. [26]

The strike experience indicates that almost all types of airline costs, even in the short run, are flexible under conditions of adversity, but this still avoids the question concerning the possibilities when operations are maintained. An example of this type occurred during the aftermath of the 1973 Middle East war, when the Arab oil producers for a time attempted to embargo crude petroleum shipments to the United States, thus jeopardizing usual domestic fuel consumption patterns. As a consequence, the Federal Energy Office devised a formula for the airlines under which carriers would limit jet fuel consumption to 1972 levels. Although some airlines, notably Braniff and National, apparently ignored the ruling and continued to operate almost normally, most of the industry did decrease utilization and grounded aircraft. Some of the cutbacks were accomplished jointly as the CAB encouraged the carriers to seek mutual capacity-limiting agreements, but still much of the reduction was achieved unilaterally. The sharpest cuts occurred in February 1974 as Trunk capacity declined from that of the prior February by 11 percent, while capacity of several individual carriers dropped even farther. Trans World's contraction, for instance, amounted to 20 percent, but its operating costs nonetheless rose by 5 percent owing to a tremendous leap in the price of jet fuel. However, had the supply reductions not been carried out and capacity levels been the same year to year, operating costs would have increased by 33 percent, or $20 million above those actually reported. Thus, sizeable cost savings were shown to be feasible even during periods of distress when operations were maintained.

Caves pointed out that airlines gave the illusion of a high fixed cost burden in a variety of ways including: the lack of an inventory, which could act as a check on output in times of falling demand; the ability to vary output without necessarily causing comparable changes in inputs; and an aversion to limiting output during recessions out of competitive considerations. But he held that these factors were not really substantive. [27] Nothing appears to have happened during the interim to dispute Caves' observations, but this is not to say that cost cutting by limiting output can be accomplished easily. The carriers' fears of traffic vulnerability during periods of competitive supply pressure are not without foundation. An example is the capacity expansion and cost-inspired restraint among the so-called North-South airlines. National was shut down by a strike from September 1975 to January 1976, during which time industry traffic was expanding strongly and its main competitors, Delta and Eastern, added abundant amounts of capacity. This supply buildup was maintained after the end of the strike, but National's output of available seats remained approximately at prior year levels because of the firm's effort to control costs. The same mode of conduct continued among these carriers until November 1976, when National abandoned its prior strategy and began to outdo its rivals in expanding capacity. In the meantime, however, National's market position had been seriously eroded. Even when allowance is made for a three-month grace period after its return to operation in order to account for poststrike traffic losses, National's share of the three-carrier traffic total during April-August 1976 slipped two percentage points, worth $25-30 million in revenue, from the comparable 1975 period. During this time, Delta and Eastern's seat output grew by over 9 percent against only 2 percent for National.

CONCLUSION

Recent evidence fails to substantiate any economies of scale among the domestic Trunks, although diseconomies do appear to afflict the Local carriers. In the determination of intercarrier cost differences, the important explanatory variables decidedly stem from management decision making rather than structural factors. Thus, despite the fact that the airlines have been regulated throughout most of their history, considerable leeway exists with regard to corporate discretion and, as a consequence, varying financial outcomes have been the result. On the issue of fixed versus variable costs, the former do not appear to represent a great burden and the airlines who have claimed otherwise probably have done so as a means of rationalizing resistance to competitive cutbacks in capacity during periods of soft demand.

NOTES

1. Robert J. Gordon, "Airline Costs and Managerial Efficiency," Transportation Economics, A Conference of the Universities—National Bureau Committee for Economic Research,

Columbia University Press for the National Bureau of Economic Research, 1965, pp. 61-94.

2. U.S. Civil Aeronautics Board, Air Carrier Traffic Statistics, October 1976, pp. 51-58.

3. John B. Crane, "The Economics of Air Transportation," Harvard Business Review 22 (Summer 1944):495-509.

4. Harold D. Koontz, "Economic and Managerial Factors Underlying Subsidy Needs of Domestic Trunk Line Air Carriers," Journal of Air Law and Commerce 18 (Spring 1951):127-56.

5. Paul W. Cherington, Airline Price Policy: A Study of Domestic Fares (Cambridge, Mass.: Harvard University Press, 1958), pp. 42-62; Mahlon Straszheim, The International Airline Industry (Washington, D.C.: Brookings Institution, 1969), p. 96; George Eads, M. Nerlove, and W. Raduchel, "A Long-Run Cost Function for the Local Service Airline Industry," Review of Economics and Statistics 51 (August 1969):259-70; William Jordan, Airline Regulation in America: Effects and Imperfections (Baltimore: Johns Hopkins University Press, 1970), p. 228; James E. McMillen, "The Effect of Scale in the Airline Industry," M.S. thesis, Massachusetts Institute of Technology, September 1971; Samuel Reid and James Mohrfeld, "Airline Size, Profitability, Mergers, and Regulation," Journal of Air Law and Commerce 39 (1973).

6. Testimony of Julius Maldutis, Jr., vice-president, Salomon Brothers, before U.S. Department of Transportation Hearing, December 1, 1976.

7. Richard Caves, Air Transport and Its Regulators (Cambridge, Mass.: Harvard University Press, 1962), p. 59.

8. Calculated from U.S. Civil Aeronautics Board, Air Carrier Financial Statistics and Air Carrier Traffic Statistics, both September 1980.

9. Ibid.

10. Ibid.

11. Ibid.

12. Calculated from Air Carrier Financial Statistics and Air Carrier Traffic Statistics, various issues.

13. Ibid.

14. Calculated from Air Carrier Traffic Statistics, September 1980; and U.S. Civil Aeronautics Board Form 41, P-10 reports, various months.

15. Calculated from Air Carrier Financial Statistics and Air Carrier Traffic Statistics, September 1980.

16. Ibid.

17. Business Week, February 16, 1976, p. 80.

18. Joseph S. Murphy, "Fiscal Management Plus Cost Control Make Northwest Great," Air Transport World, September 1976, p. 21.

19. Caves, Air Transport, p. 82.

20. The Conference Board, Roadmaps of Industry, January 1977, No. 1799.

21. Ibid.

22. Calculated from Air Carrier Financial Statistics; and Form 41, P-10 Report, 1975.

23. Air Carrier Financial Statistics, June and September 1972.

24. Ibid.

25. Ibid.

26. Ibid.

27. Caves, Air Transport, p. 82.

4

BARRIERS TO ENTRY

Since 1938 the CAB has been the sole arbiter of entry and exit within the scheduled interstate air network although, under the 1978 Airline Deregulation Act, its authority in this area is scheduled to expire by 1982. The CAB has accomplished this through a formal route certification process in which carriers apply for authority to operate or to discontinue service. By preempting the operation of market forces in this area and by recognizing existing airlines primarily, the Board for most of its history helped to insulate the dominant position of the original "grandfather" Trunk carriers. However, the protectionist climate in the airline industry changed dramatically during the later stages of the deregulation debates of 1975-78 when the Board, under Alfred Kahn, began issuing permissive authority in route cases, granting practically all petitions for route authorizations. This action encouraged carriers to bid for certifications beyond their traditional spheres and sharply escalated the pace of market entry by existing firms. Subsequently, the Deregulation Act of 1978 spurred the CAB to award scheduled authority to the former Supplemental class and newly formed carriers, as well as to accord interstate certificates to the Intrastate airlines. With regard to exit decisions, no CAB permission had to be obtained as long as adequate services were maintained by the remaining carriers. The latter provision caused an exodus of larger airlines from unprofitable routes; their places were taken in many cases by new commuter carriers.

Prior to the deregulation era, the Board did encourage the development of other classes of carriers. These included the Locals and the Commuters, but not the Supplementals whose existence has been accorded only grudging acceptance and only after considerable Congressional pressure had been exerted. The evolution of the Locals, however, had not proceeded according to plan. Set up primarily as "feeder" airlines, some Locals competed actively with the Trunks in many large city pairs, especially after 1966 when the CAB drastically expanded Local route authority and after 1978 when several acquired a more Trunk-like market structure. For instance, among the leading 200 segments, the Locals achieved market shares in excess of 10 percent in 35 segments by 1980, compared to only 4 in 1965.[1] Moreover, Republic, the largest of the Locals, actually boarded more passengers than five Trunks in 1980.[2] Thus the clear size and structural distinctions that had existed between the Trunks and Locals, while still noticeable with regard to route structure, faded somewhat with the narrowing of differences coming about through the earlier "back-door" entry and later with the removal of restrictions on market participation. As large as the gains were for the Locals, expansion by former Intrastate carriers had been even more striking. By 1980, only two years after their unleashing, Pacific Southwest, Air Florida, Southwest, and Air California had achieved at least 10 percent shares in 12 of the top 200 interstate markets and were dominant in 5.[3] Moreover, new carriers that began operations in 1980 and 1981, including Midway, New York Air, and Peoples Express, insured continued market share incursions.

Since Bain's Barriers to New Competition, conventional analysis of the entry question has focused on three measurement factors—economies of scale, product differentiation, and absolute cost barriers. The first of these examines the size needed by an entrant to achieve unit cost levels that would prevent its competing from a position of weakness. New firms, whose scale of operation generates comparatively high unit costs, will find it difficult to survive. The degree of product differentiation indicates whether the entrant will have to overcome identification advantages generally associated with the established firms. If confronted by a situation in which the product of an incumbent is strongly recognized and preferred, the new firm could be forced to engage in costly marketing strategies, which would curtail profitability, at least temporarily. Absolute cost barriers refer to those factors that cause the costs confronting a new entrant to be higher than those of the existing carriers, apart from questions of scale.[4]

NEW ENTRY INTO TRUNK OPERATIONS

For a carrier intending to establish a Trunk-like operation, barriers would be formidable even if the certification precondition were to be satisfied. As illustrated earlier in Figure 3.1, a carrier would have to supply at least two billion available ton miles, or 4 percent of total 1980 Trunk output, in order to achieve unit costs comparable to those of the typical Trunk. Caves, utilizing 1958 data, also placed the minimum necessary output for a new Trunk at about 4 percent of the total industry supply. Thus, while the absolute size requisite had increased twelvefold since 1958, the minimum requirement has expanded at roughly the same rate.[5] A concrete estimate of the minimal optimum scale would require that a new entrant serve at least 30 cities, employ about 10,000 people, and maintain a fleet of approximately 70 jet aircraft.[6] As pointed out in Table 3.1, however, the obvious difficulties involved in operating below the minimum optimal scale have become less severe over the years, since the difference in unit costs between the Trunks and Locals has apparently narrowed significantly. In any case, the 4 percent output size attached to the minimum optimal scale did exceed that of a majority of the 20 manufacturing industries studied by Bain in 1951,[7] thus implying relatively high barriers under this form of measurement.

Product differentiation would appear to present far fewer problems to potential entrants currently than at an earlier point in time. This is because of the increased standardization of the basic product and a slowdown in the pace of technological activity. While most carriers now fly essentially the same equipment and customer services are virtually identical, this was not the case earlier, particularly with respect to aircraft. New airplanes appeared with a greater frequency during the preceding two decades and this enabled some carriers to achieve product differentiation, since competing firms could match equipment innovations only after a lengthy time lag. Other marketing improvements involving in-flight amenities, for instance, could usually be copied relatively quickly.

Another potential area for product differentiation, but one that has largely been discounted, is concerned with the issue of safety. Presumably, a new airline might be forced to offer less elaborate service, and such austerity might invite questions about equipment maintenance and pilot experience. Passenger surveys have indicated great concern over safety among respondents, but the same respondents generally fail to discern any differences in this respect among the existing carriers.[8] The evidence does indicate that the certified carriers have had a better overall safety record than irregular operators. Data for the 1949-78 period on accidents per million miles flown showed a rate of only .041 for the scheduled CAB-certified carriers as against a .125 mark for the unscheduled charter airlines.[9] However, in later years, as the Supplementals were able to obtain newer equipment, the differences in the accident rate narrowed. For instance, in the 1970-78 period, the safety record of .027 for the Supplementals was only slightly behind that of the certified carriers, which recorded a .015 mark.[10]

Some airlines have been able to achieve a product advantage with respect to certain market groups. For instance, American over the years has been able to cultivate an image favored by businessmen who fly, while United, with its vast interconnected domestic route network, has established itself as the preferred carrier in many cities simply by virtue of its overwhelming number of destinations and flights offered. Even after the route certification process has been totally abandoned, probably neither of these examples will lose their potency because of their extended public awareness. Thus product differentiation does seem to pose some difficult, but certainly not insurmountable, problems for new entrants. Of course, a new entrant might be very selective in choosing markets in which to compete and thus avoid confrontations with strong, entrenched carriers. However, the discussion at this point only involves potential entry into a Trunk-like situation where such contact would be unavoidable.

With regard to absolute cost barriers in the Trunk context, the dominant issue involves the size of the capital requirement and the potential financing difficulties. As shown earlier, recent data suggest that a carrier would have to be able to make available approximately two billion ton miles annually in order to achieve minimal optimum scale. The capital cost of building such an operation, if measured by the stockholders' equity and long-term debt of Continental, whose average capital was the smallest among the Trunks in 1980, would approximate $393 million.[11] Even this amount probably understates the true investment required, since operating losses could be expected at the outset of operations. Using the same criteria in 1958, Caves estimated minimum financial requirements to be less than $20 million,[12] which, after allowing for inflation (deflated by the implicit price deflator for gross national product), suggests a nearly sevenfold increase in the amount of constant dollar capital requirements. This real cost expansion stems, no doubt, from the greater technological sophistication of the equipment and the enlarged scope of the modern Trunk operation. In any case, the sheer magnitude of the financial requirement appears to represent a formidable barrier to entry.

This is not to say that such an imposing financial obstacle to Trunk entry would prevent the formation of a Trunk-sized carrier through the consolidation of smaller airlines. Indeed the lone merger of this type consummated in the wake of the 1978 Act satisfied the major criteria implied in Trunk status. The combination of North Central and Southern, approved in the spring of 1979 and the addition of Hughes Airwest in October 1980, created an entity whose total assets, operating revenues, passengers carried, number of aircraft, cities served, and number of employees exceeded those of the smallest Trunk airline on the basis of 1980 data.[13] Only in revenue passenger miles and available ton miles did the new carrier, known as Republic, fall below the comparable volumes of the smallest Trunk operator owing to the short-hop nature of the average passenger trip and limited range of its predominant aircraft type (DC-9). During 1981 two regional operators pursued small Trunk carriers aggressively. Air Florida, in the midst of an aggressive expansion, was seeking control of Western while Texas International, after unsuccessfully bidding for National and Trans World, was able to take control of Continental in October.

LIMITED MARKET ENTRY

Given the generally high natural entry barriers that would confront a new airline seeking a Trunk-sized operation, it would be useful to examine the barriers facing carriers interested in only entering a limited number of markets since, as a practical matter, this type of entry was encouraged by the Board in the period immediately preceding and following the signing of the Airline Deregulation Act of 1978. Thus far, limited entry has probably proceeded beyond the expectations of the deregulation proponents and especially in view of the favor accorded new carriers by the financial community. These carriers include existing firms formerly outside of the mainstream, such as the Intrastate airlines, the Supplementals, and brand new carriers. The early success of some Intrastate carriers in charging fares below those of comparable interstate airlines and remaining profitable, without subsidy, while operating in a limited number of segments against Trunk competition, was evidence enough that economies of scale could accrue to a specialized carrier, provided it maintained a proper mix of routes and aircrafts and kept costly amenities to a minimum. Two such carriers, Pacific Southwest, operating in California, and Texas-based Southwest Airlines, both demonstrated profitability, although the former was the only company of this type to have maintained a prolonged profit record. However, among all Trunk, Local, and Regional carriers, Southwest, despite being less than one-fifth the size of the smallest Trunk, had achieved unit costs lower than all in 1980, except for Northwest, by virtue of its simplicity of operation and high productivity.

Having operated since 1949, Pacific Southwest has reported airline losses only once (in 1975), after its first year,[14] while Southwest, having begun operation in 1971, became consistently profitable after mid-1973.[15] Pacific Southwest at first served only 3 cities with one DC-3,[16] but flew to 15 cities with 29 aircraft by the middle of 1981.[17] The carrier had launched interstate operations between San Diego and Las Vegas and from Oakland to Reno at the end of 1978 as regulations became liberalized and was serving seven interstate segments by the summer of 1981.[18]

Southwest began service in 1971 with 3 cities and 3 aircraft and had expanded to 14 cities, including 4 non-Texas points, and 25 aircraft by 1981.[19] Southwest started its initial interstate operation early in 1979 when it commenced Houston-New Orleans service. Southwest's development is proceeding much faster than the plan of careful growth chosen by Pacific Southwest during its early years. Five years after the inauguration of service, for example, Pacific Southwest's system had only added 1 city, while its fleet size was growing from 1 to 4 planes.[20] However, had the opportunities wrought by deregulation occurred earlier, a different course probably would have evolved.

Both carriers confronted varying degrees of product differentiation disadvantages while competing against the larger established carriers. In Pacific Southwest's case, the greatest problem involved equipment. Not until 1959, for example, over a decade later than its Trunk rivals, was the carrier able to supply pressurized aircraft.[21] Pacific Southwest still survived and prospered, however, by undercutting interstate carrier prices and achieving low operating costs. Many passengers preferred to fly older equipment at the cheaper fares and the question of safety did not appear to be a factor. Jordan has estimated Pacific Southwest's share of the dense Los Angeles area-San Francisco area markets at 15 percent in 1958, which was the year before the operation by that carrier of the pressurized Lockheed Electra.[22] With the new aircraft, however, Pacific Southwest nearly doubled its market share by 1960, even though fare differentials between the two types of carriers had narrowed considerably in the interim.[23] Thus its proven viability during the years of equipment inferiority had apparently accorded Pacific Southwest the necessary respectability and public recognition, enabling it to compete against the larger interstate airlines as an equal.

Southwest's only problem with respect to product differentiation involved public recognition, since it was able to immediately provide service with modern jet aircraft. Popular approval was gained by the slashing of fares upon entry and energetic marketing in the form of advertising, which depicted the carrier as an underdog, as well as free liquor, and attractive flight attendants. Sympathy had also been generated for the carrier by a lawsuit brought by its rivals, Braniff and Texas International, which had delayed its operation for over four years. After one year of service, Southwest had already acquired 40 percent of the Dallas-Houston market,[24] but despite this, it still was not profitable, and its survival would have been jeopardized had it not defeated a later lawsuit that had attempted to force the carrier to move, with all of the other airlines, from Love Field, which was close to Dallas, to the relatively distant, new Dallas/Fort Worth Airport, which opened in 1973. The president of the company at the time, M. Lamar Muse, admitted that the necessary capital outlays involved in the transfer would have been difficult to finance.[25] Braniff and Texas International did move to the modern, but less conveniently located facility, permitting Southwest to reap a form of monopoly windfall profit in the local Dallas-Houston market after 1973, which practically guaranteed its success. By 1980 Southwest had obtained 70 percent of the whole Dallas-Houston market.[26]

Although data for the period are lacking, the original capital required of Pacific Southwest must have been minuscule, especially in light of the glut of used aircraft on the market during the period immediately following World War II. In the case of Southwest, its long-term debt and stockholders' equity at the onset of service in 1971 totaled $13 million,[27] which was also relatively modest considering the size of its Texas competitors. For instance, Braniff's capital investment at the time amounted to $278 million, while that of Texas International, a Local service airline, stood at $26 million.[28]

However, the ostensible success of the two Intrastate carriers and their later imitators should not obscure the fact that the overwhelming majority of ventures of this type failed. In his study of the California experience between 1946 and 1965, Jordan noted that only 1 carrier (Pacific Southwest), out of 16 that operated during that period, was able to remain viable continuously, and just 1 other (California Central) stayed in business for as many as six years.[29] Since Jordan's work, another California airline, Air California, has also apparently been able to achieve comparable longevity. From a humble start in 1967 serving 2 California cities with 2 used Lockheed Electras, Air California was flying 18 aircraft in 13 cities by 1981 including 4 non-California points.[30] The airline was also a highly sought-after takeover target when its parent, Westgate-California, declared bankruptcy a year earlier. However, in 1980 Air California was a high-cost operator and apparently maintained profitability by virtue of monopolies or dominant positions in several large local markets emanating from Orange County airport.

The former Intrastate carrier that experienced the most dramatic expansion in the postderegulation environment was Air Florida whose route system included European, Central American, and Caribbean points by 1981 in addition to a much broadened domestic network reaching Texas, the midwest, as well as the northeast. Of the 40 cities in its system, only 13 were in Florida, its original base, and the far-flung system was characterized as comprising five distinct operating entities.[31]

Another class of "outside" carriers capable of achieving viability within the scheduled interstate network is the Supplemental or Charter operator, whose size and degree of public recognition may have already been substantial in some cases. Although the ranks of this class of carrier have thinned considerably over the years so that only four of them conducted meaningful domestic passenger operations during 1980,[32] the Supplementals had frequently petitioned the CAB for certification to scheduled service, arguing that while the scheduled Trunks and Locals also had permission to fly charters in competition against them, they never had reciprocal rights.

World Airways, whose history dates from 1948 and whose capital investment in 1980 totaled $284 million,[33] had long sought scheduled certification on selected transcontinental routes where it would be in competition against American, Trans World, and United. After an 11-year campaign, World finally obtained permanent authorization for scheduled transcontinental service in January 1979 and began operations from Los Angeles and Oakland to Newark and Baltimore the following April with DC-10 equipment.[34] Its unrestricted one-way fare of $108 without meals went unmatched by the Big Three carriers until United, after a two-month strike in late May, introduced a $108 tariff, including food service, which was immediately matched by American and two weeks later by Trans World. World, whose program was badly undercut by the competitive response, claimed that the United action was predatory and illegal. However, early in June before a court could rule on the charge, the Federal Aviation Administration grounded all DC-10 equipment following a disastrous accident in Chicago, and when the order was lifted in mid-July, a strike against World effectively ended its initial scheduled experiment. As of mid-1981, World was again operating the daily Newark-Baltimore-Los Angeles-Oakland circular pattern and a daily Los Angeles-Honolulu round trip. Transamerica (Trans International) and Capitol were the other Supplementals that appeared well situated to accomplish limited new route entry, with the former carrier having inaugurated scheduled international service early in 1979. Capitol, by the summer of 1981, was operating two daily New York-Los Angeles round trips and a New York-Chicago-Los Angeles flight in addition to several New York-Europe services.

The success in particular of Southwest, the Texas intrastate carrier, in capitalizing on a situation in which the airline could monopolize a convenient, but largely abandoned airport, spurred interest in similar possibilities elsewhere. Southwest itself filed an application with the CAB in 1976 for new interstate carrier status, requesting permission to conduct operations from Chicago's barely used, but well-located Midway Airport, to several midwest cities.[35] Authority to serve Oakland, California's underutilized airfield (because of its proximity to San Francisco) also attracted several new certification requests.[36] The Chicago-Midway issue similarly generated multiple requests for new operating authority, including one of Midway Airlines, a proposed new carrier. In its prospectus, the organizers announced plans to provide frequent service from Midway to Cleveland, Minneapolis, and St. Louis immediately upon certification, and to Detroit, Kansas City, and Pittsburgh within two years.[37] The proposed fleet would initially contain five short-range jet aircraft and total employment would number 400 at the outset. The capital requirement for this scale of operation was initially estimated at $55 million in the first year, of which $30 million would be raised by a stock offering.[38] Salomon Brothers, the investment banking firm, had committed itself to the successful financing of the venture, provided the certification was granted under favorable terms. Thus, despite generally mediocre industry-wide profitability and a high fatality rate among new entrants of the limited market type, in the California case, important financial backing for the Midway enterprise was available, indicating that the absolute cost barrier may be only as high as the relative attractiveness of the investment. Midway Airlines subsequently inaugurated a plan of service in November 1979 after arranging for a reliable fuel supply and raising $6 million to cover equipment leases and additional costs.[39] The fledgling carrier thus became the first of its kind to operate since the 1978 Deregulation Act with service between Chicago-Midway and Detroit, Cleveland, and Kansas City. As with Southwest, Midway achieved a quasi-monopoly because almost all Chicago air travel involved busy O'Hare Airport, which was less convenient to the downtown business district. Delta had already been operating a few daily flights out of Midway, but Northwest later inaugurated service to Minneapolis and successfully scared off the fledgling carrier from that market. Midway earned its first profit during the first quarter of 1981 and was serving eight cities from Chicago with nine DC-9 aircraft by that summer.[40]

A year after the Midway start-up, New York Air, which was organized as a subsidiary of Texas International and capitalized at $33 million, began a New York (LaGuardia)-Washington (National) service in competition with the popular Eastern shuttle.[41] This operation marked a departure from the Southwest/Midway example, where direct clashes with entrenched carriers were avoided while duplicating the strategy of sharply undercutting existing fares. Nevertheless, New York Air later expanded service from New York to Boston, Cleveland, and Louisville, which except for the Kentucky destination, were all served by a formidable incumbent. A Newark-Washington (National) operation was also initiated.[42]

In April 1981, a group of former Texas International executives launched Peoples Express with a base at underutilized Newark and a capitalization of $61 million, over 40 percent of which was raised by a public stock offering. This operation initially chose to serve points including Buffalo, Columbus, Norfolk, and Jacksonville but, two months later, added Washington and Boston.[43] A new intra-Hawaiian carrier, Mid-Pacific, began service between Honolulu-Maui/Kauai with three aircraft a month earlier and had allegedly acquired 10 percent of the two markets by June.[44]

The new airline boom created such interest that the newcomers themselves became the object of competition from groups anxious to emulate their ostensible success. The most ironic example of this phenomenon occurred in Texas where M. Lamar Muse, the founder of Southwest who was later ousted after a clash with his board, formed Muse Air, backed by $36 million, and commenced operations in Southwest's original base market—Dallas (Love)-Houston (Hobby)—during July 1981.[45] Another case involved Air Chicago, which was organized by two former Midway executives. The airline established a home base at Midway Airport with $50 million in capital with a late 1981 start-up schedule.[46] Meanwhile, other new carrier projects beyond the initial planning stage late in 1981 had names like Sun Pacific, Pacific Express, and Columbia Air.

The question of cabotage, or the granting to foreign airlines the privilege of operating within the United States, became an issue in April 1979, when due to an unexpected strike by United's workers, thousands of passengers were temporarily left without air transportation to and from Hawaii. While five other domestic carriers connected Hawaii to the mainland, the loss of United service, which amounted to roughly 50 percent of the available seat miles, caused immediate disruption.[47] In this setting, the Civil Aeronautics Board allowed foreign carriers such as Qantas, Singapore, and Japan Air Lines to carry local Hawaii-U.S. mainland traffic, formerly forbidden, on their regular Pacific routes. This cabotage brought loud protests from the incumbent airlines, which wanted a full share of the windfall, and their unions. The ruling was lifted in a matter of days, but in later hearings on proposed international aviation legislation, the State Department took a procabotage position, claiming that U.S. negotiators in bilateral dealings should have maximum flexibility and might be able to gain reciprocal rights for U.S. carriers. The Transportation Department and CAB opposed cabotage except under extreme emergency conditions where passengers were stranded or businesses disrupted.[48] In any case, cabotage represents another possible opportunity for new domestic entry.

NOTES

1. Compiled from U.S. Civil Aeronautics Board, Competition Among Domestic Air Carriers, vol. VI, January 1-December 31, 1965, Tables 1 and 3; and Origin-Destination Survey, third quarter 1980, Table 10.

2. U.S. Civil Aeronautics Board, Air Carrier Traffic Statistics, December 1980.

3. Origin-Destination Survey, third quarter 1980, Table 10.

4. Joe S. Bain, Barriers to New Competition (Cambridge, Mass.: Harvard University Press, 1956), p. 85.

5. Richard E. Caves, Air Transport and Its Regulators (Cambridge, Mass.: Harvard University Press, 1962), p. 86.

6. Moody's Investors Service, Moody's Transportation Manual, 1977 (section on Western Airlines).

7. Bain, New Competition, pp. 71-86.

8. Opinion Research Corporation, Determinants of Airline Selection—U.S. Business and Non-Business Travelers, Princeton, N.J., 1969.

9. U.S. Civil Aeronautics Board, Handbook of Airline Statistics, 1973 edition, part VII, item 19A, p. 592; Supplement to Handbook of Airline Statistics, November 1975, part VII, item 19A, p. 181; Supplement to Handbook of Airline Statistics, December 1977, and December 1979, part VIII, item 19.

10. Ibid.

11. U.S. Civil Aeronautics Board, Air Carrier Financial Statistics, December 1980.

12. Caves, Air Transport, p. 89.

13. Air Carrier Traffic Statistics, December 1980; Air Transport Association, Air Transport 1981, pp. 6-7.

14. PSA Inc., various annual reports.

15. Southwest Airlines, various annual reports.

16. William A. Jordan, Airline Regulation in America (Baltimore: Johns Hopkins University Press, 1970), pp. 259, 273.

17. Official Airline Guide, July 1981 edition; PSA Inc., Annual Report 1978, p. 11.

18. PSA Inc., Annual Report 1978, p. 11.

19. Aviation Week and Space Technology, April 11, 1977, p. 30; Official Airline Guide, July 1981 edition.

20. Jordan, Airline Regulation, pp. 259, 273.

21. Ibid., p. 40.

22. Ibid., p. 312.

23. Ibid.

24. Aviation Week and Space Technology, July 3, 1972, p. 33.

25. Ibid.

26. Origin-Destination Survey, third quarter 1980, Table 10.

27. Moody's Transportation Manual 1976, p. 1366.

28. Air Carrier Financial Statistics, September 1971.

29. Jordan, Airline Regulation, pp. 17-19.

30. Ibid., p. 131.

31. Robert Joedicke, vice-president, Lehman Bros., Kuhn Loeb, Speech at Air Transport Association seminar, Seattle, Washington, June 3, 1981.

32. Air Carrier Traffic Statistics, December 1980.

33. Air Carrier Financial Statistics, December 1980.

34. Airline Executive, April 1979, p. 67.

35. Aviation Week and Space Technology, February 7, 1977, p. 30.

36. Aviation Week and Space Technology, April 18, 1977, p. 32.

37. Prospectus of Midway Airlines, A Regional Air Service, September 15, 1976.

38. Ibid.

39. Aviation Daily, August 2, 1979, p. 177.

40. Business Week, June 15, 1981, p. 84.

41. Ibid., p. 78.

42. Aviation Week and Space Technology, June 1, 1981, pp. 30-33.

43. Business Week, June 15, 1981, p. 80.

44. Stephan Halliday, vice-president, Finance, Aloha Airlines, Speech at Air Transport Association Seminar, Seattle, June 3, 1981.

45. Business Week, June 15, 1981, p. 80; Aviation Week and Space Technology, August 17, 1981, p. 44.

46. Ibid.

47. Aviation Daily, April 7, 1979, p. 39.

48. Aviation Daily, August 22, 1979, pp. 289-90.

5

THE IMPACT OF INPUT MARKETS

The climate in which airlines purchase goods and services may have a bearing on their conduct and performance. While the air transport industry can be regarded as oligopsonistic, it primarily interacts with suppliers that are also highly concentrated or even monopolistic, as in the case of the airline pilots union. When both buyers and sellers are highly concentrated, the usually close relationship between the two may lead to a breakdown in any market mechanism for goods allocation or for setting a single price. In buying a necessary input such as new aircraft, for instance, one carrier may obtain preferential treatment from an aircraft manufacturer in price or a temporary monopoly by ordering a new model early and thus have a competitive edge over a less fortunate rival. Problems may arise when a buyer confronts a stronger seller. With regard to the labor market, for example, carriers employing exclusively union personnel may have to pay higher salaries and may not deploy resources with the same degree of flexibility as others less subject to a union presence. When attempting to raise capital, airlines must compete for funds with other industries as well as among themselves, so that questions of relative strength between buyer and seller are less relevant than in the aircraft and labor markets. Nevertheless, since financial institutions must discriminate between good and bad investments when apportioning loanable funds, airlines on a sounder financial basis than others generally find their already advantageous position reinforced by having better access to credit sources. The following section will examine in greater detail the three main input markets—aircraft, labor, and capital—and their influence on airline conduct and performance, as well as Caves' prediction concerning the importance of airline size in the competition for loanable funds.

AIRCRAFT MARKET

The more recent airline/aircraft manufacturer relationship differs substantially from the early days of the industry, when vertical holding companies combined buyers and sellers of aircraft under the same corporate umbrella. During the 1930s, United Airlines and Boeing were elements of the same corporation and General Motors controlled Douglas Aircraft, together with Trans World, Western, and Eastern Airlines.[1] These arrangements held advantages and disadvantages for the airlines, depending on the quality of the aircraft product. It has been alleged, for instance, that United Airlines absorbed competitive setbacks because aircraft manufactured by Douglas were deemed superior to those of Boeing, whose equipment United was obliged to use through corporate ties.[2]

The Civil Aeronautics Act of 1938 formally banned such corporate combinations, but close interrelationships persisted in a different form. Prior to the 1970s, the dominant example had been in the area of aircraft development where the manufacturer and one or several airlines collaborated on the basic design and agreed on an initial production run with the understanding that nonparticipating carriers be excluded from early delivery positions and be subject to higher prices. The rationale for this approach was that in its absence, manufacturers ran the risk of absorbing enormous developmental expenditures without any assurance that a program could enter commercially successful production, even though following World War II, military research and development grants often mitigated the element of financial risk. However, the dimension of the danger was most recently underscored in 1971 when, in developing its L-1011 program without adequate advance commitments, Lockheed approached bankruptcy before the federal government pledged $246 million in loan guarantees.[3]

Apart from the presumed advantage gained over nonparticipants in obtaining exclusive use of new equipment at favorable prices, participating buyers stood to earn another advantage if the carriers in the agreement competed against each other. By operating the same equipment at roughly the same time, rivals would be shielded from the risk of aircraft inferiority. Operators of the Lockheed Electra in the early 1960s and the DC-10 in the late 1970s learned the competitive hazards of flying accident-prone aircraft. In 1955, when competing Boeing 707 and Douglas DC-8 long-distance jet designs became available, United Airlines unsuccessfully attempted to swing the major carriers behind the purchase of a single airplane, allegedly because of the insecurity involved in ordering the inferior model.[4] The major risk from the standpoint of the seller in the "pooled purchase" arrangement involved setting too

low a price for a new aircraft type. For instance, while Martin
beat Convair out of an order for 65 aircraft from Eastern and
Trans World in 1950, it was forced into a financial reorganization
two years later because of unmanageable cost overruns in the production of the 4-0-4 model.[5]

Commercial airframe manufacture has always been highly
concentrated and the number of firms has dwindled over time. (The
same can be said for the engine manufacturers.) Table 5.1 compares the airplane industry at the time of Caves' industry study with
the more current arrangement in terms of the existing inventories
of aircraft built by different manufacturers. Over the course of
21 years, Boeing, from a mere 7 percent in 1960, came to account
for 75 percent of the Trunk equipment on hand. Meanwhile, the
shares of Douglas (now McDonnell Douglas) and Lockheed shrank
considerably, while manufacturers such as Convair, Martin, and
Vickers, a British firm, have disappeared altogether. The ascen-
dence of Boeing was propelled by the early success of the long-
distance B-707 models and later by the shorter-distance B-727.
All versions of the latter type went on to become the best selling
airliner in history with sales in excess of 1,800 by the middle of
1981.[6] Boeing was also the first manufacturer to produce the
highly regarded wide-body jumbo jet.

TABLE 5.1

Trunk Airline Equipment Inventory
by Manufacturer, 1960 and 1981
(percentage distribution)

Manufacturer	1960	1981
Boeing	7	75
Convair	13	—
Douglas	43	18
Lockheed	24	6
Martin	6	—
Vickers	6	—
Others	1	1
Total	100	100

Sources: U.S. Civil Aeronautics Board, Handbook of Airline
Statistics, 1973 edition, Table 7b, p. 437; Pan American World
Airways, Aircraft Inventory and Orders of Selected Airlines, Fleet
Planning Dept., February 17, 1981.

Foreign penetration of the domestic market has been virtually nil after the initial success of the Vickers turboprop aircraft, first operated domestically by **Capital** Airlines in 1955. Until Eastern's purchase of the Airbus Industrie middle-distance, two-engine, wide-body A-300 in 1978, no European aircraft had been sold to a domestic Trunk carrier for 15 years.[7] However, a derivative of the A-300 did provide the principal competition for the Boeing B-767, which was ordered by United, American, and Delta in 1978 and Trans World in 1979 for delivery in 1982.

The reduction over time in the number of airframe manufacturers has apparently failed to affect negatively the relative position of the domestic carriers in the buyer/seller relationship. Ostensibly, one might hypothesize a situation in which a dominant seller could dictate terms to buyers who are given a paucity of alternatives. However, the airlines have lately become more cautious in decisions concerning equipment, which is a mood caused by the overexpansion of capacity and financial reversals absorbed in the early 1970s. This contrasts sharply with the fascination that earlier managements, which were dominated by pilot types, had for new aircraft. As a consequence, manufacturers have been unable to count on the sponsorship by airlines of new aircraft programs. The suggestion that a single airplane be manufactured by a single builder was again aired, this time by Frank Borman, president of Eastern, who called for the Air Transport Association to coordinate the specifications.[8] Before embarking on the B-767 program, Boeing vigorously but unsuccessfully pursued joint development and production arrangements with foreign manufacturers as a way to dilute the risk of the new undertaking.[9] Having failed in this effort, Boeing decided to gamble on developing an entirely new commercial transport program on its own. Meanwhile, its major domestic competitors, Lockheed and McDonnell Douglas, which were less financially secure, chose to offer derivatives of existing aircraft for the coming re-equipment phase, which promised to be substantial, given normal replacement requirements and the stringent environmental rules laid down by the federal government. Boeing judged that the principal market opportunity would focus on a transcontinental-range aircraft seating 180-200 passengers, but could not decide whether two or three engines were preferable.[10] Two large potential customers, American and United, had expressed interest in the new aircraft design, but each had indicated a preference for a different number of engines, United favoring the two-engine model and American the three-engine type. So as not to displease either, Boeing decided to offer both models, despite an estimate that the total development costs could approach $2 billion.[11] Subsequently, as traffic growth accelerated in 1977 and 1978, restoring a measure of

financial health to the industry, United made a sizeable order for
the two-engine version during mid-1978 and American, joined by
Delta, also ordered the two-engine model, but with a slightly longer
range, later in the year. The 1978 decisions for the two-engine
B-767 aircraft saved Boeing the expense of further development on
the three-engine B-777 and solidified Boeing's position as the leading aircraft manufacturer.

However, the competition for the United order between Boeing
and Airbus Industrie suggests that the buyer, not the seller, was in
the more advantageous position. For instance, Percy Wood, executive vice-president and chief operating officer at United, re-
marked that, "It's the first instance I can recall of a single carrier
negotiating with two manufacturers to get the best plane. . . ."[12]
The result was that United virtually dictated the specifications of
the B-767, which was in sharp contrast to earlier times when manufacturers played off overanxious airlines against one another to
obtain higher prices. During the negotiations, Airbus Industrie
offered three different fuselage lengths in an effort to please
United. [13] In the later deal, American was able to gain a "more
reasonable" final price from Boeing as a result of the intense
Boeing-Airbus competition. [14] Thus, despite the smaller number
of manufacturers, the airlines appear to have strengthened their
relative bargaining position, at least in the initial phases of a new
aircraft program.

The main importance of new aircraft purchases for airline
conduct and performance, however, lies not so much in the
buyer/seller relationship as in the potential advantage implicit in
the fact that the larger carriers are generally the first to place
new aircraft into service. Given the substantial financial requirements, only large carriers can afford to commit funds for unproven
aircraft and so stand to benefit in terms of product improvement,
provided the equipment fulfills its promise. Particularly if the
new aircraft represents a technological or service breakthrough,
the advantage will remain until the time when rivals can secure
competitive equipment. Occasionally there may be drawbacks in
being the first with new equipment, for example, when the new
equipment develops unforeseen problems. Also, carriers lacking
new equipment may overcome competitive difficulties through
aggressive scheduling or pricing. These strategies will be examined in greater detail in subsequent chapters.

LABOR MARKET

The impact of the labor organization on airline conduct and
performance has been dramatically demonstrated in comparisons

between two active rivals, Delta and Eastern. Within the airline industry, only Delta has escaped large-scale unionization. Elsewhere labor unions have blanketed the flight and ground occupations and have extensively covered the reservation and clerical job classifications, but the pilots comprise the lone unionized group at Delta. The latter has regularly operated over the last 18 years at profit levels in excess of the industry average. On the other hand, Eastern, which competes directly with Delta on over 80 percent of its route miles, including more than 90 markets,[15] has been a laggard in regard to earnings. For the period 1975-80, while Delta accumulated net income of $609 million, Eastern reported only $95 million in profits. During the 1965-74 span, the Delta margin had been even greater.[16]

One advantage maintained by Delta has been in the equipment area, where poor earlier planning by Eastern relegated it to a fleet of relatively older, smaller, and less efficient aircraft. Moreover, Delta, through its route system, has been able to carry a slightly higher proportion of monopoly (20 percent) market traffic than Eastern (15 percent), although both have far exceeded the industry average in that regard.[17] Nevertheless, as Table 5.2 indicates, Delta, despite paying somewhat higher average salaries, has far surpassed Eastern in productivity, enabling it to obtain a decided edge in unit labor costs. Employment costs include salaries and benefits. Employee productivity is derived by dividing revenue ton miles for all passenger and cargo services by the number of employees, and unit labor costs are produced by dividing employee costs by total revenue ton miles.

In addition to Delta's superior performance in terms of productivity, it is possible that employment costs per employee might also have been in Delta's favor had it been possible to segregate Eastern's large-scale involvement in the Caribbean and Mexico routes, where wage rates were probably lower than those of the mainland. The major advantage in not dealing with unions is not so much with regard to salaries, but in the area of work rules, where line personnel may work longer hours and where management can better fit the available labor supply to meet demand without union resistance.

The imbalances in profitability produced by labor, in conjunction with the other variables mentioned, have contributed to what has been termed an unusually belligerent competition played out primarily in the important Northeast-Florida markets and in cities, particularly Atlanta where, through scheduling escalation over the years, the two airlines carried all but 10 percent of all passengers passing through the city in 1979, despite the fact that nine other airlines operated there.[18]

TABLE 5.2

Comparative Labor Cost and Productivity Measures
for Delta and Eastern, 1975-80

	Delta (dollars)	Eastern (dollars)	Delta as a Percentage of Eastern
Employment cost per employee	27,693	27,110	2.2
Employee productivity (thousands)	76,351	72,440	5.4
Unit labor cost	36.27	37.42	(3.1)

Sources: Compiled from U.S. Civil Aeronautics Board, Handbook of Airline Statistics; 1977 and 1979 Supplements, part VII, Table 16; and Form 41 tables for 1979 and 1980.

Apart from individual carrier issues, a wider question involving the price of labor services involves the way in which the industry manages rising wage rates. Between 1970 and 1980, for instance, average airline employee compensation rose by 9.6 percent a year, while fares advanced by only 6.8 percent per annum.[19] As traffic growth inevitably slows and productivity breakthroughs become less frequent, either some means must be devised to constrain labor costs or air transportation prices must increase more steeply if the industry is to remain viable.

Forced to deal with strong unions and faced with uncertain passenger loyalty, most airlines have been loath to accept work stoppages. For their part, the representative unions, including ALPA (pilots), IAM (aircraft-servicing personnel), and the Teamsters (ground-service personnel), have successfully resisted industry-wide negotiations and instead have engaged in "whipsawing" or bargaining with individual carriers. This establishes precedents for the next round of negotiations. Nevertheless, the various measures of the relative number of job actions and lost working time indicate that the airlines are somewhat less strike-prone than other highly unionized industries.[20] This is not surprising considering the cost of a strike to an airline. Even the Mutual Aid Pact of 1958, which mitigated revenue losses for its members during a strike, did not eliminate losses. Although the provisions

and size of membership changed over the years before it was
banned by the Airline Deregulation Act of 1978, the Mutual Aid Pact
long represented a measure of strike insurance. The members
whose workers were not on strike reimbursed the shutdown carrier
with a portion of normal operating revenue, which diminished with
the length of the strike and ended once a tentative contract was
signed. When Mutual Aid payments ceased, however, the struck
carrier faced a situation in which passengers had already booked
trips on competing carriers.

The length of the strike period generally determines the speed
with which struck carriers may regain normal traffic shares.
Naturally, lengthy shutdowns necessitate a longer recovery period.
However, as shown in Table 5.3, even short strikes can take a
costly toll. In December 1975, United, the largest Trunk carrier,
experienced a 16-day strike,[21] during which time Mutual Aid
cushioned revenue losses. At the conclusion of the strike just before Christmas, the airline could count immediately only on the
return of passengers who could not find space on other carriers
and who flew on United's monopoly segments where the alternatives
usually involved complicated circuitous routings. Because of its
intense rivalry with American and Trans World, United's market
share remained depressed throughout the first quarter of 1976,
despite a full resumption of service. Where United had obtained
21.7 percent of Trunk traffic on a 20.8 percent share of available
seat miles during the first quarter of 1975, its traffic share declined by 1.1 percentage points to 20.6 percent, while its capacity
share decreased nominally. Concurrently, American's traffic
share rose by a 0.5 percentage point, while that of Trans World
increased by 0.4. Other factors obviously played some role in the
market share deterioration, but nevertheless, United reported a
loss for the first quarter of 1976 of $70.5 million, or a decline of
almost $50 million from the $20.6 million loss of the same period
in the prior year. Meanwhile, the aggregate loss for the Trunk
carriers, including United, for the first quarter of 1976 amounted
to $81.9 million, which represented a $20.4 million deterioration
from the prior year's loss of $61.5 million. These figures suggest
that United should have perhaps only lost $40 million instead of the
reported $70.5 million.

The aftershock of strikes is well known to airline managements and this has usually made them less resistant to union de-
mands. The one carrier to maintain a consistently hard-line attitude toward its contract employees has been Northwest, whose
frequent strikes have usually been long and bitter affairs. However, that carrier's resulting low-cost structure, high productivity,
and relatively high level of monopoly segments have enabled it to

TABLE 5.3

Measuring the Impact of United Strike,
December 6-21, 1975, on Traffic
Share and Net Earnings

	United as a Percentage of Trunk		Reported Net Loss (millions of dollars)	
	Traffic	Capacity	United	Trunk
First quarter 1975	21.7	20.8	20.6	61.5
First quarter 1976	20.6	20.7	70.5	81.9

Sources: Compiled from U.S. Civil Aeronautics Board, Air Carrier Traffic Statistics, March 1976; and Air Carrier Financial Statistics, March 1976.

remain among the most profitable. Nevertheless, the generally pliable attitude exhibited by most airlines has resulted in a wage structure far in excess of other oligopolistic and highly unionized industries; average annual salaries exceed advanced grades in some professional occupations. Table 5.4 compares the mean airline industry salary (exclusive of benefits) based on American, Trans World, and United with those in selected industries and occupations for 1979. It should also be noted that since the late 1960s, average airline salaries have increased much faster than those of any of the employee groups shown in Table 5.4.[22] Even when pilots, who averaged $54,700, are omitted from the figures for airlines, the industry average is comparatively high. The remaining airline workers consist of office workers, stewardesses, mechanics, ticket sellers, reservations personnel, etc., only a small portion of whom might be considered highly skilled. Yet their average salary exceeded those of the broad classes shown as well as third-level accountants.

TABLE 5.4

Average Annual Salaries of Airline Employees
and Other Selected Groups in 1979
(dollars)

Classification	Average Annual Salary
All airline employees*	24,924
Airline employees less pilots*	21,293
Private nonagricultural production workers	11,435
All manufacturing production workers	13,985
Nonsupervisory contract construction workers	17,768
Engineers III	21,931
Accountants III	19,468
Attorneys III	29,644

*Figures are based on American, Trans World, and United.
Sources: U.S. Department of Labor, Bureau of Labor Statistics, Bulletin 2070, Handbook of Labor Statistics 1980, Tables 91 and 121; airline figures from U.S. Civil Aeronautics Board, Form 41 reports, Series p. 5, and p. 10 for 1979.

CAPITAL MARKET

With regard to capital markets, the airlines compete for loanable funds not only with one another, but with all industries, so that questions of oligopoly or oligopsony are not pressing. The fact that financial institutions have finite resources requires a capital-rationing process in which credit is allotted on the basis of rate of return and safety. As an industry, domestic air transport has neither been outstandingly profitable nor among the less volatile in terms of earnings. However, while no Trunk carrier thus far has gone bankrupt, most industry mergers have involved a failing carrier.[23] Consequently, whenever internal financing has proved insufficient, the airlines have usually been able to raise outside funds, but subject to covenants generally more stringent than those affecting other industries. At the end of 1980, the Trunk carriers had 4.7 billion worth of long-term debt on their books.[24]

The implications of capital rationing by lenders for airline conduct and performance center on the relative difficulty with which individual carriers are able to obtain outside financing. Since earnings history and prospects represent the principal criteria according to which lenders distribute funds, carriers demonstrating a better record of profitability will be favored by lending institutions, while less profitable airlines will be neglected.

Outside sources have usually provided the principal funding for the recurring equipment cycles, which means that firms already trailing in profitability face further deterioration in earnings due to an inability to operate competitive aircraft if lenders deny them the necessary funds or place too stringent restrictions on management prerogatives. Carriers such as Northeast and Capital were forced to suspend equipment orders during the 1950s, [25] while in the 1970s funds for expansion were denied several airlines including Eastern, Pan American, and Trans World. [26] An irony of the capital-rationing situation is that the more profitable companies may increasingly finance expansion internally and hence rely less on capital markets.

A comparison of carriers of roughly equal size, such as Delta and Eastern, indicates how debt-level differentials can evolve. By the end of 1980, for instance, while consistently profitable, Delta carried a long-term debt burden of $165 million; Eastern, with a history of earnings instability, owed $754 million. [27] Eastern sought in 1978 to upgrade its fleet, but mainly because of very favorable financing terms, purchased 23 new European-built Airbus Industrie A-300 aircraft. The latter company, seeking to obtain a foothold in the U.S. aircraft market, first lent four A-300s free of charge to Eastern for the winter 1977-78, and then sold the 23 aircraft through European export-financing sources; one-third of the total capital involved was made available at a low interest rate of 8.25 percent. [28]

Writing in 1961, Caves expected the capital-rationing process to result in the larger carriers becoming even more dominant than they were at that time. [29] This prediction was based on trends up to 1960 that showed that the so-called Big Three carriers, including American, Trans World, and United, generally recorded better financial results than the smaller airlines, consisting of Braniff, Continental, Delta, National, Northwest, and Western. Table 5.5 indicates comparative rates of return in the 1959-65 period based on net income after special items expressed as a percentage of gross operating property and equipment. The latter is representative of physical assets. Caves apparently assumed that the forces working to redress the imbalance, such as the CAB's system of route awards that favored the smaller carriers, would be ineffective.

We explored in Chapter 3 the reasons for differentials in profitability. In any case, after 1960 and through 1965, the rate

of return for the allegedly weaker airlines consistently exceeded
that of the Big Three and would have done so even if the poorest
performer among the Big Three, Trans World, were removed
from the measurement. During this period, Trans World experienced severe equipment disadvantages due to the unwillingness of
Howard Hughes, who controlled the airline, to order adequate numbers of jet aircraft to compete with American and United.[30]

TABLE 5.5

Large and Small Carrier Net Income as a Percentage
of Gross Physical Assets, 1959-65

	Big Three[a]	Smaller Six[b]
1959	3.62	3.08
1960	1.90	0.60
1961	Negative	1.93
1962	0.56	4.24
1963	2.62	4.61
1964	4.19	7.91
1965	5.32	9.83

[a]American, Trans World, and United.
[b]Braniff, Continental, Delta, National, Northwest, and
Western.
Source: Compiled from U.S. Civil Aeronautics Board,
Handbook of Airline Statistics, 1969 edition, tables of individual
carrier income statements and balance sheets.

Since the mid-1960s, the larger carriers as a group have
only infrequently recorded a better rate of return, with the result
that several smaller airlines currently rank highest in the esteem
of investors. According to New York Stock Exchange rankings as
of mid-July 1981, the carriers that were not threatened with takeovers and had the highest price-earnings ratios included Northwest, Delta, Southwest, and Pacific Southwest. United and American, the two largest domestic carriers, lacked any earnings
upon which to base a ratio and were out of the investors' favor.

NOTES

1. Elsbeth E. Freudenthal, The Aviation Business from Kitty Hawk to Wall Street (New York: Vanguard Press, 1940), pp. 200-12.

2. Frank J. Taylor, High Horizons—The United Airlines Story (New York: McGraw-Hill, 1958), p. 110.

3. Aviation Week and Space Technology, August 9, 1971, pp. 24-25.

4. Richard E. Caves, Air Transport and Its Regulators (Cambridge, Mass.: Harvard University Press, 1962), p. 311.

5. Alexander McSurely, "Management Key to Martin Money," Aviation Week and Space Technology, January 14, 1952, p. 18.

6. Sales Department, Boeing Company, Seattle.

7. New York Times, April 9, 1978, section 3, p. 4.

8. Business Week, April 12, 1976, p. 67.

9. Ibid., p. 64.

10. Robert J. Serling, "Boeing Goes for Broke," Airline Executive, February 1978, p. 13.

11. Ibid., p. 15.

12. Harlan Byrne and Eileen Kelliher, "Huge Jetliner Order Cost United Airlines Months of Hard Work," Wall Street Journal, September 25, 1978, p. 1.

13. Ibid., p. 34.

14. Richard O'Lone, "American, Delta Order 767's," Aviation Week and Space Technology, November 20, 1978, p. 34.

15. Jim Montgomery, "Eastern Airlines Fires New Salvos in Attempt to Slow Delta's Gains," Wall Street Journal, April 12, 1978, p. 1.

16. Compiled from U.S. Civil Aeronautics Board, 1977 and 1979 Supplements to Handbook of Airline Statistics, 1973 edition and various issues of Airline Financial Statistics.

17. Compiled from U.S. Civil Aeronautics Board, Origin-Destination Survey, third quarter 1980, Table 10.

18. U.S. Department of Transportation, Airport Activity Statistics, calendar year 1979, Tables 6, pp. 58-59.

19. Air Transport Association, Air Transport 1981, p. 11.

20. U.S. Department of Labor, Bureau of Labor Statistics, Handbook of Labor Statistics 1980, Tables 169-71, pp. 417-29.

21. U.S. Civil Aeronautics Board, Air Carrier Traffic Statistics, December 1976, p. 88.

22. Compiled from Air Transport Association, Air Transport 1978, p. 33; and U.S. Department of Labor, Bureau of Labor Statistics, Handbook of Labor Statistics 1977, various tables.

76 / THE U.S. AIRLINE INDUSTRY

23. George Douglas and James Miller III, Economic Regulation of Domestic Air Transportation (Washington, D.C.: Brookings Institution, 1974), pp. 120-22.

24. U.S. Civil Aeronautics Board, Air Carrier Financial Statistics, December 1980, p. 52.

25. American Aviation, July 28, 1958, p. 54; and Aviation Week and Space Technology, June 24, 1957, p. 42.

26. Aviation Week and Space Technology, September 24, 1975, p. 35.

27. U.S. Civil Aeronautics Board, Air Carrier Financial Statistics, December 1980, p. 56.

28. New York Times, April 9, 1978, section 3, p. 4.

29. Caves, Air Transport, p. 112.

30. C. Murphy and T. Wise, "The Problem of Howard Hughes," Fortune, January 1959, p. 166.

31. New York Times, July 14, 1981, pp. D9-D10.

6

GOVERNMENT REGULATION
AND ITS DEMISE

Public regulation of business in the United States is exercised at local, state, and federal levels and covers industries accounting for roughly 13 percent of the gross national product in recent years.[1] Under legal precedents established from 1877 through the 1930s, regulations came to be applicable to any industry whose actions somehow were "cloaked in the public interest." These included natural monopolies involving electric power, gas, and telephone, where protection against price exploitation and deterioration of vital services may be warranted, and other industries utilizing a limited resource in their operations, such as radio and television broadcasting, or industries allegedly prone to "destructive" competition. The transportation industries were most inclined to be grouped under the latter designation, following the price wars among the railroads in the late nineteenth century, which endangered the financial health of many lines. The Interstate Commerce Act of 1887 created a commission to regulate the railroads, while common and contract motor carriers, as well as interstate water operators, were later brought under its control. The Civil Aeronautics Act of 1938, which was modeled on the Interstate Commerce Act, conferred regulatory jurisdiction on the Civil Aeronautics Board.

The regulatory commissions have been the subject of substantial scholarly study, but the broad issues, such as whether industry performance might be substantially different without supervision or whether the costs of regulation outweigh the benefits, have until lately received less attention than the decisions and decision-making processes of the agencies.

Perhaps the most notable early study on the impact of regulation was that of Stigler and Friedland. It was an examination made in 1962 of the determinants of regulated and nonregulated electricity rates through 1937.[2] This analysis suggested that factors other than regulation, such as per capita income, the size and density of markets, and the proportion of power generated by hydroelectric plants, explained interstate variations in average prices. They concluded that (1) regulation was ineffective because the individual utilities did not hold sufficient long-run monopoly power; and (2) regulation could not force any utility to operate at a specific output, price, and cost combination because of a declining cost curve and a lag in regulation. The Stigler-Friedland study has been criticized on methodological grounds,[3] but found support in a later analysis by Moore,[4] who concluded that actual electricity rates charged by the regulated Detroit electric utility were nearly identical to those that would have been expected from an unregulated monopolist. In contrast, Kahn, in his two-volume study of regulation,[5] questioned the Stigler-Friedland hypothesis, mainly on the ground that regulation in one locality may influence unregulated rates in another, either through competition or imitation. Kahn went on to offer numerous examples from the transportation field in support of this conclusion. One of these indicated that even though the principal thrust of regulation was in price management, agencies also exerted considerable influence by imposing service standards.[6] In addition, he pointed out that commissions generally decided where firms could operate through a licensing system for routes, wavelengths, etc.[7]

Some observers have also examined ways in which regulation may distort natural behavior. For instance, if the targeted return on investment set by the regulators is greater than the replacement cost of capital, this may generate an unnecessarily high capital investment base. Conversely, when the permissible rate of return is below the current cost of capital, this may lead to too low a level of investment. The principal work in this area was that of Averch and Johnson,[8] and later Wellisz,[9] whose conclusions have come to be known as the A-J-W effect[10] to describe incentives or disincentives to investment and output introduced by regulation. While empirical evidence has been presented on either side, it seems fair to state that the A-J-W model is probably more descriptive of monopoly rather than of nonmonopoly situations, since the same prices are set by several firms. With respect to the airlines, for instance, an industry-wide standard rate of return basically governed fare decisions between 1960 and 1977; the fact that the rate was rarely achieved is evidence of its relative height. Since the A-J-W effect infers conscious investment decisions in response to regulatory action or inaction, this would suggest that the great majority of firms expanded investment in concert in order to receive fare increases, since one firm acting alone could not influence the investment base. While airline equipment expansion has been characterized as being inefficiently rapid,[11] the preponderance of evidence indicates that investment decisions have primarily been based on the need for new equipment for route expansion and as a competitive device. Further, long-standing CAB policy, which disallowed differential fares based on the type of equipment, also served to encourage investment in new aircraft.

The general issue of the proper regulatory role has also generated a body of literature.[12] Here the question involves whether the agency essentially acts in the public interest or pursues policies designed to protect the industry in its charge. Commissioners who adopt the latter stance would claim that the two approaches are not necessarily inconsistent. For instance, the airline industry during the first half of the 1970s was accorded protection against competition by measures such as the route moratorium and capacity-limitation agreements. When these policies were implemented, their justifications contained references to their general benefits, and Robert Timm, who was chairman of the CAB in 1973-74, publicly equated the financial health of the industry with the public interest.[13] The rationale for this was based on the notion that service quality suffered and airline unemployment rose when carriers encountered financial difficulty.

Another view holds that regulation has been detrimental to the public interest because of a preoccupation with the protection of the industry. This approach originated among Marxist critics of modern capitalism, including Kolko,[14] and Baran and Sweezy,[15] who saw regulation in terms of preserving a decrepit system. However, the antiregulation stance also gained a following by the mid-1970s among libertarian proponents of competition who regarded any government intervention as counterproductive. Essentially, the complaint from both quarters concerned the preservation of any vestige of monopoly power, which nearly always had negative welfare connotations. Kahn himself sided with the libertarian position, and as CAB chairman in 1977-78, was instrumental in obtaining final approval for the Airline Deregulation Act of 1978.

For 40 years the Civil Aeronautics Act of 1938 provided the guidelines for the regulation of domestic air transport. The Introduction of this book detailed the provisions and purpose of the 1938 Act and indicated how the Federal Aviation Act of 1958 amended the earlier legislation in the area of air safety, while leaving unaffected the sections relating to economic matters. Under this mandate, the Civil Aeronautics Board, which was created to regulate the industry, intervened in most phases of carrier activity by deciding where each airline would operate and what prices would prevail. While the historical record suggests that regulation was primarily based on the idea of protecting an infant industry from destructive competition,[16] most later critics would only grudgingly accept such a proposition, and all would argue that, whatever the initial merits, regulation had long outlived its usefulness.

This reasoning was articulated by academics, including Caves, Cherington, Jordan, Kahn, Miller and Douglas, and Eads,[17] but did not gain important political support until 1975, when the so-called Kennedy Report[18] demanded airline deregulation. During 1977 Kahn was appointed chairman of the CAB and obtained majority support of his views among other members. In a series of precedent-shattering decisions, the Kahn Board eased market entry by issuing route certificates to virtually all applicants and authorized scheduled interstate service by charter carriers, intrastate operators, and newly formed airlines.

The new entry and the threat of additional entry resulted in a proliferation of discounts, which caused a decline in average fares in 1978, while national consumer prices were rising by 8 percent.[19] Whether it was the result of price-cutting and/or favorable economic conditions, airline traffic in 1977 and 1978 grew rapidly as did profits. In this climate and with strong White House backing, Congress overwhelmingly approved the Airline Deregulation Act of 1978, which amended the 1958 Act, and set in motion complete deregulation through sunset provisions. However, since the Kahn Board acted under the old legislative mandate, it was apparent that the new law had not been needed to effect the bulk of the change that the critics of airline regulation had articulated. Nevertheless, the new law institutionalized the new course and also served as a model for proposed deregulation of the trucking and railroad industries. Moreover, where the old law offered regulators a wide latitude in policy matters, the new legislation specifically avoided terms that could be construed as industry protective options.

The Airline Deregulation Act of 1978 was signed into law on October 24, 1978[20] and stressed competition as an objective. Its Declaration of Policy was in sharp contrast to that embodied in the earlier legislation. While the 1938 document, reiterated in 1958, offered ambiguity with respect to carrier rivalry, the 1978 Act was more direct on the subject of competition. For example, where Section 102(d) of the Federal Aviation Act spoke generally of promoting "competition to the extent necessary to assure sound development of an air transportation system . . .,"[21] the later act substituted an entirely new set of articles with four (out of ten) devoted to the subject of competition:

> The placement of maximum reliance on competitive market forces and on actual and potential competition to provide the needed air transportation system and to encourage efficient and well-managed carriers to earn adequate profits and to attract capital. . . .
> Section 102(a)(4).

The prevention of unfair, deceptive, predatory, or anti-competitive practices in air transportation and the avoidance of unreasonable industry concentration, excessive market domination, and monopoly power and other conditions that would tend to allow one or more air carriers unreasonably to increase prices, reduce services, or exclude competition in air transport. . . . Section 102(a)(7).

The encouragement, development, and maintenance of an air transportation system relying on actual and potential competition to provide efficiency, innovation, and low prices, and to determine the variety, quality, and price of air transportation services. . . . (Section 102(a)(9).

The encouragement of entry into air transportation market of new carriers, the encouragement of entry into additional air transportation markets by existing air carriers, and the continued strengthening of small air carriers so as to assure a more effective, competitive airline industry. . . . Section 102(a)(10). [22]

In summary, during the interim period before deregulation, the new law required the Board to act more quickly on route applications, allowed for some automatic entry, encouraged new carrier formation, and established an unregulated band for price adjustments. The termination of the CAB and the transfer of its remaining functions to other agencies was scheduled for 1985. Before then, Board authority over route matters was to cease after 1981, while jurisdiction over all pricing activity would halt after 1982. By the end of 1983, the Board was directed to review compliance with the deregulation directives and draw up a plan for its own demise. In the event that the Board felt that it should continue, it was instructed to present a case to Congress, which would decide on a course of action.

During 1981, with the approval of the Reagan administration, moves were afoot to advance the CAB's sunset. Alternative plans were proposed by the Department of Transportation, CAB, and Congress. While general agreement existed with regard to transfer to the Transportation Department of responsibilities for airline data collection, intercarrier agreements, and international rate jurisdiction, disagreements over the imposition of labor protective provisions and antitrust protection threatened to bog down early passage of such a bill. [23]

PRICING INTERVENTION

While the initiation of price changes has almost always been the responsibility of the carriers, the CAB remained the ultimate arbiter in the final determination of rates through 1978. After 1978, the CAB played a decreasing role, tending toward its complete withdrawal scheduled for the end of 1982. The broad regulatory power in airline passenger pricing had been defined in Sections 403 and 404 of Title IV and part of Section 1002 in Title X of the Civil Aeronautics Act of 1938, which was continued virtually intact by the later Federal Aviation Act of 1958. These articles required that existing tariffs be filed with the Board, as well as advance notice of changes, while CAB was provided with the authority to approve or disapprove carrier petitions based on criteria also developed by the Board. Under the original legislation, no tariff change could be undertaken without permission, but pricing seemed to be only infrequently the focus until the mid-1970s, when a decline in productivity, coupled with sharp fuel cost escalation, brought pressure for frequent rate increases. It was in this climate that CAB pricing practices came under the intense scrutiny of economists and politicians, and the Airline Deregulation Act of 1978 was largely a reaction to the position of the Board, which was perceived to be protective of the industry and anticonsumer.

The consequence of this was a sharp discontinuity in regulatory philosophy. The contrast could be best noticed in an examination of the different versions of Section 1002(e), where the basic rate-making guidelines were stated. The earlier legislation offered the following concerning those factors that should be taken into consideration:

> The effect of rates upon the movement of traffic; the need in the public interest of adequate and efficient transportation of persons and property by air carriers at the lowest cost consistent with the furnishing of such service; such standards respecting the character and quality of service to be rendered by air carriers as may be prescribed by or pursuant to law; the inherent advantages of transportation by aircraft; the need of each air carrier for revenue sufficient to enable such air carrier, under honest, economic, and efficient air management, to provide adequate and efficient air carrier service.[24]

The above section was amended by the 1978 legislation as follows:

The criteria set forth in section 102 of this Act;*
the need for adequate and efficient transportation
of persons and property at the lowest cost consistent with the furnishing of such service; the effect of
prices upon the movement of traffic; the desirability
of a variety of price and service options such as peak
and off-peak pricing or other pricing mechanisms to
improve economic efficiency and provide low-cost
air service; and the desirability of allowing an air
carrier to determine prices in response to particular competitive market conditions on the basis of
such air carrier's individual costs.[25]

Where the early legislation mostly offered only general direction to the regulators, the later statute not only emphasized the desirability of low fares, but indicated areas in which innovation in
pricing should be encouraged.

The practical operation of the rate-making process had been
governed by the CAB "rules of practice," which defined the prepara-
tion, filing, complaint, and decision procedures. For instance, a
30-day advance notice generally applied to rate proposals, meaning
that new tariffs could not take effect at least until such time had
elapsed. During this period, interested parties wishing to support
or oppose the filing could do so. These groups might have included
other carriers, consumer groups, members of Congress or the
executive branch, airport operators, etc. Between the filing date
and time of intended effectiveness, the Board voted and issued the
decision. If the Board for any reason failed to act in time, the proposal was considered approved and took effect on the prescribed
date.[26] Until the mid-1970s, carrier disapproval of the rate hike
filings of another was rare, while discount proposals usually drew
resistance. Opposition to fare increases had traditionally been the
business of groups outside the industry.

The Board also established fare levels and other price policy
after holding formal proceedings. Two such inquiries, the General
Passenger Fare Investigation (GPFI) between 1956 and 1960 and the
Domestic Passenger Fare Investigation (DPFI) from 1970 to 1974
resulted in the issuance of guidelines and orders governing both fare
structure and price levels. In the latter investigation, the Board
ruled on nine issues, the first three of which were decided on the

*The reference is to the Declaration of Policy, which empha-
sized the new commitment to competition. Four parts of this section are shown earlier in the chapter.

basis of written communication between the Board and the carriers, while the final six areas or "phases" were settled after public hearings resembling a judicial proceeding where witnesses could be cross-examined. [27]

A third, but rarely used, rate-making procedure employed by the Board involved calling representatives of the airlines together in an attempt to narrow differences when, for instance, many carriers had submitted proposals for fare increases. This approach was last utilized in 1969. [28]

If a CAB price ruling had to do with a structural issue, the order became binding on all carriers unless an exemption could be obtained. In phase nine of the DPFI, for example, the Board decided that the ratio of first-class fares to those for coach should rise in stages from the 130 percent prevailing in 1974 to between 150 and 163 percent, depending on distance, by 1977. All carriers flying equipment in a dual configuration were forced to alter their tariffs in accordance with this decision.

On matters related to fare levels, carriers were not bound to raise prices but had to reduce rates, if the Board so ruled. When the Board voted to grant a fare increase, the carriers, acting as oligopolists, quickly introduced the price rise because the industry was convinced that price elasticity was less than unity. This meant that revenue losses due to the lower traffic volumes would be more than offset by higher yields per passenger. As the kinked demand curve theory suggests, one holdout against the increase could defeat the general revenue gain, but there existed strong pressure against such behavior because the other carriers would then be forced to drop the new price, leaving all worse off, provided that the inelastic price assumption was correct.

By the end of 1972, the Board's Bureau of Economics had transformed the general guidelines handed down during phases six through eight of the DPFI into a formula capable of dealing with carrier requests for tariff revisions. The newly created cost-based, rate-making machinery would measure the impact of a new fare proposal in terms of its effect on the prevailing rate of return on investment in the industry. For instance, if the formula determined that a request for a fare increase would push the return on investment beyond the Board's definition of the 12 percent standard, the filing would be denied. However, since the carriers were privy to the same expense and revenue data base as the Board and were acquainted with the formula, much of the mystery surrounding fare decisions presumably was removed since the carriers would generally know when a fare increase could be secured. The new mechanism appeared to make it easier for the carriers to obtain rate relief, especially during the inflationary period following the 1973-74

fuel price escalation. From December 1973 through the end of
1978, 15 general rate increments worth 35 percentage points were
granted.[29] Thereafter, while 17 separate increases were allowed
through July 1981 by the CAB, implementation became selective due
to competitive considerations. Delta and U.S. Air, for instance, refused to raise fares in several instances and thus deterred whoever
competed with them from doing so. Also the threat of entry and the
new entry itself proved to be an obstacle in the execution of rate
hikes. The result after 1978 was a proliferation of price anomalies
wherein it often became cheaper to fly longer distances than shorter
ones.

Early in 1976, the industry-filing strategy changed from one
in which relatively large, but infrequent increases, were requested
to one that petitioned for small raises whenever the rate machinery
permitted. The shift to filings for small but frequent rate increases
stemmed from a dissatisfaction with the speed with which the Board
was acting and its failure to take anticipatory cost increases into
account.[30] While the increases granted from 1973 to 1975 averaged
4.5 percent, those awarded from 1976 to 1978 averaged only 2.5
percent each. The total of 12 fare increases granted from 1973 to
1977 exceeded the number gained by the carriers between 1938 and
1972,[31] indicating the new prominence of pricing in carrier activity.

In addition to creating the new rate-making machinery, the
DPFI also mandated that first-class fares increase relative to coach
rates. During the investigation, opponents of the decision had argued that first-class service could become extinct and subsequent
evidence seemed to bear this out. As a percentage of total Trunk
traffic, first-class volume accounted for 16.4 percent in 1969 but
had dropped to 11.7 percent by 1974.[32] The incidence of two recessions during this period undoubtedly contributed to the decline
as corporations probably discouraged first-class travel as a cost-
cutting device. First-class fares rose to 160 percent of regular
coach between 1975 and 1978, which was a period of economic expansion, and the ratio fell again from 10.0 to 7.2 percent.[33] Thus,
while the average annual decrease of the pre-DPFI period amounted
to 0.9 percentage points under largely unfavorable conditions, the
decline was maintained at that rate even during the post-DPFI span
under favorable economic conditions, but higher fares, suggesting
unexpected price sensitivity among first-class users. With first-
class load factors at 35 percent, compared to 61 percent for coach
in May 1978,[34] several Trunk carriers filed to reduce the 150-163
percent first-class to coach price ratio set by the DPFI in an effort
to lure travelers back to first class and free space in the coach
compartment. By this time, the low-fare procompetition philosophy
of the Board was probably at its peak and approval for 120-130 percent ratios was readily given, thus vacating the DPFI standard.[35]

The undoing of the first-class/coach ratio was not the only casualty of the shift in the regulatory climate that ensued at the conclusion of the DPFI. In fact, except for the cost-based, rate-making machinery, the impact of the DPFI was short-lived as successive Board chairmen and members moved with the political winds toward positions that ran counter to the 1970-74 directives. Since many of the DPFI findings had been decided by slim majorities, a new policy course encountered little resistance. By 1976 only two CAB members had heard as much as the final portion of the DPFI, except for G. Joseph Minetti, who had heard the entire proceeding but had voted against most majority stands. New appointments to the Board appeared to be conditioned on a candidate's position toward the new direction as Presidents Ford and Carter both favored deregulation.

Perhaps the earliest sign of a shift in the CAB's pricing policy occurred in the area of discount fares, which had been severely restricted by the DPFI. The Board concluded during phase five that full-fare passengers were probably overcharged because of revenue dilution from discounts, and it sought to limit their usage. In its ruling, the Board revoked discounts that were discriminatory and required carriers to submit a profit impact test for future proposals. The former criteria eliminated youth and family plan fares, while the Discover America program had been considered unreasonable and unprofitable. However, Discover America, which involved relatively long-haul travel and minimum length of stay restrictions, was reinstated in 1975 and other nondiscriminatory discounts gained approval as carriers sought to encourage traffic growth, which had turned sluggish due to adverse economic conditions.[36] Meanwhile, the Board's profit impact test became something of a farce as the claims of carriers that their programs had great potential for generating revenue were accepted at face value. However, the requirement was not officially removed until mid-1978.[37]

At that time, a rule was also issued that vacated the DPFI condition that carriers file uniform fares by mileage on a formula basis. This was in response to filings from new carriers desiring low-fare entry to markets with solidly entrenched incumbents and from incumbents wishing to introduce new, cheaper classes of service as a competitive tool. Under the DPFI standard, such price/service quality options would have been impossible, but it also created conditions in which longer trips might be less expensive than shorter ones.

The final repudiation of DPFI came shortly before passage of the Airline Deregulation Act of 1978 and, in effect, legitimized an unregulated pricing zone that had been rejected in the last phase of the earlier investigation. The upward flexibility in rates was limited to 5-10 percent of the standard industry fare level, dependent on the number of carriers authorized to provide service in the particular market, while the floor was set at 50-70 percent, based on whether a peak or off-peak period was involved.[38]

When the Airline Deregulation Act of 1978 came into effect, its substantive pricing aspects had already been established through the efforts of the Board during the 1975-78 period. These included the unregulated range for rate changes and the rate-making rules emphasizing low fares and service quality options. All that the new legislation did was to reiterate the prevailing regulatory positions and set a timetable for complete deregulation, which would take place at the end of 1982, in the case of pricing.

REGULATION OF ENTRY AND EXIT

While the 1978 Airline Deregulation Act called for the end of route regulation by the end of 1981, the exercise of such control had been decreasingly in evidence under the climate created by the Kahn Board beginning in 1977 and virtually nonexistent by the time of the legislated expiration date. However, for 40 years, regulation of entry and exit was the principal element in government management of the airline industry. Entry into the industry was first officially accomplished in 1938 at the time of the approval of the Civil Aeronautics Act when the CAB, through its "grandfather" clause, granted permanent status to the carriers holding mail route contracts operated during 1938.[39] The 18 carriers that received certification in this way constituted the domestic industry and later became known as Trunk airlines since their route systems tended to transcend regions. Although the original number had already dwindled to 16 before World War II through suspension and consolidation, it was not until 1952 that any significant merger activity further reduced Trunk membership. By 1978 additional consolidations had cut the total to 10, not counting Pan American whose domestic involvement remained nominal. However, the Board authorized additional entry by allowing carrier classes beside the Trunks to acquire special certification. These included: the Local service group, admitted on an experimental basis in 1943 and permanently in 1955; the Supplementals, which gained provisional authority to provide nonscheduled service through Congressional intervention in 1962 and permanent rights by 1966; the all-cargo carriers, which were certified in 1949; and the Commuter group, which first gained official recognition in 1952.[40] In addition, the Supplementals were awarded "grandfather" rights along with the scheduled airlines in the deregulated all-cargo market in 1978.[41]

The rules on exit were liberalized by the Airline Deregulation Act of 1978 and generated the most controversy after passage. Under the old legislation, the Board usually allowed carriers to abandon markets only after a quasi-judicial proceeding that could be time consuming and expensive. The 1978 Act, however, simply required a 90-day advance notice filed with the Board and the local airport authorities;[42] this procedure was used until the end of 1981 when CAB jurisdiction over route matters ceased. The Board retained authority to force an extension of service for indefinite periods if it found "essential air service" to be disrupted because a substitute carrier could not be found.[43] However, subsidy payments would be available if such service caused losses. Essential air service was defined in terms of a minimum allowable number of departures linking the subject community to a hub city.

Until the ascendance of the Kahn Board in 1977, applications for new entry into scheduled service by the Supplementals, Intrastate carriers, and new entities had been repeatedly rejected by the Board whose behavior in this area stemmed from a long-held attitude that the legislative mandate to "foster sound economic conditions" required protection of the certified carriers from competition. Nevertheless, through its later specialized entry authorizations of the Locals, Supplementals, and newly organized airlines, the Board encouraged a large increase in the number of firms in the industry. After mergers and exits from attrition are subtracted, the Board, by December 1980, included 63 carriers under its jurisdiction not counting the Commuter-class airlines.[44]

The Federal Aviation Act empowered the CAB to foster the development of the airline system through granting authority to operate routes to new or existing airlines on whose initiative such requests were made. However, the ability of the Board to revoke an operating certificate was less straightforward, since the enabling legislation intended route authority to be permanent in an attempt to insure a measure of industry stability. Under Section 401(g) of the Federal Aviation Act, operating authority could be reduced or removed only if an operator failed to obey Board directives or else if the carrier itself desired a decrease in authority. An example of the latter involved the voluntary transfer of hundreds of small markets from the Trunks to the Local service carriers, which in turn transferred markets to Commuter airlines. The Board could also award temporary rather than permanent authority in a market as a means of testing a carrier's performance. In adjusting industry route authority, the statutes nevertheless failed to provide the Board with firm directives on criteria in selecting one carrier over another. The one guideline regarding route-authorization criteria could be found in a vaguely worded but frequently quoted section of the Declaration of Policy of the Federal Aviation Act, which charged the Board to provide for:

> Competition to the extent necessary to insure the sound development of an air transportation system properly adapted to the needs of the foreign and domestic commerce of the United States, of the Postal Service, and of the National Defense.[45]

As a consequence, the individual cases generally were decided on the basis of whatever evidence seemed most compelling at any point in time to a majority of the Board membership. Frequently, criteria adopted to determine a case were rejected in a similar case. Thus, a system of ad hoc decisions developed in which precedent was mentioned only where it rationalized a current judgment. Apart from the route award process with regard to entry and exit, Board approval was also required on mergers and acquisitions, transfers of operating authority between carriers, and on multilateral capacity-limiting agreements, but the initiative in all of these matters still resided with the carriers.

Shortly before leaving the CAB to join the Committee on Wage and Price Stability in 1978, Kahn offered some confirmation for this arbitrary behavior in an address to the American Bar Association:

> I have been told by people who have been at the CAB a long time that in the past the Board would often choose among competing applicants for the right to operate a particular route in secret sessions, held in a closed room from which all staff were rigidly excluded; that somehow out of that process emerged a name attached to the route in question; that the Chairman—or perhaps his assistant—would then pick up the telephone and call the General Counsel and tell him who the lucky winner was, and nothing more. Then a lawyer on the General Counsel's staff, amply supplied with blank legal tablets and a generous selection of cliches—some, like "beyond-area benefits," "route strengthening" or "subsidy need reduction," tried and true, others the desperate product of a feverish imagination—would construct a work of fiction that would then be published as the Board's opinion. Need I add that any resemblance between it and the Board's actual reasons for its decision would be purely coincidental.[46]

Given the ambiguity of the statutes, the Board was given ample leeway in the determination of any adjustment in operating authority. For instance, a carrier might be awarded nonstop turnaround certification in a market or be required to make intermediate stops within a given city pair or else be saddled with a long-haul restriction forcing the carrier to operate beyond the prescribed segment with the same aircraft, thus denying it the right of turnaround service. The latter two measures were designed to provide incumbent carriers with protection against serious traffic diversion. Certification could also be permissive or mandatory, and temporary or permanent. Permissive authority left the implementation of an award to the discretion of the carrier, while mandatory certification required that authority be utilized in a prescribed manner. Once a route decision was promulgated, however, the Board generally avoided interference with carrier prerogatives regarding the number of flights, type of equipment operated, or the kinds of amenities offered. The Board occasionally monitored carrier behavior after the receipt of new route authority as a means of evaluating performance and as a guide in subsequent proceedings. Moreover, the CAB under Alfred Kahn announced, in 1978, a policy under which new route awards might be forfeited in favor of a "back-up" carrier in the event of poor service delivery. [47] This stance was reiterated by Kahn's successor, Marvin Cohen, who indicated that the Board might decertify a carrier if the incumbent failed to offer sufficient low-fare service options. [48]

There existed a set of standard procedures in the route application process. Typically, carriers filed requests for new authority, but the Board was not obligated to take any action if the case was considered unimportant or if the current workload was too heavy. At the discretion of the Board, individual applications might get lumped into a general area proceeding involving many applicants and routes. If the Board did decide to hear a petition, it was assumed that the Board acknowledged that new authority was warranted and a prehearing conference was held in which the issues and extent of the case were defined. The record of the prehearing deliberations was then made public so that all interested parties could have an opportunity to participate in the subsequent public hearings, which might involve oral testimony and the presentation of exhibits by all participants to support their respective positions. In due course, the presiding law judge issued an initial decision at which time further arguments could be filed with oral arguments and/or exhibits presented directly to the Board, which then rendered a final decision. That verdict could be appealed to the Board by disappointed parties and recourse was also available in the courts. On international route matters, Board decisions remained subject to presidential approval, ostensibly owing to foreign policy considerations. The length of cases typically varied from a few months to several years.

The 1978 legislation altered the ground rules for the route application process in several important respects during the interim 1979-81 period. Perhaps the most basic involved the transfer of the burden of proving the worth of a petition from the applicant to the opponent.[49] That is, once the applicant was found to be "fit, willing, and able," the adversary had to show the proposed certification not to be consistent with public convenience and necessity, where the petitioner formerly carried that burden. Another significant modification had to do with strict time limits placed on the Board for the determination of applications. Under the previous legislation, it had been possible for route cases to be virtually open-ended affairs but, under the 1978 legislation, final adjudication had to be reached within 240 days from the date of application.

Among the criteria evaluated by the Board in route cases, perhaps the most important involved the question of competition, assuming the market was large enough to support more than one carrier. The so-called "presumption doctrine," meaning a presumption that competition would be favored in markets where the traffic level could support two or more carriers, was specified in a 1943 case:

> While no convenient formula of general applicability
> may be available as a substitute for the Board's dis-
> cretionary judgment, it would seem to be a sound
> principle that, since competition in itself presents
> an incentive to improved service and technological
> development, these would be a strong, although not
> conclusive, presumption in favor of competition on
> any route which offered sufficient traffic to support
> competing services without an unreasonable increase
> of total operating cost.[50]

A side benefit of increased competition was thought to be its impact in generating traffic, since increased service in a market could induce growth apart from what would occur normally from economic or demographic developments. Despite the "presumption doctrine," however, there were occasions, such as during 1970-75, when the Board sought to limit the spread of competition through the so-called route moratorium. This indicated that the attitude of a particular Board combined with prevailing economic conditions, rather than the legislation itself, dictated the degree to which the pursuit of competition was pressed.

The Board also based its awards on the need to strengthen certain undersized or financially weak carriers, although it was true that occasionally applications were rejected because carriers appeared too small to provide adequate service or compete effectively with larger airlines. Two writers have suggested that the Board followed a conscious policy of equalization in which route awards acted as the principal agent of the transformation.[51] In point of fact, the Trunk carriers have grown less comparable but not so much with regard to size as in financial strength. Especially during the 1970s, many of the smaller Trunk airlines gained the approbation of Wall Street, while some of the largest came close to bankruptcy. Caves, writing in 1961, incorrectly foresaw the largest carriers becoming dominant financially even though the carrier-strengthening criteria had already been well established in route cases.[52] The "grand design" thesis on equalization appears to lack strong foundation in fact, given the fairly steady turnover of Board membership, but the process has nonetheless advanced, whether deliberately or not.

The strengthening criterion in route cases was also applied in the matter of subsidy abatement. Almost from the beginning of its stewardship of the CAB budget, Congress requested that the CAB reduce subsidy payments to the airlines, which had reached a high of $83 million in 1963.[53] These federal allowances had been extended as a cross-subsidization device to enable carriers to provide service to unprofitable points. Apart from the grants paid to Northeast until that carrier was absorbed by Delta in 1972, no Trunk carrier received subsidy after 1957. The process of subsidy withdrawal for the Trunks not only involved the acquisition of new profitable routes, but the shedding of smaller, unprofitable segments, which were usually assigned to the local service carriers, most of which still receive subsidy. During 1966 the Board made a dramatic gesture toward reducing the subsidy paid the Locals by voiding numerous multiple-stop restrictions that had been placed on them, thus enabling these carriers to compete directly with Trunks in many dense short- and medium-haul markets.[54] By fiscal year 1969, the subsidy paid the Local service carriers had fallen by 40 percent from the 1963 peak; however, it rose again with the advent of the 1969-70 recession.[55] The subsidy bill for fiscal 1980 amounted to $83 million, equaling the 1963 peak.[56]

In explaining decisions, the Board often stressed the importance of route integration. For instance, if a carrier already operated in a market but with a one-stop restriction, it would already have an identity on both sides of the segment despite its lack of nonstop authority. The granting of nonstop rights would improve the flexibility of the carrier's route system, as well as add convenience to the public, provided that the market was underserved. Consideration was also presumably given to the integrative capability of the various applicants. Carriers that already served markets on either or both sides of the sought-after authority possessed an ability to carry passengers from either city to more distant points via single plane service. If the Board were to award the route in question to a carrier without this capability, passengers traveling outside of the local market would be confronted with the inconvenience of changing planes, airlines, or airports. Other less general issues in route cases that fell under the "strengthening" heading involved helping carriers overcome a lopsided seasonality problem by awarding a north-south route to a predominantly east-west carrier or aiding carrier fleet utilization by granting a long-haul certification to a carrier that had an abundance of long-haul aircraft. A related point was that a carrier without sufficient equipment to serve a desired market might claim in its application that suitable aircraft had been ordered or could easily be leased. Some carriers seeking market entry in the late 1970s, when price discounting became a CAB policy objective, sought to ingratiate themselves with the Board by offering price/quality options in route applications. A typical example entailed "no-frills" flights at one low price as opposed to the standard offering of first-class and coach services at different prices.

The motives of carriers in applying for new routes were diverse. The basic inducement, of course, was the fact that expansion of a route network enlarges the intangible assets. Moreover, the cost of prosecuting route cases was usually minuscule compared to the future value of a route. Also a defensive element was involved: a carrier might apply for a route not necessarily out of deep interest but simply in order to preempt a rival.

The record indicates that route case applications were responsive to the business climate. During the recession-plagued 1970-75 period when no new approvals were given, an annual average of 52 applications were nevertheless received.[57] Conversely, during the mostly recession-free decade of the 1960s, the CAB processed an average of 103 formal route applications per year.[58] Typically, when traffic and profits were strong, carriers felt encouraged to expand operations and the Board generally became more willing to grant new authority, since there existed no imminent financial danger to the carriers. The Board also utilized the new certification process to dampen industry profitability that threatened to exceed the rate of return criteria. During periods of economic difficulties, carriers were more reluctant to embark on any expansion and the Board similarly limited route mile increases.

The most dramatic example of Board restraint occurred when an unofficial moratorium during the 1970-75 period brought the route award process to a standstill. The moratorium arose out of a concern by the Board chairman and other members over excess industry capacity, a condition brought about by a period of wholesale expansion of route authority and wide-body equipment deliveries in the face of falling demand during the 1969-70 recession. At the behest of Chairman Browne and Chairman Timm after him, the Board simply ignored new route applications during the period.[59] While traffic levels improved in 1972 and 1973, a majority of the Board still maintained that overcapacity posed a financial threat to the industry and encouraged route transfers and capacity-limiting agreements in addition to the route moratorium so as to curb supply. However, by 1975, with the departure of Robert Timm as chairman and amidst mounting criticism, both the route moratorium and the capacity agreements were terminated.

During recessions, the route adjustment process involved transfers, suspensions, or deletions of authority, all of which could be characterized as carrier-strengthening devices. However, because of regulatory lag where cases could take years to resolve, retrenchment efforts frequently stretched into an economic recovery while route expansion programs continued even as an economic downturn began to restrict traffic and carrier profitability. In the latter case, certification and serving additional route miles usually intensified the financial problems of the new entrant and its rivals.

Route swaps or transfers represented an attempt by carriers to reorganize and strengthen route systems through the exchange of less well-integrated routes for better integrated ones. The concept was endorsed during the period of the route moratorium by Chairman Timm, who in 1973 urged the carriers to take route improvement into their own hands.[60] However, of the seven major plans filed with the Board between 1973 and 1974, only four were approved.[61] Board objections to the proposals included the criticism that certain carriers might gain too much power in an area while rendering little public benefit. Other parties protested that the CAB, not airline management, was charged by Congress with determining route structure, or that some smaller carriers whose systems were narrow would be placed at a disadvantage since they had few routes to exchange.

PRODUCT REGULATION

By fostering an oligopolistic industry structure and simultaneously helping to restrain price rivalry throughout most of its history, the CAB encouraged airlines to channel whatever competitive energies they possessed toward the product area, which was left relatively uncontrolled. Rivalry concerning capacity, where the carriers competed in offering passengers greater scheduling convenience and better equipment, constituted the most important form of this nonprice jousting. Other sources of intercarrier rivalry were in-flight and ground amenities. Over the years, airline product competition was often vigorous and this, more than any other factor, was at the root of the industry's repeated inability to achieve the rate of return on investment set for it by the CAB. During the 1970s, the industry profit rate exceeded the target only in 1978. [62]

Despite the fact that airline prices generally remained above marginal cost in the short run, strenuous efforts at achieving product differentiation through service improvements forced costs to rise toward the price level. Since this was the case, it would have been appropriate for the Board to prevent service inflation in the interest of industry profitability. However, Caves' earlier observation that the Board had been reluctant to meddle in airline product matters, with some notable exceptions, remained valid through 1981. [63] The Airline Deregulation Act of 1978 thus had little to undo in the product area as opposed to the extensive rewriting of the original pricing and entry/exit guidelines.

The Federal Aviation Act of 1958, in Section 102 of Title I, clearly empowered the CAB to act when product competition became destructive, but the Board's apparent reluctance to interfere in this area probably stemmed from the notion that, by allowing product competition, sufficient incentives would be provided to ensure that the carriers maintained decent service levels. Since pricing already had come under effective control, the extension of similar stringency to the product would have rendered the industry completely noncompetitive and thus contrary to the spirit of the legislative mandate. By choosing to permit product competition, the agency evidently sought to avoid a condition of price rivalry that might be destructive or predatory. It has also been suggested that formulating rules governing service would be more difficult than doing the same for price. [64] Nevertheless, failure of the CAB to blanket the product field has been termed a regulatory imperfection. [65]

This is not to say that the Board never felt the need to step in to halt certain industry-product practices when they threatened to financially undermine some carriers or when they simply were deemed wasteful and the airlines involved could not or would not extricate themselves voluntarily. [3] The Board had the power to impose tariff-filing requirements on food and liquor services, which could either be approved or suspended. Aside from direct involvement, however, clearly the most potent CAB weapon affecting product

competition was the Board's control of the entry/exit process; the
potential for new route entry acted as an inducement for incumbent
carriers to maintain service levels at a point that would deter the
Board from revoking an existing authority or certifying a new entrant. Of course, the traffic growth within a market might have
been such that its sheer size could induce the Board to select a new
competitor regardless of prior service levels.

One of the early examples of CAB product intervention involved the rejection of a filing in 1952 by United to provide four-
across seating instead of the five-across arrangement in coach that
had prevailed since the introduction of that type of service in 1948.
In its decision, the Board found the proposal to be potentially destructive, since all competitors would have to match the lower density seating plan. This would result in higher unit costs, which
might render the coach experiment uneconomic and destroy it as a
low-cost alternative to first class.[66] Another early instance of
Board influence on airline product competition had to do with the
purchase of new equipment. The Board, in a series of opinions on
price differentials, penalized carriers flying inferior equipment
while rewarding those owning more advanced aircraft. This was
accomplished by allowing the carriers with the newer planes to apply a surcharge to the normal fare while preventing airlines with
the older aircraft from reducing fares. The effect of these Board
actions was to speed the introduction of new equipment regardless
of whether the airlines could structurally or financially digest the
rapid aircraft turnover. Among the grounds used to justify this
policy was the charge of the Civil Aeronautics Act to encourage the
air transport network to be "properly adapted to present and future
needs of the foreign and domestic commerce of the United States,
of the Postal Service, and of the National Defense."[67] Apparently
the Board felt that it was responsible for promoting technological
advance in aircraft, as well as the normal regulation of the industry.

The examples of direct involvement in airline product policies
have been more prominent in the recent period than in the past, perhaps owing to a heightened sensitivity of the Board to the financial
problems of the carriers during the economically disruptive and
recession-prone 1970s. The so-called "great lounge war of 1970-73"
has been described in detail in another context, but basically involved
the CAB in extricating the participating carriers from a situation in
which no airline was willing to act unilaterally to replace nonrevenue-
yielding passenger lounges with saleable seats which, by 1973,
strong traffic demand had made desirable. The Board eventually
voted to force the carriers that insisted on retaining the coach
lounges to charge $10 extra per passenger. Only Continental,
among the four competing carriers, failed to remove the lounges,

but Continental, unlike the others, flew in only one important market—Chicago-Los Angeles. However, Continental won a stay of the
order in the courts, thus enabling it to maintain a service advantage
without having to impose a surcharge. Late in 1974 a "liquor war"
broke out on the East Coast-Florida routes when National, seeking
to recover its market share lost during a long strike, started to
offer free drinks to coach passengers in addition to those in first
class. Eastern matched it, while Delta had already been supplying
free champagne with its meal service. When this costly "frills"
competition threatened to spread throughout each carrier's system,
the Board, which had only recently awarded the industry a 4 percent
increase, acted to end it. It issued a warning to the effect that it
viewed the "obviously uneconomic practices" with alarm and would
monitor the situation closely. In a thinly veiled threat, the Board
went on to say that future fare increase requests might not be ap-
preciated. The statement by the Board had the desired effect on
National and Eastern and each withdrew the service early in 1975.
However, Delta continued to offer free champagne with its food
service. [68]

During phase 6B of the DPFI, the Board intruded on product
competition by discouraging the carriers from offering extra space
as a service amenity. Carriers might provide only five-across
coach seating on narrow-bodied aircraft instead of the six recommended by the Board and, by so doing, increased the industry load
factor. However, the Board decided to penalize this presumed inefficiency by counting the foregone seats in calculating the load factor for rate-making purposes. Thus, with the reported load factor
at 55 percent, which was the minimum level required for the filing
of a fare increase, the "real" rate may have amounted to only 53
percent, which would have ruled out a price rise filing.

Perhaps the most important intervention in airline product
rivalry ever embarked upon by the Board involved the approval of
multilateral capacity reductions by American, Trans World, and
United on several long-haul routes beginning in 1971 and lasting
until 1975. Although some of the capacity agreements remained in
force for 3.5 years, their popularity was always limited. The
smaller carriers and the Supplementals, for instance, felt threatened by the "diversion" potential and criticized the agreements
throughout the 1971-75 period as an unnecessary and harmful
capacity-control device. They contended that unilateral constraint
was both possible and practical. The Justice and Transportation
Departments both complained about the anticompetitive aspects and
the flouting of the antitrust statutes. Further expressions of dissatisfaction came from cities whose nonstop service was reduced
and from labor organizations whose members felt threatened by the

real and potential layoffs arising out of the extension of the agreements. The Air Transport Association (ATA), the scheduled airline trade group, could take no position because of the split on the
issue among its members.

Apart from the strenuous support of the Big Three carriers,
the sole advocates of the capacity control idea seemed to be the CAB,
three of whose members' votes gave official sanction to the agreements. Although the initial agreements were voted under the chairmanship of Secor Browne, the later chairman, Robert Timm, became the champion of the idea and tried his utmost to gain acceptance for the scheme.

With the economy rebounding from the 1969-70 recession, industry profits in general were naturally bolstered so that improved
earnings were registered in 1972 and 1973, thus removing the main
argument in favor of the agreements. In addition, as we have noted,
the later anti-inflation drive singled out the regulatory agencies for
fostering inefficient and anticompetitive practices. These events,
combined with alleged improprieties by Chairman Timm and a pro-
agreement ally on the Board, seemed to have doomed the agreements even before the court struck them down in April 1975.

While capacity-limiting agreements appear to have lost their
relevance in a climate dominated by deregulation, it is conceivable
that we have only seen their temporary demise. Their resurrection
might possibly be achieved in connection with fuel conservation if,
for instance, mandatory consumption quotas were to be set for industries or in the cases of airport gate-space constraints and local-
ly imposed flight curfews.

NOTES

1. Based on computation from several years of national in-
come data after a definition given in F. M. Scherer, Industrial
Market Structure and Economic Performance (Chicago: Rand
McNally, 1970), p. 519.

2. George Stigler and Claire Friedland, "What Can Regulators Regulate? The Case of Electricity," Journal of Law and Economics 5 (October 1962):1-16.

3. Scherer, Industrial Market Structure, pp. 537-38.

4. T. G. Moore, "The Effect of Regulation on Electrical
Power Prices," unpublished paper delivered at North American
Regional Conference of the Econometric Society, San Francisco,
December 1966.

5. Alfred E. Kahn, The Economics of Regulation: Principles
and Institutions (New York: John Wiley, 1971), vols. I and II.

6. Ibid., vol. II, pp. 109-11.

7. Ibid.

8. Harvey Averch and Leland L. Johnson, "Behavior of the Firm Under Regulation Constraint," American Economic Review 52 (December 1962):1052-69.

9. Stanislaw H. Wellisz, "Regulation of Natural Gas Pipeline Companies: An Economic Analysis," Journal of Political Economy 71 (February 1963):30-43.

10. Kahn, Economics of Regulation, vol. II, p. 49.

11. Richard E. Caves, Air Transport and Its Regulators (Cambridge, Mass.: Harvard University Press, 1962), p. 359.

12. Friedrich A. Hayek, The Road to Serfdom (Chicago: University of Chicago Press, 1944), pp. 88-100; Lee Loevinger, "Regulation and Competition as Alternatives," The Antitrust Bulletin 11 (January-April 1966):104-8; James R. Nelson, "The Role of Competition in the Regulated Industries," The Antitrust Bulletin 11 (January-April 1966):7-8, 17-21; Waldon H. Hamilton, Price and Price Policies (New York: McGraw-Hill, 1938); Milton Friedman, Capitalism and Freedom (Chicago: University of Chicago Press, 1962), ch. 9; Walter Gellhorn, Individual Freedom and Government Restraints (Baton Rouge: Louisiana State University Press, 1956), ch. 3.

13. Robert Lindsey, "CAB Seeks a Role in Flight Schedules," New York Times, December 6, 1973, p. 1.

14. Gabriel Kolko, The Triumph of Conservatism (New York: Free Press of Glencoe, 1962).

15. Paul A. Baran and Paul M. Sweezy, Monopoly Capitalism (New York: Monthly Review Press, 1966).

16. Edgar Gorrell, "The Civil Aeronautics Act of 1938 and Democratic Government," Journal of Air Law 9 (October 1938): 700-10.

17. Caves, Air Transport and Its Regulators; Paul Cherington, Airline Price Policy (Boston: Harvard Graduate School of Business, 1958); William Jordan, Airline Regulation in America (Baltimore: Johns Hopkins University Press, 1970); Kahn, Economics of Regulation, vol. II; George Douglas and James Miller III,, Economic Regulation of Domestic Air Transport: Theory and Policy (Washington, D.C.: Brookings Institution, 1974); George Eads, The Local Service Airline Experiment (Washington, D.C.: Brookings Institution, 1971).

18. U.S. Senate, Report of the Committee on the Judiciary, 93rd Cong., 2d sess., Subcommittee on Administrative Practices, 1975.

19. Calculated from U.S. Civil Aeronautics Board, Air Carrier Financial Statistics, December 1978; and U.S. Department of

Commerce, Bureau of Economic Analysis, Economic Indicators, March 1979.

20. Albert R. Karr, "Carter Signs Airline Deregulation Law; CAB Will Grant Routes More Generously," Wall Street Journal, October 25, 1978, p. 2.

21. Airline Deregulation Act of 1978, Section 102, 72 Stat. 740, 49 USCA 1303.

22. Commerce Clearing House, P. L. 95-504, Airline Deregulation Act of 1978, S. 2493-2 and S. 2493-3.

23. Aviation Daily, July 15, 1981, p. 78.

24. Airline Deregulation Act of 1978, Section 1002(e), 72 Stat. 788, 49 USCA 1482.

25. Commerce Clearing House, P. L. 95-504, Airline Deregulation Act of 1978, S. 2493-38.

26. Paul S. Cherington, Airline Price Policy (Boston: Plimpton Press, 1958), pp. 74-75.

27. Douglas and Miller, Economic Regulation, p. 154.

28. Ibid., p. 153.

29. Compiled from various issues of Aviation Daily.

30. Aviation Week and Space Technology, January 5, 1976, p. 24.

31. U.S. Civil Aeronautics Board, Handbook of Airline Statistics, 1973 edition, part VIII, pp. 531-45.

32. Computed from U.S. Civil Aeronautics Board, Air Carrier Traffic Statistics, December 1969 and December 1974.

33. Ibid., December 1975 and December 1978.

34. Ibid., May 1978.

35. David Griffiths, "First Class Fare Reductions Filed," Aviation Week and Space Technology, April 24, 1978, p. 33.

36. William H. Gregory, "CAB Economic Policies Shifting," Aviation Week and Space Technology, February 17, 1975, p. 20.

37. David Griffiths, "CAB Sets Broad Changes in Domestic Fare Rules," Aviation Week and Space Technology, July 17, 1978, p. 29.

38. Ibid.

39. Caves, Air Transport, p. 127.

40. Douglas and Miller, Economic Regulation, pp. 111-12.

41. Aviation Daily, March 2, 1978, p. 11.

42. Commerce Clearing House, P. L. 95-504, Airline Deregulation Act of 1978, Amendment to Section 401(j) of Federal Aviation Act of 1958, 49 USC 1371(j).

43. Ibid.

44. U.S. Civil Aeronautics Board, Report on Airline Service, Fares, Traffic, Load Factors and Market Shares, July 1979, Table C-2.

45. Section 102(d) of the Federal Aviation Act of 1958.

46. Reported in Aviation Week and Space Technology, August 14, 1978, p. 9.

47. U.S. News and World Report, March 6, 1978, p. 42.

48. Aviation Daily, January 24, 1979, p. 129.

49. P.L. 95-504, Airline Deregulation Act of 1978, Amendment to section 401(d) of Federal Aviation Act of 1958, 49 USC 1371(d).

50. Transcontinental and Western Air, Inc., et al., Additional North-South California Services, 4 CAB 373, 375, 1943.

51. Samuel Richmond, Regulation and Competition in Air Transportation (New York: Columbia University Press, 1962), p. 237; William Fruhan, The Fight for Competitive Advantage: A Study of the U.S. Domestic Trunk Air Carriers (Boston: Harvard Business School, 1972), p. 161.

52. Caves, Air Transport, p. 184.

53. U.S. Civil Aeronautics Board, Handbook of Airline Statistics, 1973 edition, p. 216.

54. Eads, Local Service Airline, pp. 150-76.

55. Calculated from Handbook of Airline Statistics, 1973 edition, p. 221.

56. U.S. Civil Aeronautics Board, Air Carrier Financial Statistics, September 1980, p. 3.

57. Calculated from U.S. Civil Aeronautics Board, Annual Reports to Congress, fiscal years 1970-76.

58. Ibid., fiscal years 1960-70.

59. Charles Schneider, "CAB Moratorium on Route Cases Easing," Aviation Week and Space Technology, October 20, 1975, pp. 14-15.

60. Robert Timm in speech to United Airlines' President's Conference, January 15, 1973.

61. Aviation Daily, July 2, 1975; July 8, 1975; August 19, 1975; September 5, 1975.

62. Air Transport Association of America, Air Transport 1981, p. 2.

63. Caves, Air Transport, p. 232.

64. Kahn, Economics of Regulation, vol. I, p. 22.

65. William A. Jordan, "Airline Capacity Agreements—Correcting a Regulatory Imperfection," Journal of Air Law and Commerce 39 (Spring 1973):196.

66. Aaron Gellman, "The Regulation of Competition in United States Domestic Air Transportation: A Judicial Survey and Analysis, Part II," Journal of Air Law and Commerce 25 (Spring 1956): 158-60.

67. Caves, Air Transport, pp. 241-42.

68. Aviation Daily, November 14, 1974, p. 73.

7

AIRLINE PRICING

BACKGROUND

As opposed to the competitive model in which price is independent of producer control and that of monopoly where the lone
producer sets the price comfortably above marginal cost, oligopoly
pricing is not only the most prevalent form within modern capitalism, but by far the most complex. Included among the phenomena
determining the degree of rivalry in oligopolies are the number of
firms, conditions of entry, cost and market share imbalances, and
the extent of product differentiation. In theory, a small number of
rivals protected by formidable entry barriers, with small differences in costs and market shares manufacturing an undifferentiated
product, would gravitate toward the monopoly model, while firms
in the opposite condition would indicate that the industry was competitive, and that price would more closely approximate marginal
cost.

With regard to industry size, logic suggests that recognition
of interdependence and joint profit-maximizing action are easier to
obtain among a few firms than many. Moreover if barriers to entry
were low, incumbent firms might be loath to raise prices much
above marginal cost out of fear that this would entice entrants,
which might reduce earnings per firm and perhaps destabilize the
industry. More active pricing rivalry could arise from disparities
in unit costs where, for instance, a low-cost operator might reduce
prices below marginal cost to drive out a high-cost opponent with
limited staying power. Product differentiation is a factor in oligopoly pricing in the case where a superior product commands a
premium or an inferior good is priced at a discount. However,
since the structural factors influencing the degree of rivalry are
rarely one-way, and since market behavior may defy logic, predictions of actual industry conduct should always be hedged.

In the airline industry, the largest markets typically include no more than two or three rivals selling a largely undifferentiated product. Moreover, until the late 1970s, entry barriers were formidable, due to high absolute cost requirements but mostly because of the protection accorded the incumbents by the regulatory agency. Despite such conditions, certain elements did encourage competition. These included the inequalities among carriers in cost and market share, which determined relative strength or weakness.

While appreciating the structural restraints imposed on airline rivalry, Caves attributed whatever competition that existed primarily to carrier size and market share disparities and recognized the subordination of pricing rivalry to product rivalry.[1] Strict supervision by the CAB of tariffs and, until 1977, a reluctance to experiment were probably decisive in forestalling rivalry based on pricing strategy. On the other hand, initiative in product competition remained relatively free of impediments under regulation. The fact that pricing became more prominent as a competitive device after 1977 initially stemmed directly from a reversal of CAB policy in which carriers were encouraged to offer price/service quality options. Later when new entry became rampant, pricing assumed the dominant role in airline rivalry.

The following section presents some examples of early price competition, traces the progression of this rivalry from relative passivity to its present importance, and evaluates its impact in the marketplace. In addition, a hypothesis is presented on the cyclical nature of airline prices, and certain observations and predictions of Caves involving the course of price levels and the importance of pricing as a competitive tool are examined.

COMPETITIVE PRICING

Some of the more interesting earlier competitive pricing examples during regulation involved instances where marginal carriers in a market, usually by reason of inferior equipment or restrictive route authority, established a discount fare that went unmatched. These included cases in which jet aircrafts confronted outmoded propeller equipment or where a carrier with a one-stop restriction on a segment had to compete against rivals having a nonstop certificate. One well-documented example of a carrier attempting to overcome a severe competitive disadvantage involved Capital, which is now defunct. Late in 1948, the airline had instituted the first domestic scheduled coach-class service between New York and Chicago.[2] Previously, only first-class service had been offered by the scheduled carriers on this segment and Capital, operating under a one-stop restriction through Pittsburgh and with older equipment against three competitors operating with nonstop authority, carried less than 1 percent of the local passengers.[3] Thus Capital had little to lose when it offered a reduced meal service and higher seating density at a 33 percent discount, since service on either side of Pittsburgh would have been maintained in any case. The price/quality alternative offered by Capital went unmatched until mid-1949, when Trans World introduced an identical price but with nonstop flights. By March 1950, however, Capital had increased its New York-Chicago traffic share to 8 percent.

The apparent success of the initial coach experiment inspired Capital to introduce the new class of service to several more segments and enabled it to move from a position of near bankruptcy during 1947-48 to a point at which new equipment purchases could be financed.[4] Beginning in 1948, coach class accounted by 1950 for 14 percent of scheduled Trunk revenue passenger miles,[5] indicating a growing acceptance throughout the industry of a new type of service that had evolved out of desperation. However, Capital never really overcame its adverse position and was merged into United in 1961 under the so-called "failing business doctrine" promulgated by the CAB.

As the first generation of jet aircraft began to be delivered in large numbers around 1960, it was forecast that general price reductions would result out of a competitive scramble to popularize jet air travel, particularly among the large segment of the adult population who had not yet flown.[6] A Gallup survey had estimated this percentage at 53 percent as late as 1970,[7] and the market potential ten years earlier must have been far greater. Caves, whose study incorporated events only through mid-1961, viewed this prediction on declining fares skeptically, since the direction of fares had, up to that point, never turned downward even during periods of soft demand. Moreover, between 1958 and 1960, which covered the initial jet introduction period, the average composite price for the Trunk carriers actually rose by 8 percent, or nearly 11 percent after adjusting for the effects of an unfavorable shift in the first-class/coach mix.[8] By the end of 1960, jets carried 42 percent of domestic Trunk traffic, while two years later this share had grown to 68 percent.[9] Thus, Caves' observation was apparently based on an interpretation of the underlying structural factors as well as some early evidence.

Despite the more rapid movement toward a greater percentage of cheaper coach traffic within the Trunk total, an increase in the general price level nonetheless proceeded through 1962, at which point the predicted reversal began to take place. Average fares then fell continuously until 1969. From 1962 to 1968, the composite

price declined by an unprecedented 16 percent, or by 8 percent if
an adjustment were to be made for the traffic mix change.[10] What
seemed to have happened was that the 1960-61 recession, which
severely depressed traffic volume, probably distracted the carriers
from marketing programs they might have had for the new aircraft.
Trunk revenue passenger miles only increased by 5 percent between
1959 and 1961 while capacity was growing by over 14 percent, resulting in a sharp load factor deterioration.[11] Instead of pursuing
discount fare schemes, the carriers applied surcharges to jet operations and also were granted two significant fare increases within a
three-month period in 1960. A further price rise occurred early
in 1962. However, once the recession was over, a number of discount programs were launched in 1963, including a three-class service experiment by Continental, a new family plan fare by American,
and a Visit USA tariff introduced by some local service carriers.
All of these filings were promptly matched throughout the industry.
The next wave of discounts occurred in 1966 and consisted principally of a standby youth fare and the Discover America excursion
program, which offered a 25 percent reduction from regular coach
fares in almost all markets, subject to certain restrictions involving length of stay and days of travel.[12] The 1963-68 period was
also unique in that no general fare increases were applied for.

Due to the favorable price climate and generally healthy economic conditions, traffic growth, during the five-year span, averaged 17.5 percent a year.[13] Such rates had not been achieved since
the "infant" stages of the immediate postwar period. The carriers
thus prospered as traffic growth far outpaced price reductions,
while the operating efficiencies of the jet aircraft served to hold
down costs. The latter had afforded the carriers leeway in experi-
menting with discount programs in the first place. Trunk operating
expenses per seat mile declined by 20.9 percent from 1960 to 1968.[14]
In doubting the possibility of a general price decrease, Caves apparently underestimated the marketing ingenuity of the industry, nor
did he appreciate the magnitude of the unit cost savings associated
with the new equipment.

It has been mentioned that equipment inferiority can give rise
to pricing competition. However, price differentials also material-
ized in markets through equipment superiority where the CAB allowed
a carrier operating advanced aircraft to levy a surcharge on the
normal fare. This occurred late in 1958 when National, which first
provided turbojet service, raised coach fares to first-class rates
and placed a surcharge on regular first class.[15] In 1970, the CAB
rejected a similar attempt by Trans World to establish a surcharge
on its B-747 service on the grounds that load factor erosion would
occur and that long-run operating savings eliminated the need for
the higher charges.[16]

Perhaps the most conspicuous example of a price/service quality option was the price and amenity differential between first-class and coach service first introduced in the late 1940s. Other types included the surcharges levied on superior aircraft, off-peak discounts, the requirement of advance purchase and/or minimum length of stay for certain rebate plans, and multistop versus non-stop service. However, until 1977, such programs were not unique to individual markets but were offered throughout the industry. During the DPFI, the CAB institutionalized its distaste for rates tailored to markets by establishing a cost-based formula for tariffs based on fixed terminal and mileage charges tapered to reflect higher short-distance costs. The Board also rejected pleas for a discretionary pricing band free of CAB supervision. These actions had the effect of standardizing rates according to mileage. This meant that all 500-mile segments, for instance, would have an identical fare.

As discussed earlier, the impact of the DPFI was short-lived due to the trend toward deregulation. However, the transformation in the directives on entry and pricing was so dramatic that by June 1980, it was possible to fly the 2,475-mile New York-Los Angeles segment without restriction for $99, which equaled the comparable tariff on the 418-mile New York–Cleveland segment.[17] In addition, due to the unique features of certain fare actions, matching by rivals became less certain.

One of the first examples of an unmatched pricing initiative involving a price/quality option in the new regulatory environment occurred in August 1977, when Allegheny gained permission to implement "Simple-Saver" fares in nine markets where that carrier operated under restricted authority. Allegheny's justification emphasized the opportunity afforded the potential passenger for low-priced transportation "provided only that he is willing to make at least one stop en route and probably change flights."[18] The package provided for a 30 percent discount from regular coach but was available on only 35 percent of Allegheny's seats in any particular market. The latter provision was designed to deter competition with nonstop authority, since the potential for diversion would apparently be limited. Allegheny tried very hard in its fare petition to emphasize that its plan would not injure the incumbent carriers. The airline explained that they might lose more from full-fare passengers paying only the discount fare than from diversion of traffic to Allegheny. Table 7.1 presents some market share results in those city pairs in which Allegheny carried a greater than 1 percent share before the experiment. In each of the three markets, Allegheny increased its market share, and in Boston-St. Louis the two percentage point improvement was accomplished despite a schedule reduction. Allegheny halved its Boston-St. Louis trips from 2 daily

TABLE 7.1

Impact of "Simple-Saver" Fare in Selected Markets,
Fourth Quarter 1976 to Fourth Quarter 1977

	1976	1977	Change
Boston-St. Louis			
Allegheny	1,240	1,690	36%
Industry	20,830	20,730	(1)%
Allegheny percentage	6	8	2 pts.
Chicago-Providence			
Allegheny	180	1,110	511%
Industry	8,880	11,140	25%
Allegheny percentage	2	10	8 pts.
New York-Louisville			
Allegheny	5,170	6,140	19%
Industry	29,610	32,540	10%
Allegheny percentage	17	19	2 pts.

Note: Traffic is expressed in terms of origin-destination local passengers.

Source: Computed from U.S. Civil Aeronautics Board, Origin-Destination Statistics, Table 10, fourth quarters 1976 and 1977.

two-stop and 1 three-stop round trips to 1 two-stop and 0.5 three-stop frequencies, while Trans World, the main nonstop carrier in the market, went from 3 to 2.5 nonstops but increased daily two-stop service from a .5 to 1.5 daily round trips.[19] Allegheny's greatest gains occurred in the smallest segment—Chicago-Providence—where its traffic grew fivefold with a rise in market share of eight percentage points. Here Allegheny flew 1 daily three-stop round trip against service involving change of plane connections in the prior year, while the major carrier, United, operated 2 daily nonstop round trips but eliminated a lone two-stop operation.[20] In the largest market shown—New York-Louisville—where Allegheny already held a 17 percent share, two percentage points were added over the course of the year although the quality of the schedule declined. While American, the principal rival, maintained 2 daily nonstops and 1.5 one-stop round trips in both years, Allegheny went from 3.5 one-stops and 0.5 two-stops to 2 one-stops, 0.5

two-stops, and 1 three-stop. [21] Since in its petition Allegheny estimated costs per additional passenger at between $4 and $9, depending on the market, net profit may have amounted to from $46 to $60
for each new passenger carried. [22] Obviously, some potential travelers probably substituted "Simple-Saver" for full-fare travel, resulting in revenue losses, and Allegheny did increase flight frequencies; hence costs in two of the three markets rose. But overall,
the experiment must have been satisfactory, since the carrier later
petitioned the CAB to extend the tariff to six additional markets.

Because oligopoly and the presence of the CAB inhibited competitive price behavior in the interstate network, the best examples of
price competition before deregulation appeared in intrastate markets
which were beyond the jurisdiction of the CAB where regional carriers
encountered larger interstate airlines. During the 1975-78 period,
exponents of the cartel hypothesis of airline behavior emphasized
the contrasts between intrastate and interstate pricing to support
their case. With barriers to entry generally lower within the intrastate context, successful price competition represented one of the
keys to survival for a new entrant since the incumbents already possessed consumer recognition and usually maintained an edge in service levels. Conversely, the high entry barriers existing in the interstate system allowed the incumbents there to follow a system of
administered pricing.

In California, prior to 1965, entry and exit on purely intrastate routes were virtually unfettered, and downward price adjustments could be instituted without regulatory permission. [23] Although,
after a change in the law in 1965, the California Public Utilities Commission acted with practically the same powers as the CAB. Until
1965 when the intrastate incumbents also gained a measure of protection from new entry, price rivalry was active among the intrastate carriers. The basis for the competition was the inferior
equipment initially operated by the intrastaters, which numbered
16 between 1946 and 1965. [24] For instance, in the large Los Angeles-
San Francisco market, the typical intrastate carrier was unable or
unwilling to operate the largely pressurized, turbine-powered aircraft flown by the established interstate airlines until 1959, when
Pacific Southwest, the lone intrastate carrier to operate throughout
this period, completely changed its fleet from relatively outmoded
DC-4s to advanced Lockheed Electras over a two-month period. [25]
During most of the 1950s, the intrastate carriers charged coach
fares 22 to 26 percent below those offered by the larger interstate
carriers, notably United and Western. When Pacific Southwest
inaugurated Electra service in 1959, the disparity in quality ended,
but a fare differential of 10 percent nevertheless persisted. Only
by 1962, when Pacific Southwest had already achieved significant

market share inroads, did the interstate carriers resort to discounting; this virtually eliminated the price variation. While price
competition effectively subsided by 1965 in favor of service rivalry,
the ability of Pacific Southwest to operate without the requirement
of cross-subsidizing unprofitable segments enabled the interstate
carriers better to resist pressures to raise fares during the inflationary 1970s. Moreover, evidence suggests that the California Public Utilities Commission was less pliant than the CAB on petitions
for fare increases. For instance, while the standard economy fare
on the Los Angeles–San Francisco segment, which was lower to
begin with, rose 108 percent between 1965 and 1978, the fare on a
comparable mileage bloc such as Dayton–St. Louis increased by 150
percent. [26] The significance of this is that prices within the California markets in general remained well below similar interstate
segments throughout the postwar period, thus supporting the domestic industry cartel hypothesis, which held that interstate fare rigid-
ity led to price levels far above minimum attainable marginal costs.

The apparently successful entry of the Texas intrastate carrier, Southwest, into the Dallas-Houston market involved active
competitive pricing at the outset, but achievement of viability by
Southwest could only partially be attributed to price rivalry. Although certified by the Texas Aeronautics Commission in 1968,
Southwest began service only in 1971 due to litigation brought by the
incumbent interstate carriers, Braniff and Texas International.
Contrary to the early California example, the Texas regulatory
body was empowered to control entry and exit but not price. [27] Initially, Southwest established a $20 one-way coach fare in the mar-
ket against a $26 rate charged by the interstate carriers. However,
although service levels were comparable, this 23 percent differential did not result in the rise in market share anticipated by Southwest, and with losses mounting, the carrier raised its price to that
of the interstate carriers. At the same time, however, Southwest
did maintain a $10 fare on an unpublicized late night "ferry" flight
that gradually became very popular. Toward the end of 1972, this
fare was raised to $13, and weekend service at that price was
sharply increased. Braniff and Texas International reacted by
slashing their weekend and weekday coach fares to $13, starting
what the president of Southwest termed an "insane price war." [28]
By the time this episode ran its course, a two-tier system of a $25
fare for weekdays and $15 for nights and weekends was established.
However, the price war and the new off-peak fare, which was under
$20, apparently succeeded in tapping a substantial market of travel-
ers who previously made the 240-mile journey by surface modes.
Between 1972 and 1973, for instance, while traffic growth in ten
comparable interstate markets averaged 4 percent, the rate of

increase on the Dallas-Houston segment exceeded 20 percent.[29]
Together, the new fare package and the traffic surge enabled Southwest to earn its first profit during the second quarter of 1973.[30]
Later in the same year, Southwest enjoyed a quasi-monopoly situation and became consistently profitable as Braniff and Texas International moved operations to the two newer, but less accessible airports serving each city, while Southwest continued to serve the older
but convenient airports in both Dallas and Houston after fighting a
lawsuit intended to get it to move also. The primary significance
of the price rivalry in the Dallas-Houston case was not its impact
on market share but the effect that reduced fares had on generating
traffic. While exploring various pricing alternatives out of competitive necessity, the Texas carriers stumbled upon the price
threshold at which many travelers were willing to forsake automobiles and buses for air transport. The fact that Southwest subsequently prospered, however, was undoubtedly due more to the
unique circumstance, whereby the former incumbents relinquished
the most convenient facilities, than to any inherent marketing skills
on the part of Southwest.

Although pricing as a competitive device had been deempha-
sized by the oligopolistic industry structure and the intention of the
CAB, efforts to promote pricing rivalry were particularly vigorous
during the period leading up to the enactment of the Airline Deregulation Act of 1978. It has been pointed out that when Robert Timm re-
signed as CAB chairman late in 1974, the regulatory climate changed
drastically from one protective of the industry to one favoring consumerism. Throughout the 1975-78 period, a virtually continuous
but one-sided debate raged concerning the merits of airline regulation. Most of the carriers and their labor unions were arrayed
against the Executive branch, a great majority of Congress, and
various consumer groups. Against these odds, the fact that the deregulation law was not enacted until 1978 was a tribute to the lobby-
ing power of the airlines and unions. The main criticism leveled
at the industry was the lack of price competition; the tradition of lower intrastate fares was used to demonstrate how the CAB was shel-
tering the industry from competition. The Subcommittee on Administrative Practice and Procedure of the Committee on the Judiciary
under Senator Kennedy held hearings and assembled the principal
documentation in support of the view that the airlines had been protected from competition by the CAB.

While the struggle over deregulation continued, the CAB, which
had been slightly reconstituted, took action late in 1976 to stimulate
competition by greatly liberalizing rules affecting charter flights so
that passengers no longer had to belong to an affinity group or buy a
ground package with a charter fare. Moreover, length of stay re-

quirements were eliminated, as were minimum prices.[31] In fact,
the only feature distinguishing charter from scheduled travel was a
30-day advance purchase provision. While the Trunks still maintained more charter operations than the Supplementals, the new rule
not only increased the chances for passengers to be diverted to the
latter, but also meant that the Trunk carriers would have to juggle
their own fleet mix merely to handle low-yield traffic, which would
be affected by passengers shifting from scheduled flights to the new
system.

To defend itself against the attractiveness of the new charter
fares, American, early in 1977, filed a so-called "Super-Saver"
tariff on its most vulnerable transcontinental markets—New York-
Los Angeles/San Francisco. These offered great discounts but required an advance booking just like the new type of charter fares.
Trans World objected to this on the grounds that the timing was poor
since the peak season was approaching while United, which had only
recently embarked on a large charter program to capitalize on the
liberalized charter rules, complained for obvious reasons.[32] But
both carriers nonetheless matched American's fares, which the
Board approved. The fares soon spread to all transcontinental
routes, as well as the Arizona-East Coast markets, because travelers found it cheaper to be routed through New York on the East
Coast and Los Angeles or San Francisco on the West Coast than to
fly directly from points like Boston and Philadelphia or San Diego
and Phoenix, which originally had not been included in the "Super-
Saver" program. By April 1978, the fare became available nationwide because of the threat of diversion, among other reasons.
Table 7.2 indicates the impact on traffic of the "Super-Saver" in
the New York-West Coast markets for 1977.

TABLE 7.2

Total Trunk and New York-West Coast Traffic
Growth, 1977 vs. 1976
(percent)

	Scheduled New York-West Coast	Scheduled Trunk	Charter Trunk
January-March	(1.7)	6.2	30.8
April-December	23.6	7.9	(1.7)
Year	18.6	7.5	4.5

Note: Traffic is based on revenue passenger miles.
Sources: New York-West Coast from U.S. Civil Aeronautics
Board, Origin-Destination Surveys, Table 8, first and fourth quar-
ters, 1976 and 1977; Trunk from U.S. Civil Aeronautics Board,
Air Carrier Traffic Statistics, 1977 monthly issues.

The "Super-Saver" fares generated a high level of traffic growth after implementation late in April 1977. While during the January-March period, the rates of change were slightly negative for the two New York-West Coast markets and up by 6.2 percent for the total Trunks, the rise in the former amounted to three times that of the latter between April and December. Meanwhile, Trunk charter traffic was up by 31 percent during the earlier period when the liberalized rules had not been undercut, but down by 2 percent between April and December, reflecting the new price competition from the scheduled side. The apparent success of the "Super-Saver" was hailed by industry critics and even won converts within the industry to the desirability of large discounts. This quickly encouraged more price/quality options such as "Super Coach," "Super Jackpot," "Chickenfeed," and "Peanuts" fares with the encouragement of the CAB, which had, by this time, completely reversed its position and advocated consumerism under Alfred Kahn.

Accompanying the proliferation in discount fares was a radical change in the route award process, which was designed to keep fares low by easing new entry. With the landmark Improved Service to Wichita Case, which was decided in March 1978, the Board started issuing permissive authority.[33] This meant that instead of selecting only one applicant for a route, several or all applicants were granted operating certificates; the aim was to encourage carriers to apply for desirable routes, given the higher likelihood of a successful application. Presumably the threat of new entry would act as a check on high administered prices in any market, since the prospect of supranormal profits held an obvious attraction for a potential entrant. In reality, the actions of the Kahn Board accomplished de facto deregulation in advance of the Act, which was not signed into law until October 1978, but the precedent-shattering policies carried out by the CAB in 1977-78 indicated that the old Federal Aviation Act of 1958 could have accommodated several basic positions concerning regulation. More specifically, the new provisions governing route authority in the Airline Deregulation Act of 1978 made it highly unlikely that the regulatory body would ever revert to an approach protective of the industry.

For all intents and purposes, the permissive entry made possible by the Improved Service to Wichita Case and supplemented by the dormant carrier provision and expedited administrative procedures enabled existing and new carriers to quickly enter any desirable markets. Almost immediately, intrastate airlines such as Pacific Southwest and Air Florida branched out beyond state borders, bringing with them simple one-class, sharply discounted fares, which the incumbent operators did not always match because of quality differences based on meals, first-class service, etc. Established carriers including Trans World and United rushed into markets involving Florida, which allegedly would smooth seasonal problems afflicting both airlines.

Where the older carriers coveted new markets, the decision to go forward was generally based on a pricing policy in which revenues generated at an expected load factor and price would only be required to cover variable costs as opposed to fully allocated costs. This was ostensibly the case with Eastern's entry into the New York-Los Angeles/San Francisco markets in June 1980 where the incumbents—American, Trans World, and United—were willing to tolerate lower fare offerings of two former Supplementals (already there with few flights) but felt compelled to match Eastern's low fare package since Eastern had scheduled nearly as many operations as each incumbent. The Eastern entry immediately precipitated a wild price war as Eastern's initial results at the matched fares were abysmal. By the middle of June, the unrestricted coach fare for the 2,500-mile trip had plunged to $99 before rising to $129 for the remainder of the summer. Although the fully allocated break-even load factor probably hovered around 90 percent due to the low fares, Eastern defended its actions by claiming that the losses incurred were smaller than what would have occurred had the equipment been placed elsewhere that summer.[34] A year later, however, Eastern had halved its presence in the two markets.

New entry by established carriers was not universally as raucous as the transcontinental episode. For instance, in New York-Dallas, which Delta entered in December 1980 against American and Braniff, Delta charged the existing fares and only resorted to capacity-controlled discounts six months later due to unsatisfactory load factors. Apart from the transcontinental and Florida examples, price as a competitive weapon was most evident upon the entry of new carriers such as Midway, New York Air, and Peoples Express who offered spartan, point-to-point service and whose small, nonunionized operations permitted them to offer sharply lower fares. In Newark-Norfolk, for instance, Peoples Express, in May 1981, introduced a flat $35 fare, 57 percent under the prevailing tariff, while New York Air was charging $59 between New York and Cleveland or 56 percent below the previous base set by United.[35] In both cases the incumbent matched the upstart price but in the dense Eastern "shuttle" markets—New York-Boston/Washington—Eastern allowed New York Air a $10 fare advantage on weekdays based on service quality differences. Eastern reasoned that its no-reservation, guaranteed seat service was worth more to the frequent business traveler than the New York Air service, which offered far fewer flights but provided food and drinks on the short trip.

Despite the new entry and the theory behind the deregulation thrust, namely the notion that oligopoly pricing and a pliant CAB had forced consumers to pay unnecessarily higher fares, the results during the initial period after deregulation showed unprecedented increases in aggregate prices. From the second quarter of 1978 to that of 1981, domestic industry prices rose by 55 percent,[36] exceeding the consumer price index increase of 40 percent[37] and equaling the total growth during the 20-year period between 1957 and 1977.[38] Average prices did rise more slowly in the entry targeted markets such as New York–Los Angeles, which saw a 36 percent increase over the 3-year period, and in New York–Columbus where prices rose by 27 percent.[39] However, not only was the CAB's cost-based price-making formula still in place during this span, but fare flexibility provisions were also operative, which enabled the carriers to pass on cost increases and more when competitive conditions permitted. Thus, as fuel prices exploded by 182 percent between 1978 and 1981[40] and other costs rose while a recession dampened traffic demand, the carriers scrambled to cross-subsidize their infiltrated losing markets by raising rates in those (far more numerous) segments whose oligopolistic structure was still intact.

CYCLICAL ASPECTS OF AIRLINE PRICING

Although several observers including Caves have drawn conclusions about the behavior of airline prices during business cycles,[41] the subject has yet to undergo any systematic analysis. The presumption regarding the issue has been that prices move counter to economic activity: during expansion, average fare levels tend to fall in real terms, while the reverse occurs in recessionary times. This alleged inverse relationship conflicts with the competitive notion that, during an economic slowdown, firms move to decrease prices in order to stimulate demand. However, since oligopolistic firms in pursuit of joint profit maximization are apt to coordinate pricing activities, decisions to alter prices will mainly be contingent on the presumed elasticities of demand. If demand is thought to be price elastic, for example, there will be a tendency to reduce prices, since total physical sales volumes would more than offset lower prices, resulting in an increase in revenue. Inelastic demand would induce firms to increase rates at every opportunity.

Time-series regression analysis is one method of examining the nature of the relationship between airline price movements and the economic cycle. This method is utilized here. It is necessary that data be available for several alternating periods of expansion and contraction. Since economic activity during most of the 1960s was practically devoid of recession, the analysis was performed separately for the 1952-61 and 1969-78 periods, which contained three and two recessions respectively and were both subject to similar regulatory review.

The discontinuity in time periods facilitates a comparison of impressions on the alleged relationship made by earlier writers such as Caves and Cherington, whose frame of reference preceded the later period. Another important matter is the periodicity of the data. Discrete inputs would be preferable to annual figures which, by averaging movements within the year, could mask the interaction of the variables. However, while several coincident economic indicators are available monthly, industry price data may only be obtained quarterly from public sources, thus limiting the investigation to a quarterly basis. The airline price time series also has to be smoothed to eliminate a seasonality problem in which third quarter rates tend to be lower than the rest of the year due to a disproportionate share of pleasure travelers, who utilize discount fares more often than do business passengers. Table 7.3 presents the results of a simple regression having four-quarter moving average Trunk passenger per revenue passenger mile deflated by the consumer price index as the dependent variable and total industrial production as the explanatory variable representing aggregate economic activity. For the 1952-61 period, the presumed inverse relationship between airline price movements and the economy was seemingly confirmed as both the correlation coefficient (r) and the t-statistic had negative signs. However, the low $\bar{R}^2$ of .14 and small F-value of 5.85 implied very weak causality between the two variables. By comparison, the diagnostic signs measuring the 1969-78 price/cycle linkage surpassed those of the earlier period in every respect. Not only did the $\bar{R}^2$ measure a relatively strong .673 with a healthy F-value of 74.11, but the correlation coefficient (r) and t-statistic also indicated a more convincing relationship between the economy and airline price. Moreover, the latter equation produced a lower standard error.

Under the presumption that response time in pricing is reduced due to a slowness to perceive economic events and regulatory lag, the same regressions were run with the industrial production variable lagged one quarter. However, the results were inconsistent. For the earlier period, the fit between the variables improved slightly ($\bar{R}^2$ = .14 to $\bar{R}^2$ = .19) while for the more recent period, the $\bar{R}^2$ deteriorated from .67 to .60. The wide differential in results between the two periods nevertheless remained.

TABLE 7.3

Measures of Correlation and Determination of Macroeconomic
Activity and Average Airline Prices

Measure	1952-61	1969-78
r	-.374	-.820
$\bar{R}^2$	.140	.673
t-statistic	-2.42	-8.61
F-value	5.85	74.11
Standard error of estimate	.09	.04
Number of observations	38	38

Sources: Input data for airline prices calculated from various issues, Air Carrier Financial Statistics; economic data from Business Conditions Digest, various issues.

Any study of the presumed relationship would be incomplete without a review of the important events of the two periods. Of the four major identifiable pricing actions in the 1952-61 span, for instance, three occurred in the middle of recessions,[42] ostensibly in response to pressure on earnings. However, the first successful attempt at a fare increase during the period was a $1 per ticket rise obtained in April 1952[43] not out of concern for falling traffic, which was not in evidence, but to cover cost increases. During the post-Korean War recession of 1953-54, the carriers sought another general price rise, but were rebuffed by the CAB.[44] The agency did award an across-the-board fare increase of 4 percent plus $1 per ticket early in 1958[45] shortly before the trough of the severe 1957-58 recession, when traffic slumped badly. Later in the year, despite the resurgence in economic activity, the CAB allowed the carriers to tighten restrictions on certain discount fares, which added another 3.5 percent to average industry prices.[46] The final general rate increase of the period amounted to about 5 percent effective in mid-1960 during the time of the 1960-61 recession.[47] Thus it would appear that the major upward fare measures and attempted actions mostly occurred in response to adverse economic conditions and were undertaken in an effort to maintain profitability. Yet the weak regression results for 1952-61 generally fail to reflect this. Inflation, which might have reduced the fare increases, could not have been a factor since the annual rate of change of the consumer price index averaged only 1.4 percent during the period.[48]

Perhaps the strongest force at work during this time was the steady growth of coach class traffic, which diluted average yields. Prior to 1952, higher yield first class accounted for 81 percent of Trunk revenue passenger miles but by 1961, the share had declined to 42 percent.[49] Indeed, had this movement not occurred, real average fares at the end of the period would have been 10 points higher than the 1952 level, instead of 1 point lower. The greatest upward thrust in the coach share came between 1952 and 1954 and 1959-61 when 13 points each were added.[50] The first increase drew its impetus from earlier experimentation which started to snowball, competition from Supplemental carriers whose fares were cheaper, and also from a need to stimulate traffic growth, which had faltered during the 1953-54 recession. The later change coincided with the first deliveries of jet aircraft, which were fitted in a dual first/ coach configuration. Had the traffic structure been more stable, the individual fare actions probably would have been more visible in the time series and consequently would have been reflected in the regression results. However, since the large coach share movements apparently coincided with general fare increases, the latter became less visible. The fact that these disruptions occurred and diluted the yield so that real average prices tended to decline during recession periods indicates that the inverse relationship between prices and business activity was probably stronger than indicated in the regression and in keeping with the oligopolist notion of administered pricing.

The 1969-78 period was subject to an entirely different set of forces but probably the same conclusions could be drawn. The regression results appear to confirm the idea that airline prices moved counter to aggregate economic activity. As with the earlier example, however, such a determination requires that more information be considered. Of the 38 quarters from 1969 to 1978, 11 of the discrete periods were officially designated recession periods.[51] The first fare increase occurred at the start of the 1969-70 downturn with the next increase two quarters after the trough,[52] as airline traffic remained depressed even though aggregate economic activity had already turned up. A further small rate rise was approved in September 1972 under the CAB's own initiative, arising from phase seven of the Domestic Passenger Fare Investigation. The next round of rate expansion occurred during the 1973-75 recession mainly in response to runaway fuel costs. Three increases totaling 15 percent were granted between December 1973 and November 1974.[53] Upon the completion of the DPFI in December 1974 (which, among other things, formulated a rate-making mechanism by which escalating costs could automatically be passed through, given certain conditions), ten rate increases, none higher than 3 percent, were awarded from 1975 through 1978,[54] which was a span of nearly constant economic growth. The 1969-78 period also witnessed occasional bursts of discounting. One relatively mild episode of this type occurred late in 1975 after the recession and a number of rate increases depressed traffic. A later series of discount proliferation starting in April 1977 took place in a fairly healthy economic setting mainly under the prodding of the CAB, which had adopted a pro-competitive stance.

Contrary to the 1952-61 experience, shifts in the traffic structure appeared to be minor. The coach share of total traffic from 1969 to 1978 expanded by 10 percentage points,[55] much less than the nearly 40-point change earlier. Inflation, however, was far more severe as the consumer price index grew by an average 6.5 percent a year[56] against only 1.4 percent per annum in the prior period measured. This alone could perhaps explain the quadrupling of the number of fare increases, which the new DPFI standard made easier to obtain after 1974. Once airline fares were tied directly to costs by the DPFI, real prices failed to rise but at least remained constant for two years until substantial discounting became widespread by late 1977. This indicates that administered pricing remained the rule in the airline industry, since fare increases were implemented whenever possible without regard to the repercussions in demand. While government regulation tended to constrain upward price movements during periods of adequate profitability, rate changes, rather than being used as a competitive instrument, became a means by which the carriers kept pace with cost inflation.

CONCLUSION

Given the high degree of market concentration in the air transport industry and the support of the regulatory authority, the tendency toward interdependence in pricing remained high until changes in regulation occurred toward the end of the 1970s. Until then, rate competition had occasionally occurred and had a generally salutary effect. This resulted from competitive imbalances where marginal carriers were able to carve out a profitable niche in markets by offering options generally involving lower service quality but at a reduced price. Prior to the deregulation phase, perhaps the most significant example of price competition involved the California case where, beyond the jurisdiction of the CAB, unregulated entry encouraged intrastate price rivalry at least through 1965 when the California regulatory authority raised entry barriers. This situation provided a unique opportunity to view side by side the results produced by the differing regulatory approaches. The fact that coach price levels within California remained consistently lower than rates charged on comparable interstate routes indicated that entry and the threat of entry could successfully thwart the administered pricing practices extant on routes under the aegis of the CAB. This lesson was not lost on the critics of federal airline regulations, whose arguments made ease of entry the cornerstone of the Airline Deregulation Act of 1978. However, interstate airline pricing was not without some beneficial side effects with regard to consumer interests. For instance, the carriers' efforts to popularize air travel with the advent of jet aircraft through a variety of discount offerings, caused real average fares to fall drastically between 1963 and 1968, producing high rates of traffic growth in the process. Similar events occurred in 1977-78, but these later price reductions probably would not have taken place except for the prodding of the CAB, which was then obsessed with promoting competition.

While regression analysis results apparently confirmed a presumed inverse relationship between airline price movements and the business cycle, a documentation of the major pricing actions reinforced the notion that price increases clustered in periods of sluggish demand and poor earnings. The fact that regression results for the periods studied differed concerning degrees of significance between the variables may have been due to distortions in the data, such as the impact on prices of the shift toward more coach traffic in the 1952-61 period. Nevertheless, the overall impression of this and other evidence on airline industry rate-making policy is one of general adherence to oligopolistic-administered pricing. It remains to be seen what effect the Airline Deregulation Act of 1978, with its stress on freer entry, will have on this situation in the long run. The initial results through 1981 have indicated a breakdown in pricing discipline where new entry has occurred. But given the enormous increases in the overall price level since 1978, oligopolistic pricing was apparently still alive and well throughout the vast majority of domestic markets.

NOTES

1. Richard E. Caves, Air Transport and Its Regulators (Cambridge, Mass.: Harvard University Press, 1962), p. 376.
2. Paul Cherington, Airline Price Policy (Cambridge, Mass.: Harvard University Press, 1958), pp. 187-203.
3. Ibid.
4. Ibid.
5. U.S. Civil Aeronautics Board, Handbook of Airline Statistics, 1973 edition, Table 26, p. 34.

6. "Cherington Foresees Airline Fare Cuts," Aviation Week, April 20, 1959, p. 40.

7. "The Incidence of Air Travel in the General Population" (Princeton, N.J.: Gallup Organization, July 1970), p. 2.

8. Handbook of Airline Statistics, Table 80, p. 88.

9. Ibid., Table 11E, p. 450.

10. Ibid., Table 80, p. 88.

11. Ibid., Table 15, p. 23.

12. Ibid., part VIII, pp. 541-42.

13. Ibid., Table 15, p. 23.

14. Ibid., Table 14, p. 22; Table 63, p. 71.

15. R. H. Cook, "Fare Case Unaffected by Jet Surcharge," Aviation Week, February 2, 1959, p. 43.

16. Harold Watkins, "TWA Asks for Surcharge, Higher Tariffs for Peak Season," Aviation Week and Space Technology, March 23, 1970, p. 30.

17. Reuben Donnelly Corp., Official Airline Guide, June 1980.

18. Allegheny Airlines, Inc., Justification in Support of Simple-Saver Fares, May 1977.

19. Reuben Donnelly Corporation, Official Airline Guide, November 1976 and November 1977.

20. Ibid.

21. Ibid.

22. Allegheny Airlines, Inc., Simple Saver Fares, May 1977.

23. California State Constitution, State of California, Public Utilities Code and Related Constitution Provisions (Sacramento: California Office of State Printing, 1965), pp. 13-17.

24. William A. Jordan, Airline Regulation in America (Baltimore: Johns Hopkins University Press, 1970), p. 15.

25. A. M. LaMond, "An Evaluation of Intrastate Regulation in California," Bell Journal of Economics 7 (Autumn 1976):649-50.

26. Official Airline Guide, July 1965 and July 1978.

27. Simat, Hellieson & Eichner, Inc., An Analysis of the Intrastate Air Carrier Regulatory Forum, vol. 1, January 1976, p. 13.

28. Erwin Bulban, "Third Airline Joins Cut-Rate Fight Between Braniff and Southwest," Aviation Week and Space Technology, February 26, 1973, p. 30.

29. U.S. Civil Aeronautics Board, Docket 28068, Service to Harlingen Case, Exhibits HRL-R-256 and TXIA-SRT-2.

30. "Commuter Airline Turns First Profit," Aviation Week and Space Technology, August 6, 1973, p. 30.

31. "Eased Charter Rules Worry the Skeds," Business Week, September 20, 1976, pp. 34-35.

32. Laurence Doty, "American Fare Bid Draws Fire," Aviation Week and Space Technology, February 21, 1977, p. 24.

33. U.S. Civil Aeronautics Board, Improved Authority to Wichita Case, Docket 28848, 78-3-78.

34. Airline Executive, May 1981, p. 13.

35. Business Week, June 15, 1981, p. 79.

36. Compiled from U.S. Civil Aeronautics Board, Interim Financial Reports, second quarter 1978 and second quarter 1981.

37. U.S. Department of Commerce, Economic Indicators, July 1978 and July 1981.

38. U.S. Civil Aeronautics Board, Handbook of Airline Statistics, 1973 edition and 1979 Supplement, part II, Table 73.

39. TWA Pricing Department.

40. Air Transport Association, Air Transport 1980, p. 12 and various 1981 issues of Aviation Daily.

41. Caves, Air Transport, p. 377.

42. Handbook of Airline Statistics, pp. 534-37.

43. Ibid.

44. Ibid.

45. Ibid.

46. Ibid.

47. Ibid.

48. Economic Report of the President, February 1978, Table B-42, p. 220.

49. Handbook of Airline Statistics, p. 34.

50. Ibid.

51. U.S. Department of Commerce, Business Conditions Digest, September 1978.

52. Handbook of Airline Statistics, p. 543.

53. Ibid. and Handbook Supplements.

54. Aviation Week and Space Technology, and Aviation Daily, various issues.

55. U.S. Civil Aeronautics Board, Airline Traffic Statistics, December 1970 and June 1978.

56. U.S. Department of Commerce, Economic Indicators, September 1978, p. 23.

8

PRODUCT COMPETITION

BACKGROUND

In the airline industry, public regulation reinforced the oligopolistic structure through a long practice of blockading entry, but failure to restrain product competition allowed for seemingly anomalous behavioral patterns. On the one hand, models describing product quality in a competitive environment under regulation correctly hypothesized that, given price constraint, supranormal profits would be dissipated in vigorous service rivalry.[1] Between 1962 and 1980, for instance, the rate of return in the airline industry averaged only 6.7 percent,[2] while the Aaa corporate bond yield amounted to 7.1 percent and the Baa 8.0 percent[3] over the same period. At the same time, the typical large city-pair setting consisted mostly of two or three carriers bidding for market share. However, the intensity with which they appeared to compete with regard to service quality frequently belied the existence of a tight oligopolistic structure. Microeconomic theory suggests that the recognition of interdependence, which would allow for uncontested allocation of market share, is an inverse function of the number of firms. Thus, while acknowledging the active service rivalry within the industry, the academic critics of regulation, who formulated applications of the nonprice competitive model to the airlines,[4] were at a loss to explain the intensity of service quality rivalry. They also chose to ignore the welfare implications of this type of competition in arguing that the public had been shortchanged due to a lack of active price rivalry.

Failure to conform to the oligopolistic model of passive behavior was generally stated in terms of industry immaturity or explained as a result of regulation: the CAB, by ostensibly offering a protection as a friendly regulator, encouraged reckless competitive behavior. White suggested that perhaps an S-curve mentality

dominated the thinking of airline planners.[5] While such explanations were not without merit, they generally failed to appreciate,
especially during the earlier phases, that scheduling involved only
one aspect of the pervasive role of aircraft in product rivalry.
Moreover, the influence of airline-marketing departments within
the corporate structure has been vastly underrated.

Among the various industries, air transportation is perhaps
unique in that aircraft, the principal capital asset of each firm,
plays a direct and dominant role in the competitive framework.
Whereas most consumers approve or disapprove goods produced
by capital equipment, the end product in the airline industry is the
seat contained in the capital equipment. The type, size, age, and
particularly the deployment of aircraft by each carrier appears to
be crucial in the determination of a firm's market share. Carriers offering more attractive aircraft and schedules maintain an
obvious edge over rivals since air travelers typically may choose
from at least two operators in a market. Naturally, other wholly
independent modes of product competition, such as in-flight
amenities and ground service, also figure in the overall outcome.
Nevertheless, the success or failure of strategies regarding the
purchase of aircraft and their scheduling rate high in the financial
performance of an airline.

It has been suggested that the pace of new aircraft development has slowed, thus placing more of a burden on scheduling
tactics in airline rivalry. This factor in addition to other matters
involving a changing environment in the industry and its effect on
airline product competition and divergent degrees of rivalry among
different carrier groups are analyzed below. The last topic requires a test of a Caves' hypothesis, proposed nearly 20 years ago,
concerning the intensity of competition within an east-west group
of carriers and a north-south grouping.[6]

TECHNOLOGY AND COMPETITION

While equipment quality remains an important element of
product competition, the intensity and effectiveness of such rivalry
has diminished considerably in recent years. During the earlier
period of industry development, rapid advances in aircraft technology enabled carriers frequently to obtain great advantages over
rivals with regard to speed, comfort, or cost economies. As
presented in an earlier section, the great improvement in market
share achieved by Capital between 1955 and 1958 associated with
its installation of the advanced Vickers Viscount turboprop aircraft
in several competitive segments represented one example of this.

In the latest period, however, a combination of forces, including economic dislocations and financial difficulties within the industry and among some manufacturers, sharply curtailed the introduction of new equipment. Table 1.4 illustrated the competitive ramifications of the changed pace of aircraft introductions. Among the top 100 markets, for instance, there were swings in traffic shares greater than ten percentage points in 54 percent of the markets between 1955 and 1958. However, less than 20 percent of the top markets experienced similar changes in the 1975–78 period.[7]

Table 8.1 summarizes aircraft developments in the modern era. As indicated in the table, only 8 new passenger aircraft types, most of which were of the wide-bodied type, were put into domestic service in the 1970s, compared to 20 and 25 in each of the two preceding periods. Most of the newly introduced wide-bodied aircraft types were designed and contracted for in the late 1960s. These included the Boeing 747, Lockheed 1011, and McDonnell Douglas' DC-10 and later derivatives of all three types. The only exception was the European Airbus A-300, which was first operated in domestic service by Eastern late in 1977.[8]

TABLE 8.1

Stages of Introduction of New Aircraft Types, 1936–79

Period	Number of New Aircraft Introduced	Manufacturers with Most Introductions
1936–49	17	Douglas (7) Lockheed (5)
1950–59	20	Lockheed (5) Douglas (5)
1960–69	25	Boeing (9) Douglas (7)
1970–79	8	Boeing (3)

Source: U.S. Civil Aeronautics Board, Handbook of Airline Statistics, 1973 edition and 1975, 1977, and 1979 Supplements.

The curtailment in new aircraft introductions had several causes. First, the initial deliveries of the jumbo jets unfortunately coincided with the 1969-70 recession, which depressed demand and caused the industry load factor to drop under 50 percent in both 1970 and 1971.[9] Instead of the almost steady double digit increase in traffic of the late 1960s, revenue-passenger-mile growth for the industry averaged less than 1 percent a year from 1969 to 1971,[10] negating the optimistic traffic projections upon which purchases of the wide-bodied aircraft had originally been justified. The resulting glut of capacity had a predictably negative impact on profits. The second key development involved sharp fuel price rises in the aftermath of the 1973 Middle East war, and again late in the decade. Between 1972 and 1974, the price of domestic jet fuel rose by 105 percent,[11] causing operating expenses to soar. One consequence of the sudden escalation of fuel cost was that carriers tended to abandon plans they may have entertained for further wide-bodied aircraft purchases though moderate traffic growth had resumed in 1972 and 1973. Another explosion in fuel prices between 1978 and 1980 of 128 percent had more of an impact on post-1980 ordering plans.[12] The third important event was the deep 1973-75 recession, which stunted traffic volumes even more severely than had the prior business slowdown. Moreover, the nonmaterialization of new equipment orders would probably have caused one large airframe manufacturer—Lockheed—to go bankrupt except for the intervention of the federal government in the form of a massive loan guarantee.

Apart from the economic dislocations during 1970-75, another limiting factor involved the effect of the wide-bodied aircraft on consumers. The main appeal of the jumbo jets was their spaciousness. Moreover, many carriers remodeled the interiors of their narrow-bodied aircraft to create the so-called "wide-bodied look," which made maximum use of available fuselage space. Although surveys showed that wide-bodies had a definite edge with respect to perceived passenger comfort,[13] subsequent events indicated that this advantage was not overwhelming and could apparently be neutralized by a competitive increase in flight frequencies of narrow-bodied craft. Earlier innovations, which featured pressurization and jet speed, represented technological improvements that were more difficult to counteract quickly in a competitive environment.

It would be useful at this point to examine consumers' reception and competitive responses to the introduction of the wide-body in an actual market setting. Two markets where the new equipment competed with narrow-bodies were New York-Dallas and Chicago-Dallas. Both fulfill the requirement for such an inquiry since one

TABLE 8.2

New York-Dallas Flight Frequencies and
Market Share, 1970-75

| | Daily Round Trip Flights | | | Local Passenger Share (percent) | |
| | American | | Braniff | | |
Period	Narrow	Wide	Narrow	American	Braniff
1970-4	5.5	0	4	70.6	29.4
1971-2	3	1	4	67.0	33.0
1971-4	3.5	1	4.5	63.9	36.1
1972-2	4.5	1	6	63.1	36.9
1972-4	3.5	2	6	61.6	38.4
1973-2	3.5	2	7	60.6	39.4
1973-4	5.5	1	7	58.7	41.3
1974-2	7	0	8	58.5	41.5
1974-4	7	2	9.5	55.5	44.5
1975-2	7	2	9	60.9	39.1
1975-4	9	0	10	59.9	40.1

Sources: Tabulated from Reuben Donnelly Corp., Official
Airline Guide; and U.S. Civil Aeronautics Board, Origin-
Destination Survey, various issues.

of the two rivals—Braniff—never fielded a wide-body in either market, while the other—American—experimented with B-747s and
DC-10s. The fact that both segments involved only two carriers
also simplifies the analysis. Tables 8.2 and 8.3 indicate scheduling changes and traffic share in two quarter intervals during the
early 1970s. The two variables are not strictly comparable with
regard to timing as each is not available on the same basis as the
other. Schedules generally are not consistent within a quarter,
while the market share data can only be calculated quarterly from
published sources. The schedules indicated in the tables thus reflect the February and November timetables or midpoints of the
second and fourth quarters rather than the quarter as a whole.

TABLE 8.3

Chicago-Dallas Flight Frequencies and
Market Share, 1971-74

| | Daily Round Trip Flights | | | Local Passenger Share (percent) | |
| | American | | Braniff | | |
Period	Narrow	Wide	Narrow	American	Braniff
1971-4	7	0	5.5	69.8	30.2
1972-2	5	2	6	66.4	33.6
1972-4	6	1	6	65.0	35.0
1973-2	5.5	1	6.5	59.7	40.3
1973-4	7	0	7.5	60.4	39.6
1974-2	7	0	10	55.7	44.3
1974-4	11	0	11	56.7	43.3

Sources: Tabulated from Reuben Donnelly Corp., Official Airline Guide; and U.S. Civil Aeronautics Board, Origin-Destination Survey, various issues.

In the New York-Dallas market, American first introduced a B-747 early in 1971. Prior to that, American had flown 5.5 daily narrow-bodied round trips against 4 for Braniff. When introducing B-747 service, American eliminated 2.5 daily narrow-bodied flights since a B-747 provided approximately the same number of seats as 2.5 B-727-200s. Still outnumbered in terms of seats but now with parity in flight frequencies, Braniff was able to push its market share from 29.4 to 33.0 percent from the fourth quarter of 1970 to the second quarter of 1971. The next major scheduling change took place a year later as American, probably in response to erosion of its share, increased its narrow-bodied frequencies to 4.5 and substituted a smaller DC-10 for the B-747. Meanwhile, Braniff's narrow-bodied flights rose to six round trips a day, thus achieving frequency superiority, and its market share improved to 36.9 percent. In the fourth quarter of 1972, American traded a narrow-body for a second DC-10 but suffered a further diminution in market share. During September of 1972 and through the following March, American was troubled by a system-wide work-rule slowdown by its pilots, who were dissatisfied with the course of their labor contract discussions.[14] This caused American to absorb unusual schedule delays and must have alienated many passengers even beyond the period of the slowdown. Through the second quarter of 1974, when American withdrew its wide-bodied service, perhaps in response to the escalation in fuel price, Braniff maintained its edge in frequency by staying a step ahead of American in scheduling and succeeded in building its market share to 41.5 percent, or 12.1 percentage points higher than the mark before the introduction of the B-747 by American. Had Braniff remained at the lower share level, it would have carried 11,000 fewer passengers during the second quarter of 1974. American reinstituted wide-bodied service in the fourth quarter of 1974 with two DC-10s, using Dallas as an intermediate stop in a transcontinental night coach program. However, Braniff responded by raising its daily frequencies to 9.5 and saw its market share rise to 44.5 percent. Its share fell back to 40 percent once a scheduling equilibrium without wide-bodies was finally achieved in 1975. By then Braniff was operating one more daily round trip than American, thus reversing the competitive situation in 1970 and in the process achieving a significant improvement in share.

Because the introduction of wide-bodied planes by American in the Chicago-Dallas market occurred a year later than the New York-Dallas case, both rivals had the benefit of some experience. American had cut back 2.5 narrow-bodied flights when instituting B-747 service in New York-Dallas and apparently lost in share as a consequence. This time, however, American maintained its total frequencies at 7 by substituting two DC-10s for two narrow-bodies, while Braniff was adding a one-directional flight. Despite the small change in the relationship of relative frequency, Braniff's market share rose by over three percentage points, implying a negative reception for American's DC-10s. The labor difficulties that beset American during this period may also have played a role in its market share deterioration. Subsequently, American reduced wide-body service to one round trip and eliminated it altogether by the fourth quarter of 1973. At that point, Braniff's market share had grown to 39.6 percent or 9.4 percentage points higher than the level before the start of American's wide-body program. During the second quarter of 1974, Braniff suddenly turned to an aggressive scheduling strategy by adding 2.5 round trips and was able to add nearly 5 more points in traffic share. American shortly responded with an increase of 4 frequencies, however, and an equilibrium was finally reached but at a scheduling level that seemed unwarranted, based on traffic volumes. Due to the 1973-75 recession, traffic in the Chicago-Dallas market had declined by 18 percent between the fourth quarter of 1973 and the same period a year later,[15] which was the period in which the scheduling escalation took place.

In both instances of wide-body versus narrow-body rivalry, the alleged appeal of the wide-body equipment was never apparent. Fearing the worst, the nonwide-body carrier, in this case Braniff, sought to undermine the appeal of the advanced aircraft by increasing its number of flights. In this way Braniff was able to offer improved scheduling convenience in the marketplace and appeared to be successful. Obviously this analysis ignores other types of marketing competition. Nor does it ascertain whether or not Braniff's efforts were directly converted into an improved financial performance. Nonetheless, it can be fairly stated that American must have absorbed a setback at the conclusion of both episodes since its overall schedule, and hence expenses, grew, but it concurrently lost substantial ground in market share. The two examples underline what has been said concerning the marketing significance of the comfort feature of the wide-body equipment, namely, that the aircraft size breakthrough has not been accorded the highly favorable consumer response given earlier basic innovations, such as pressurization and speed.

Despite the relative paucity of new aircraft models in the 1970s, equipment deliveries proceeded but these were primarily based on the need to replace aging, inefficient aircraft rather than to obtain competitive advantage. The disruption owing to fuel prices in particular caused a discontinuity in the types of equipment purchased. For instance, before the steep increase in fuel costs at the end of 1973, most of the deliveries during the 1970-73 period were of the wide-bodied variety, with the reverse occurring afterward. Of the 283 aircraft received by the Trunk carriers from 1970 through 1973, 65 percent were either B-747s, DC-10s, or L-1011s.[16] However, from 1974 through 1978, when another fuel price problem appeared, only 27 percent of 323 deliveries were for gas-guzzling wide-bodies, while 70 percent were for the Boeing 727-200, which had been first introduced in 1967 and subsequently achieved the distinction of becoming the volume leader in commercial aviation.[17] With its three engines consuming 1,600 gallons per hour,[18] and its 130-seat capacity and cost-efficient 500-mile average flight length, it was a type of aircraft that satisfied basic requirements for the 1970s, that is, satisfactory fuel economy and seating appropriate to market size. It should be noted that the generation of aircraft being designed to serve the 1980s and 1990s will have only two or three engines, for fuel economy, and will be in the 150-200 seat range to accommodate the moderate traffic growth expected by then. This contrasts sharply with the ebullient projections that precipitated the development of the earlier wide-bodied equipment.

CAPACITY COMPETITION

In the pursuit of the competitive edge, the overriding presumption of airline rivalry is that if you "fly the schedules (seats), you get the passengers." All things being equal, this assumes that a 50 percent share of seats or frequencies should yield a return equivalent to 50 percent of the traffic in a market. However, by offering more convenient schedules than its rivals, a carrier might obtain a greater than proportional market share. More convenient schedules generally imply a greater than 50 percent capacity share. Scheduling strategy is based on the so-called S-curve, which hypothesizes that a capacity share beyond some threshold point, say 55 percent, should earn a disproportionate traffic share, perhaps 60 percent. In practice, other variables complicate this relationship. Some of these factors would include the effects of alternative forms of product rivalry, such as in-flight and ground service, price competition, and relative "city power." The latter refers to the following each carrier commands in a particular city and is generally a function of the level of service provided to all destinations. However, passenger surveys have repeatedly confirmed scheduling convenience as the main determinant of traveler preference in airlines, and the S-curve concept has been long established among airline strategy managers.

Prior to the heavy onset of price/service quality options after 1977, airline schedulers were loath to incur a noticeable two-to-one or even three-to-two nonstop frequency disadvantage in a market, while less visible five-to-four or similar handicaps were frequently tolerated. Attempts by one carrier to gain an advantage in capacity had often led to excess capacity situations as rivals matched each upward movement and then became fearful of exposing themselves as demand declined as during a recession. The Chicago-Dallas situation in 1974 is an example of this. After the explosion of fuel prices in 1973-74, the strategy of "capacity loading," in which a carrier attempted to gain an S-curve advantage became a more costly experiment given the high probability that a rival would respond in kind. Unless new volumes could be generated, traffic levels would remain split along original lines, thus causing a decline in each competitor's load factor, while the cost of the new capacity would add to operating expenses, leaving the contestants in a worse situation than before. As a result, the pursuit of market shares in general tended to be discouraged as a marketing goal. In summarizing the strategy presumably followed by American after 1973, R. L. Crandall, then senior vice-president of marketing, declared to his own management that:

> We have sought to exercise as much restraint as possible and, at least as importantly, have done everything possible to indicate to our competitors that we are very anxious to encourage capacity restraint. There has been a downward drift in American's share of available seat miles underscoring that our emphasis has recently been on share gap and load factor, not on market share. [19]

The increased use of various price/service quality strategies after 1977 also caused the capacity-loading tactic to lose emphasis. Under the prodding of the CAB, which was intent on promoting competition, carriers were better able to enter new markets but were less apt to seek scheduling parity than to gain a foothold by providing a less popular departure or "no-frills" service at lower fares, which were not universally matched by the incumbents. This developing aspect of airline rivalry was explored in Chapter 7.

In order to keep pace with rising demand, while minimizing fuel and other volume-related costs, the carriers began to increase the number of seats in existing equipment to complement the normal additions from new aircraft deliveries and higher utilization rates. To illustrate the magnitude of the move toward denser seating, American, from the end of 1973 to the end of 1977, increased the number of seats on each type of equipment in a range of 5 to 56 and the annual number of seats available for sale were equivalent to an amount that would be provided by seven DC-10s. [20] United's increases in seats over the same period ranged from 4 to 31 per aircraft and provided the equivalent of five B-747s a year. [21]

Another effort to increase profitability, developed after 1973, involved route "rationalization" or what one observer termed "self-monopolization." [22] This was simply the shifting of resources from less promising markets to those deemed more propitious. Crandall alluded to this when he noted American's efforts to improve its market share and increase its load factor in preference to "slugging it out" through competition in capacity, while a Trans World statement concerning its scheduling strategy for 1977 was even more direct:

> In 1977 we in scheduling will be working to identify those flights or segments where the last three or four years' track record, and early results in 1977, indicate that those services probably will never turn profitable in the near term future. Once identified, these services will be prime candidates for cancellation next year and beyond as we require planes for more potentially profitable areas of our system. [23]

Trans World, toward the end of 1977, introduced the so-called
"super coach" idea: a multiple-flight, dual-configuration service in
two large but unprofitable markets—Chicago-Los Angeles and New
York-Denver—was eliminated in favor of a sharply discounted all-
coach, dense seating service at a much reduced frequency level.[24]
This price/service quality alternative reduced TWA's market share
in Chicago-Los Angeles from about 15 to 7 percent and in New York-
Denver from 30 to 18 percent.[25] However, the move succeeded in
turning large losses within those markets to small profits even
though competing carriers matched the price reduction without reducing their service in the Chicago-Los Angeles segment. This
occurred because the break-even load factors were achieved thanks
to the combination of the new fares and the reduced capacity. Thus,
not only were new travelers attracted by the discount prices, but
passengers from nearby points were also more willing to accept
less direct service to pass through the "super coach" segment.
For instance, many Chicago-San Francisco travelers chose a
Chicago-Los Angeles-San Francisco routing in order to take advantage of the discount, which amounted to 40 percent of the regular
coach fare on the Chicago-Los Angeles segment. In the New York-
Denver market where United at first chose not to match the innovation due to its dominant frequency pattern, TWA succeeded in divert-
ing from it a substantial number of price-sensitive passengers.[26]

The effects of the so-called route rationalization process and
its unravelling may be seen in Table 8.4, which records the aggre-
gation of each domestic carrier's traffic distribution according to
market share during the 1973-77 and 1978-80 periods. Table 8.4
indicates that 15.1 percent of all industry traffic in 1977 was obtained in markets where the carriers in total held a share of less
than 30 percent. This measure may be difficult to understand, but
simply involves segmenting each carrier's volume by markets according to the share obtained. If Continental, for instance, cap-
tured 25 percent of the Chicago-Los Angeles market, that traffic
would be placed in the under-30-percent category, as would Delta's
29 percent share of the New York-Miami market or American's 20
percent share of New York-Washington. The under-30-percent
category is shown separately to represent that portion of traffic
acquired where the carrier was more apt to be a marginal competitor. On the other hand, where an airline can capture at least
60 percent of the traffic in a market, the presumption is that the
carrier must be earning above normal profits. Naturally there
may be exceptions to both suppositions. For instance, markets
served by three or four carriers generally require that the traffic
share of at least one competitor fall below 30 percent, but if the
capacity share can be kept proportionately lower, thus allowing for

a positive share gap, steady profits may accrue to the successful airline. At the higher end above a 60 percent traffic share, profitability could be threatened if the carrier obtained the high traffic share by means of an even higher share of capacity. In such an unusual circumstance, operating expenses might exceed revenues.

TABLE 8.4

Percentage Distribution of Domestic Industry
Traffic according to Market Share, 1973-80

Market Share	1973	1977	1978	1980
Less than 30%	16.7	15.1	16.0	23.6
30-59%	32.8	34.4	33.8	36.0
60-89%	25.6	25.3	26.3	23.5
90% and over	24.9	25.2	23.9	16.9

Source: U.S. Civil Aeronautics Board, Origin and Destination Statistics, Table 10, 1973, 1977, 1978, and 1980 issues.

The one segment to decline noticeably during the 1973-77 period was the under-30-percent group, which must have included a great number of markets of doubtful profitability. Exit from such markets apparently proceeded according to the dictates of profit-maximization. Analysis of the other three segmentations is less straightforward. Between 1973 and 1975, for example, route rationalization moved forward as the group with a quasi-monopoly of 60-89 percent and the more pure monopoly traffic both grew at the expense of the group with 30-59 percent. After 1975, however, the directions were reversed as the categories above 60 percent declined relative to the 30-59 percent group. The difference may be explained by the lifting of the route moratorium in 1975 at which time the CAB again began to hear route cases and award new operating certificates. This process had been placed in limbo after 1970 when the Board decided to protect incumbent carriers against increased competition. Since new service authorizations are primarily based on a presumption of inadequate service and/or a lack of competition, new market entry would have to have been concentrated in the 60 percent and over market share grouping. The CAB under Alfred Kahn's chairmanship and Congressional support for some form of deregulation also added impetus to the erosion of the dominant share markets. Nevertheless, the fact that the 60-percent-plus shares declined only modestly between 1975 and 1977, while that of the under-30-percent group continued to drop, indicates that new entry probably did not check the rationalization process during this period.

By 1978 the low extreme had gained slightly at the expense of the 90-percent-plus group indicating some deregulation impact, but by 1980 the movement toward greater market segmentation appeared to be enormous. From a roughly 50-50 percent position between the two highest and two lowest bands, the split moved to 60-40 percent in favor of the smaller market shares. The true extent of the market share shifting during the two years after passage of the Deregulation Act was somewhat muddled in that several new scheduled interstate carriers including Air Florida, Pacific Southwest, Southwest, World, Capitol, etc. became part of the CAB origin-destination surveys only in 1979, which meant that traffic distributions in such intrastate markets as Los Angeles-San Francisco and Dallas-Houston had excluded a key competitor prior to 1979. For example, in the former city pair where United had held 48 percent of the passengers in the third quarter 1978 survey without Pacific Southwest being counted, this share dropped to 28 percent two years later when Pacific Southwest was revealed to be the dominant carrier with 32 percent of the market.[27] Similarly, in Dallas-Houston where Southwest reportedly had maintained the lion's share since 1973, Texas International with 51 percent and Braniff at 47 percent were purportedly the leaders in the 1978 survey, but these shares dropped to 12 and 15 percent respectively once Southwest was officially revealed to have held 71 percent of the business in 1980.[28]

Nevertheless, other evidence indicates that much of the movement toward greater share dispersion was real. In the large transcontinental markets, for instance, new entry caused most incumbent traffic to fall from the 30-59 percent category into the under-30-percent group. In the New York-Los Angeles and New York-San Francisco markets, American, Trans World, and United saw their collective share drop from near 100 percent to around 75 percent due to the entry of Eastern, Pan American, Capitol, and World beginning in 1979.[29] Moreover, where Braniff with 41 percent and Delta with 57 percent had split the Chicago-Houston market in 1978, six carriers were sharing the traffic in 1980 with only one carrier accounting for more than 30 percent (Delta).[30]

PATTERNS IN PRODUCT COMPETITION

In analyzing competitive patterns within the industry, Caves hypothesized that the large transcontinental east-west carriers,

namely American, Trans World, and United, tended to recognize
their mutual interdependence and therefore engaged in less heated
rivalry with one another than was the case with the predominantly
eastern-based north-south airlines—Delta, Eastern, National, and
Northeast (before 1972).[31] Thus the latter group presumably was
more prone to the "slugging-it-out" approach to competition in
capacity than the east-west group whose behavior tended more toward a peaceful coexistence model. To demonstrate his point,
Caves compared the relative load factor movements of the two groups
during the late 1950s. At the onset of the 1957-58 recession, the
load factors of both groups declined from prior year levels, but that
of the north-south carriers dropped further than that of the east-
west group. Moreover, while the load factor of the east-west carriers improved during the economic recovery of 1959, that of the
north-south airlines slipped further due to increases in capacity in
excess of traffic growth.[32] These facts were presented by Caves
to support the notion of two distinctly different patterns of conduct
regarding capacity that existed in the industry.

A shortcoming of Caves' analysis involved his failure to take
account of strike activity in the late 1950s. For 1958 in particular,
when Eastern sustained a strike that lasted over a month,[33] the
north-south load factor for the year appeared higher than normal,
since Eastern's total capacity excluded a full month of available seat
miles. Thus, in other circumstances, the group would have shown
an improvement for 1959 though most likely not so great as that of
the east-west group. Under a pattern of peaceful coexistence, carriers could more easily adjust joint capacity to demand conditions
than where rivalry was more severe. In the latter situation, carriers resisted unilateral reductions in capacity when demand soft-
ened and tended to expand schedules to capture a greater market
share during an economic expansion.

Table 8.5 expands Caves' findings through comparison of the
load factors of the same two carrier groups for the pre-deregulation
1969-77 period and the 1980 result is shown as a matter of interest.
With Trans World and United expanding into Florida during 1979,
American's enlargement of its Dallas hub, and Eastern and Pan
American's (National) incursions on the main transcontinental segments in 1980, the east-west, north-south differentiations had lost
much of their relevance by 1980. Although the north-south carriers
were reduced from four to three by the merger of Delta and Northeast in 1972, the data through 1977 supported the notion of more intense product rivalry within the north-south group. The period
under observation contained three recessions when load factors
should have dropped. Initially, however, the experience of 1969
seems to contradict Caves' position, since the east-west load factor

declined more sharply than that of the north-south and even fell
slightly in 1971. Moreover, the rebound in the load factor for the
east-west group in 1973 only registered 3.5 percentage points as
against a 4.8 point improvement for the north-south carriers. The
relatively poorer east-west performance during the earlier portion
of the period may be partially explained by the preponderance in deliveries of the new generation of wide-bodied aircraft to the east-
west carriers.

TABLE 8.5

East-West and North-South Carrier Load Factors, 1969-80
(percent)

	1969	1971	1973	1975	1977	1980
East-west	51.0	48.5	52.0	55.4	58.6	59.3
North-south	49.3	47.4	52.2	53.0	54.7	58.9

Note: Carrier load factors have been adjusted by author for
all industry strikes and other service disruptions.
Source: U.S. Civil Aeronautics Board, Air Carrier Traffic
Statistics, December 1969-December 1980.

One advantage enjoyed by the east-west carriers was the
transcontinental limit on capacity described in Chapter 6 in which
American, Trans World, and United, with CAB approval, carried
out joint reductions of capacity in four long-haul markets. This
agreement obviously enabled those carriers to limit pressure on
load factors and also pointed out the more cooperative side of their
marketing behavior. Eastern had been able to enter into a similar
arrangement on its New York-San Juan route with American and
Pan American, but those carriers did not compete to any extent
against Eastern on the mainland.
After 1973 comparative load factors reverted more to the
pattern described for the earlier period by Caves. Despite the start
of a severe recession in November 1973, industry traffic volumes
held up until mid-1974 due to domestic gasoline shortages, which
diverted a considerable amount of short- and medium-distance automobile travel to the air. At the same time, the airlines were allowed to limit capacity by mutual agreement as a fuel-saving device,

but again, most of the accords involved the east-west carriers. Thus, while the east-west group was able to curtail available seat miles by 7 percent, the north-south carrier decline amounted to only 3 percent in 1974.[34] Thereafter, the gap between the load factors grew larger each year through 1977 even though all of the agreements concerning capacity had been ended by government order in April 1975.[35] While never dormant, competition among the north-south carriers began to increase after the absorption of Northeast by Delta late in 1972. Almost immediately, Delta made a strong bid to improve on Northeast's former weak position in the New York-Florida markets by heavily expanding schedules.[36] Later, when National sustained two long strikes in 1974 and 1975, both Delta and Eastern increased capacity in an attempt to make travelers leave National, which had been strikebound for four months in each year. After National's second strike, it apparently was compelled to bring its capacity more into line with the levels offered by Delta and Eastern, which resulted in another increase in capacity. All told, north-south available seat miles increased 17 percent between 1973 and 1977 compared to only 6 percent for the east-west group, while the traffic growth difference was much narrower at 23 and 19 percent, respectively.[37]

Other evidence supported the notion that the north-south carriers suffered from greater instability. Table 8.6 indicates percentage differences between the highest and lowest performer in each group for selected measures in 1977, which is the only recent year with statistics free of significant distortion from strikes and before the entry splurge blurred directional distinctions. Presumably, the greater the spread in the main performance variables among rivals, the more likely was the possibility that the worst operator would resort to disruptive marketing techniques to improve its lot. In each of the variables shown, the north-south group produced larger variation between their best and worst performers than was the case within the east-west bloc. For instance, Delta's high domestic profit ratio of 15.38 percent versus National's 3.12 percent was far greater than United's 9.73 percent as against 2.79 percent for Trans World.[38] With respect to unit costs, National's .31¢ rate was only two-thirds that of Eastern, while those of United and Trans World were quite close.[39] The employee productivity measure involved National and Eastern, on the one hand, and United and American on the other, but produced a similar result.[40]

The significance of differing competitive patterns within the same industry seems obvious from a theoretical standpoint; namely, that the less interdependent firms should earn lower than normal profits and run a higher risk of business failure than those companies behaving more cooperatively. However, in this instance, the

facts do not support this conclusion, at least regarding profitability. Although Northeast apparently would have gone bankrupt had it not been absorbed by Delta in 1972, the allegedly more combative north-south group consistently surpassed the transcontinental carriers in terms of rate of return on investment and on sales. From 1972 through 1977, for instance, the average return in investment for Delta, Eastern, and National combined was nearly twice that of American, Trans World, and United, even though the differences in the latest two years were narrower.[41]

TABLE 8.6

Ratio of Best to Worst Performer for
Selected Measures by Carrier Group, 1977
(percent)

Carrier Group	Rate of Return on Investment	Operating Expenses per Available Ton Miles	Passenger Revenue per Employee
North-south	393	67	124
East-west	249	98	108

Sources: Computed from U.S. Civil Aeronautics Board, Interim Financial Report, December 1977; Form 41 reports.

The fact that the profitability of the north-south carriers was regularly greater than that of the east-west group in the later period contrasts with conditions in the earlier period when Caves performed his analysis.[42] However, the wide variation in the rate of return, especially within the north-south group itself, indicates that relative profitability involves other variables as well. Perhaps the best thing to be said about this exercise is that the intensity of competition alone is insufficient as a profit determinant since firms with lower load factors achieved higher profitability. Therefore, an investigation of varying competitive patterns under oligopolistic conditions, while interesting with regard to how they evolve, appears to have yielded little toward an explanation of financial results. As indicated in Chapter 3, relative profitability may be a function of many factors, including employee and equipment productivity, the ratio of fixed to variable costs, and the share of total revenue attributable to cargo operations.

CONCLUSION

Since the jets replaced the piston equipment during the 1960s, resulting in a substantial increase in the speed of air travel, the impact of aircraft technology on product competition abated considerably as the types of new aircraft decreased in number relative to the past and features affecting consumers failed to gain a following comparable to earlier innovations. While the introduction of widebodied equipment brought with it great technical advances, for instance, the evidence suggests that, at least with respect to domestic service, the comfort and spaciousness of such aircraft have been far overshadowed by the long-established consumer preference for scheduling convenience.

The fact that market share fluctuations had been much less pronounced up to the deregulation phase than in the earlier periods, however, reflected not only the reduced impact of the new equipment but also the high operating costs, which apparently dampened enthusiasm for the "slugging-it-out" approach to product competition. Particularly after the escalation in fuel prices during the winter of 1973-74, segments of the industry sought to limit capacity expansion in general and reduced their competitive behavior or left markets where they were weak and diverted equipment to safer segments, instead of resorting to protracted wars of uncertain outcome over capacity. Indicative of the less expansive mood on the part of the carriers after 1973 is the fact that adjusted Trunk available seat miles rose only 12 percent during the 1973-77 period compared to 17 percent from 1969 to 1973.[43] Moreover, a significant portion of the later increase resulted from the relatively inexpensive method of adding seats to existing aircraft. The movement toward route rationalization, which was essentially anticompetitive, occurred at a time when great efforts to revitalize rivalry among carriers were being pressed by the CAB. This suggests that the industry might have become less competitive had the CAB remained passive in awarding routes and in pricing policy after 1977.

The issue over whether a dichotomy exists within the industry concerning the intensity of product competition was raised by Caves, who concluded that the north-south airlines generally carried on a more lively rivalry than the large east-west carriers. Caves held that imbalances in size, market share strength, or financial condition were more prevalent among Delta, Eastern, and National than among American, Trans World, and United. Later evidence on the changes in relative load factor supported this conclusion even though one of the sources of the instability was eliminated when Delta absorbed Northeast in 1972. However, the logical extension of this conclusion, which has to do with assuming greater profitability for

the east-west carriers, could not be confirmed since such a simplistic analysis omitted consideration of other apparently equally important variables. Moreover, recent changes in the industry structure have virtually obliterated the earlier distinctions of competitive groupings, which renders such analysis moot in the deregulated context.

NOTES

1. George J. Stigler, "Price and Non-Price Competition," Journal of Political Economy 76 (January-February 1968):149-54; G. C. Archibald, "Profit-Maximizing and Non-Price Competition," Economica 31 (February 1964):13-22.

2. Computed from various editions of U.S. Civil Aeronautics Board, Handbook of Airline Statistics and Air Carrier Financial Statistics.

3. Economic Report of the President, January 1981, Table B-65.

4. George W. Douglas and James C. Miller, III, Economic Regulation of Domestic Air Transport: Theory and Policy (Washington, D.C.: Brookings Institution, 1974); John C. Panzar, "Regulation, Service Quality, and Market Performance: A Model of Airline Rivalry," Ph.D. dissertation, Stanford University, 1974; A. S. DeVany, "The Effect of Price and Entry Regulation on Airline Output, Capacity, and Efficiency," Bell Journal of Economics 6 (Spring 1975):327-45; Gary J. Dorman, "Airline Competition: A Theoretical and Empirical Analysis," Ph.D. dissertation, University of California, Berkeley, 1976; Richard Schmalensee, "Comparative Static Properties of Regulated Airline Oligopolies," Bell Journal of Economics 8 (Autumn 1977):565-76; Lawrence J. White, "Quality Variations When Prices Are Regulated," Bell Journal of Economics and Management Science 3 (Autumn 1972):425-36.

5. Lawrence J. White, Quality, Competition and Regulation: Evidence from the Airline Industry, presented at American Telephone & Telegraph Conference on Regulation, Dartmouth College, September 1971.

6. Richard E. Caves, Air Transport and Its Regulators (Cambridge, Mass.: Harvard University Press, 1962), pp. 25-27.

7. Data for 1955-58 from ibid., p. 26; data for 1975-78 calculated from U.S. Civil Aeronautics Board, Origin-Destination Survey, Table 10, various issues.

8. Aviation Daily, November 21, 1977, p. 115.

9. Air Carrier Traffic Statistics, December 1971.

10. Handbook of Airline Statistics, 1973 edition, Table 16, p. 24.

11. Air Transport Association, Air Transport 1977, p. 7.

12. Air Transport Association, Air Transport 1980 & 1981, p. 12.

13. Gallup Organization, A Study of the U.S. Air Traveler Conducted for American Express, August 1975, pp. 15-16.

14. "What Ails American Airlines," Business Week, May 12, 1973, pp. 134-36.

15. Origin-Destination Survey, Table 10, fourth quarter 1973 and fourth quarter 1974.

16. General Electric Corp., Aircraft Engine Group, Aircraft Operating Indices, Table 1, various issues.

17. Ibid.

18. Ibid., Table 7, various issues.

19. Remarks of R. L. Crandall, senior vice-president, American Airlines, to management meeting, May 3, 1978.

20. Compiled from American Airlines, Domestic Operating Statistics, Flight and Traffic Statistics, Report 911-253-34, various issues.

21. Compiled from United Airlines Inc., Operating Statistics, various issues.

22. Julius Maldutis, "Airline Industry Monopoly Power Revisited," Salomon Brothers Stock Research Department, March 1, 1978, p. 3.

23. Trans World Airlines, 1977 Marketing Plan.

24. Aviation Daily, July 12, 1977, p. 50, and November 23, 1977, p. 130.

25. Origin-Destination Survey, first quarter 1977 and first quarter 1978, Table 10.

26. Ibid.

27. Ibid., third quarter 1978 and third quarter 1980.

28. Ibid.

29. Ibid.

30. Ibid.

31. Caves, Air Transport, pp. 344-45.

32. Ibid.

33. Handbook of Airline Statistics, 1973 edition, part VIII, item 14, p. 574.

34. Air Carrier Traffic Statistics, December 1974.

35. C. E. Schneider, "Capacity Pact Blocked by Court," Aviation Week and Space Technology, April 28, 1975, pp. 31-32.

36. "Delta Joins the New York-Florida Scramble," Business Week, July 29, 1972, pp. 40-42.

37. Calculated from Air Carrier Traffic Statistics, December 1973 and December 1974.

38. Ibid., December 1977.

39. Ibid.

40. Computed from U.S. Civil Aeronautics Board, Form 41 Schedules.

41. Calculated from U.S. Civil Aeronautics Board, Quarterly Interim Financial Report, various issues.

42. Handbook of Airline Statistics, 1965 edition, part IV, pp. 242-51.

43. Air Carrier Traffic Statistics, December 1969, December 1973, and December 1977.

9

AIRLINE PERFORMANCE

Because of its visibility as an important service industry, its quasi-utility status, and its high level of concentration, air transport has been one of the more frequently analyzed industries. During the deregulation debate of 1975-78, the industry and the Civil Aeronautics Board came under particularly intensive scrutiny as the political process attempted to identify some areas of resource misallocation that could easily be portrayed as inflationary. Critics of the prevailing system charged that overpricing took place and that airline service was not sufficiently attuned to market demand. Aside from the merits of the case, the criticism proved highly attractive politically and the result was the Airline Deregulation Act of 1978, which sought to substitute free market forces in spheres formally controlled by the regulatory authority. The object was to remove government influence, which was presumed to be protective of the industry to the detriment of the public interest.

The purpose of this chapter is to provide a reevaluation of some areas of airline performance that bear directly on the welfare issues and were at the core of the 1975-78 dialogues. Included are an examination of air transport profitability among its different groups and in comparison to other industries, the issue of equity of the airline price structure, and how the airlines rate with other industries in the area of promotion.

INDUSTRY PROFITABILITY

Since accounting practices are seldom applied uniformly among firms in the same industry, and far less commonly between industries, analysis of comparative rates of return is very difficult. Differing treatment of depreciation and inventories are only two sources of bias in reported profits, while varying amounts of assets

145

and debt levels may materially distort the denominator of the equation for the rate of return. Stockholders' equity, net assets, or capital and surplus usually comprise the base of the equation. With regard to the average rate of return in the airline industry, the Civil Aeronautics Board, for rate-making purposes, includes interest expenses with final net income in the numerator; the former is important due to the industry's relatively large debt burden. The investment base, in this recent definition, comprises stockholders' equity, current notes payable, long-term debt, advances from associated companies, advances from nontransport divisions, unamortized premium on debt, and unamortized debt expense. [1]

Table 9.1 details the CAB's recent figures on the rates of return of the various airline groups. Perhaps the most obvious point is the consistent advantage that the smaller Trunk average had over the Big Four during the 1962-80 period. In most instances, the Local service record was also stronger than that of the Big Four. The experience of 1962-80 contrasts with the period prior to 1960 during which the Big Four regularly outperformed the smaller carriers. It was in this earlier setting that Caves, in 1962, predicted decreasing viability for the smaller carriers. However, the group emerged from the 1960-61 recession apparently with less damage and, largely because of the CAB's policies for strengthening routes and their own cost control efforts, achieved a position of superiority during and after the recession-free decade of the 1960s. The Local carrier group also benefited from continuing subsidies on service to unprofitable hinterland points and, especially after 1966, from even more favorable route awards than those accorded the smaller Trunk group. [2] This latter policy reflected concern by Congress over subsidy payments. The increased profitability of the smaller carriers raises the issues of optimum size and economies of scale. As indicated in Chapter 3, the smaller Trunks achieved the lowest unit costs by 1976, whereas those of medium size had done so by 1958.

The usual measure of adequate profits is a comparison of the rate of return with the prevailing long-term interest rate, the implication being that the assets of unprofitable industries, if liquidated, might earn a higher yield if invested in securities. In fact, during only eight years of the 1962-80 period did the industry's rate of return exceed Moody's Aaa corporate bond rate, indicating subnormal performance on the part of the industry. [3]

On two occasions (1960 and 1971), the Board established a rate of return standard for the industry, which offered stockholders profits comparable to those from investments involving similar risk in order to insure access to capital markets. The technique for developing the standard involved estimation of the cost of debt and

TABLE 9.1

Rate of Return, Income after Taxes before Interest
Expense as a Percentage of Total Investment,
Trunk and Local Service Carriers, 1962–80
(percentage)

	Total Domestic Trunks	Big Four*	Other Trunks	Locals
1962	3.6	2.3	7.4	10.2
1963	4.9	4.0	7.1	8.6
1964	9.6	7.6	15.4	9.9
1965	11.6	9.4	17.5	11.2
1966	10.4	7.5	17.6	7.7
1967	8.9	7.9	11.5	3.9
1968	5.8	4.2	9.3	0.8
1969	5.3	5.1	5.6	(2.9)
1970	2.3	0.1	6.5	0.7
1971	4.4	3.6	5.8	4.0
1972	6.0	5.0	7.8	7.1
1973	5.9	3.5	10.1	9.3
1974	8.7	6.9	11.5	12.2
1975	3.0	0.3	6.7	4.9
1976	7.5	6.0	9.5	9.8
1977	9.1	5.9	12.8	13.8
1978	12.8	12.4	13.6	14.0
1979	7.1	6.0	8.1	8.2
1980	5.7	5.3	6.2	11.6

*American, Eastern, Trans World, and United.

Note: Investment base definition was altered slightly between 1965 and 1966.

Sources: U.S. Civil Aeronautics Board, Handbook of Airline Statistics, 1973 edition, part VI; Supplements to Handbook 1975, 1977, and 1979; Air Carrier Financial Statistics, December 1979 and December 1980.

equity capital and the debt/equity ratio. The 1960 standard was issued at the end of the General Passenger Fare Investigation and set a 10.5 percent rate for the Trunks, while the later determination, issued during the Domestic Passenger Fare Investigation, established a 12.0 percent rate.[4]

Achievement of the standards has proved elusive for the industry, although certain individual carriers have consistently exceeded them. During the 1960s, the 10.5 percent standard was surpassed once and nearly matched once, while the later figure was also exceeded once but not even approached in any other year during the 1970-80 period. Since both standards entered into the rate-making process, it might be argued, especially by upholders of the "client" hypothesis, that the CAB raised the standards beyond legitimate levels to make it easier for the carriers to obtain price increases. However, at least with respect to the 1971 decision, the Board had rejected a bid by a group of six carriers which sought a 13.6 percent standard.[5] In point of fact, critics of the industry have for the most part acknowledged the unsatisfactory airlines' profits but would have contended that an excess rate of return could be frequently achieved if the carriers had not engaged in costly and frivolous service rivalry.

Comparison of the industry's profitability with that of other industries requires reliance on common definitions of accounting income and investment, which in practice are rarely completely comparable. Unless one has access to detailed balance sheets and income statements and is able to sort out product lines, accounting improvisation, and cumulate individual performances into industry totals, conclusions can only be general. Table 9.2 presents crude comparisons based on material from the Citibank Monthly Economic Review, which, in its April issue, discloses return on net worth, defined as stockholder equity, book net assets, or capital and surplus, and net income as a percent of sales (profit margin) for manufacturing and nonmanufacturing industries, including air transportation.

With regard to return on net worth, air transport appears to have held its own in 1960-69, but not during 1970-80, implying a greater vulnerability to recession since the latter period contained three business downturns against one at the start of the earlier era. Airline performance during the 1960-69 period was aided by sharply declining unit costs following the introduction of jet aircraft. However, compared to the rate of return in the similarly regulated trucking industry, that for the airlines trailed badly in both periods. One factor limiting airline income is its relatively large debt structure whose servicing has proven to be a great drag on earnings. The profit margin comparisons indicate a pattern similar to the

net worth examples; the airlines appeared to perform relatively
well in the earlier period but unsatisfactorily later.

TABLE 9.2

Average Return on Net Worth and Sales, Air Transport
and Selected Industries, 1960-69 and 1970-80
(percentage)

	Return on Net Worth		Profit Margin	
	1960-69	1970-80	1960-69	1970-80
Air transport	12.4	7.8	3.9	1.8
Total manufacturing	12.2	14.3	5.8	5.0
Trucking	17.0	14.3	3.3	3.5
Trade	12.1	13.5	2.3	2.3

Source: Compiled from Citibank, Monthly Economic Review,
various issues.

An aspect of airline earnings that the averages mask is the
great volatility that has characterized profitability under the
Citibank definitions. For example, while the airline rate of return
on net worth between 1960 and 1980 ranged from negative 5.0 percent in 1980 to a peak of 27.5 percent in 1965 for total manufacturing, this rate has moved less than nine percentage points from a
low of 9.9 percent in 1961 to a high of 18.4 percent in 1979.[6] The
range of rate of return in wholesale and retail trade was an even
narrower five points over the 21-year period. The irregularity of
airline earnings apparently stems from an inability to quickly adjust output to changes in demand. The lead time needed for equipment deliveries and the addition of seats to aircraft cause demand
to outrun supply during business upturns, while reluctance to ini-
tiate service cutbacks for fear of the competitive consequences
limits the ability to adapt to declining demand.

These characteristics create situations in which airline supply at any given time may be better suited to past or future demand
than to the current level. The airlines also appear to be more
prone to inflexible input prices, particularly with respect to labor
costs.

Another way to compare airline financial performance against that of other industries is to examine prices of common stock in relation to earnings per share. This price-earnings (P-E) ratio provides a rough gauge of investor's estimates of various companies and industries. For instance, if the industry norm measures a P-E ratio of ten, firms above that mark would appear to command more respect than companies below. The key variables affecting the ratio level would include the capital appreciation prospect and the dividend record, both of which are functions of the earnings record. Although certain individual carriers have appealed to investors from time to time, the aggregate P-E ratio for the airline group has rarely surpassed the all-industry averages. The main reason for this appears to be the erratic pattern of industry profitability and a poor dividend record resulting from earnings instability. In the 1973-80 period chronicled by Business Week, for instance, the airline P-E ratio exceeded that of the industry composite only once.[7] Moreover, in August 1981, 11 of the 19, or 58 percent, of the airlines listed on the New York Stock Exchange failed to pay a dividend on their common stock, while only 11 percent of the other listed securities omitted dividends.[8]

PRODUCT PRICE

During the deregulation debate of the 1975-78 period, perhaps the principal criticism leveled at the industry was that interstate fares were too high. This was charged in the Report of the Senate Subcommittee on Administrative Practice and Procedure of the Committee on the Judiciary.[9] The report did not view barriers to entry as being prohibitive. Minimal product differentiation, too, should have allowed air transport to be more competitive even though it was conceded that individual markets could never support more than a few carriers. However, as the CAB restricted entry, the contention was that fares were fixed at levels higher than minimum attainable marginal costs and thus caused a welfare loss. This, in turn, induced active nonprice competition, particularly in the area of capacity expansion, which was viewed as wasteful since it resulted in increased costs and prevented the industry from earning more than a normal profit. The report concluded that reduced official entry barriers would reduce fares because of the threat of new competition, and this would induce the carriers to reduce nonprice rivalry. Passenger load factors would then rise in response to price decreases and restrained capacity growth, and profitability would improve. Thus the carriers would be better off, and air travelers would benefit from price relief without any serious diminution in service. Proponents of deregulation hoped for a more fragmented industry, which would be forced to keep prices close to a competitive ideal by the removal of administrative restrictions to entry.

The basis of the overpricing argument was the intrastate experience, where fares in markets outside of CAB jurisdiction were generally lower than those on interstate segments of comparable distance. Two markets in particular (Los Angeles-San Francisco and Dallas-Houston) were cited. In California, for instance, the regular intrastate one-way day coach fare on the 338-mile Los Angeles-San Francisco segment was $28 in July 1978 or 48 percent less than the $54 charged for a trip of equal length between St. Louis and Dayton.[10] In the 240-mile Dallas-Houston segment, the $28 regular coach price was 35 percent less than the comparable fare levied on the 237-mile Detroit-Milwaukee route.[11] In both examples, specialized intrastate carriers had committed themselves to the lower fares not only owing to competition, but also because their lean cost structures permitted them to do so. Intrastate airline businesses were generally based on participation in a few dense markets with a single type of aircraft operating "no-frills" service under high utilization. These operators also benefited from less erratic weather conditions, no requirement of a massive computerized reservations system or large-scale promotion activity, and less restrictive labor work rules. By contrast, the Trunk carriers operated across wider areas, encompassing short- and long-haul markets, which necessitated different equipment types. We have discussed how the Texas carrier in question, Southwest, during 1972-73, having failed to attract sufficient business with cut-rate fares, raised prices to the interstate levels and then accidentally discovered the threshold discount price at which high traffic generation was achieved. Subsequently, Southwest was handed a quasi-monopoly by its competitors and the courts. With regard to California, however, one intrastate carrier, Pacific Southwest, has been nearly always profitable for 30 years while charging fares well below comparable interstate rates. Yet, while Pacific Southwest and later Air California have been successful, 15 other California intrastate carriers failed during that period.[12] Despite the high turnover, many of the important California markets were well served, but only because several interstate airlines, including United, Western, and Trans World, continued to maintain service even though intra-California operations were only infrequently profitable for them.[13]

From the experience gained thus far, it appears that the necessary conditions for viability in a low-fare environment must include high passenger load factors and high equipment utilization as well as tight cost control. Based on the intrastate examples, the proponents of deregulation believed that reduced fare levels would provide for the former, while the carriers would find the means to limit expenses once survival was at stake. However, with regard to low fares promoting extra traffic, the presumption on price elasticity may not universally hold. Reactions to the heavy discounting of the 1977-78 period were uneven. Table 9.3 compares traffic and price changes in two short-haul markets between the second quarters of 1977 and 1978 when total industry enplanements were up by 15 percent on a 2 percent decline in average prices and an expanding economy.[14] These markets were selected because the proponents of deregulation extrapolated the experience of short-haul segments susceptible to diversion of ground modes to air in relating the intrastate experience. Presumably the shorter the distance, the greater the community of interest and the possibilities for generating air traffic. As discussed earlier, the most important pricing event of the period in question was the implementation at the end of March 1978 of a "Super-Saver" fare featuring discounts of 30-50 percent on regular fares in all markets. The fare, while restrictive in terms of requiring an advance purchase and a minimum stay, was seen as a breakthrough in low-cost travel, holding particular promise for visits to friends and relatives and vacation travel. It is also important to recall that the CAB approved five separate fare increases averaging 1.6 percent each between July 1977 and May 1978.[15] Further, favorable economic conditions may have been responsible for a 10 percent industry-wide traffic increase.[16]

TABLE 9.3

Traffic and Prices in Two Short-haul Markets,
Second Quarter, 1977 and 1978

	Los Angeles-Las Vegas		St. Louis-Kansas City	
	Local Passengers	Yield per Mile	Local Passengers	Yield per Mile
1977	172,720	13.90¢	43,650	13.34¢
1978	219,880	14.29¢	48,780	14.52¢
Change (percent)	27.3	2.8	11.8	8.8

Sources: U.S. Civil Aeronautics Board, Origin-Destination Survey, Table 10 and Data Base 1a, second quarters 1977 and 1978.

Traffic growth in the 227-mile Los Angeles-Las Vegas market appeared to respond to the "Super-Saver" program since passenger volumes rose by 27.3 percent and the average fare increased by only 2.8 percent. If allowances are made for the economically inspired growth and the general fare increases, traffic might have risen by 17 percent on a 5 percent price decline, indicating a high elasticity factor of 3.4. The 5 percent price dilution arose from the increased use of the discounts in the later period. Clearly, this type of market should have responded favorably given the vacation orientation of any market involving Las Vegas. The 229-mile St. Louis-Kansas City market behaved differently, as the number of passengers rose by 11.8 percent and prices grew by 8.8 percent. Utilizing the above adjustments would have cut both elements, so that there would have been virtually no change in traffic and price. However, the fact that average fares increased by a percentage slightly greater than the total of the general price rises implies a somewhat higher percentage of full-fare passengers than in the original traffic mix and hence a lack of response to the "Super-Saver" discounts. The relative steadiness of the traffic composition in the St. Louis-Kansas City market would also lend credence to the notion that economic factors alone caused the traffic growth.

Perhaps the main significance of the inconsistent reaction to the sharp price discounts was that in markets like St. Louis-Kansas City where substantial traffic growth failed to materialize, carriers would still have to rely primarily on the traditional nonprice devices to enlarge individual volumes and secure revenue gains, since competition is intensified under conditions of sluggish demand. When demand softens and pricing alternatives have little impact, load factors generally come under pressure as rivals hesitate to eliminate flights for fear of losing market share. In such situations, the impulse to raise fares increases, especially when productivity improvements are difficult to obtain. If a joint reduction in capacity could be obtained within a market, a welfare loss would result from deterioration in service. Thus the comparison with intrastate conditions is inappropriate since it implies uniform price elasticity, which is not demonstrable.

Despite the questions raised, nothing in the above directly addresses the fundamental issue of interstate overpricing. Some doubt has been cast on the basic assumptions of the proponents of this view but not about the issue itself. In the following, however, a case will be made for the notion that interstate airline fares have not been exorbitant and indeed may have been kept too low under regulation. Part of the problem with the overpricing claim is one common to most assaults on big business, namely, the assumption that unfair market power exists where sellers are few, which is based on an unrealistic ideal of competition. With regard to the airlines, criticism has been intensified by a general belief in the "client" theory of regulation; but this too may be incorrect. According to some critics, the regulators have protected industry interests to the detriment of public welfare. A logical extension of this idea is the assumption that the CAB has encouraged rate increases. If this were true, airline price increases should have outpaced or at least matched those recorded in other oligopolistic but unregulated consumer industries. Table 9.4 compares airline price movements with changes in wholesale prices of three four-digit SIC industries manufacturing consumer products. Limitations in the length of the latter time series preclude going back earlier than 1957 and the three are among the few available from that date.[17] However, average airline prices in 1957 were barely changed from immediate postwar levels when, due to widespread government subsidy, the CAB chose to regulate airline profit rates by modifying the subsidy level rather than the price level. Further, rapid traffic expansion caused passenger load factors in excess of 60 percent, and these remained comfortably ahead of the break-even point during practically the entire decade of the 1950s. Thus there was little reason to suppose that air fares were inflated in 1957. Critics might point out that intrastate California fares during that period were also below comparable interstate rates, but this may be countered on the grounds of the simpler, specialized operation, as well as the inferior equipment used on intrastate flights. Pacific Southwest, the intrastate carrier, operated unpressurized, piston aircraft until 1959. Nevertheless, as Table 9.4 indicates, the average price increase over the 23-year period was much less pronounced in the airline industry than that of the two industries shown, as well as all of the aggregate indexes. There are difficulties in comparisons of this sort, including changes in the weighting of products within industries and in productivity. The airline price index was particularly influenced by the addition of promotional fares in its product mix and by cost economies resulting from introduction of jet aircraft. However, even assuming no new product or operating efficiencies occurred during the period, it seems difficult to believe that the airline price rise could have exceeded that of either the chewing gum or cigarette industries, which must also have undergone productivity improvements. If one assumes that air fares were reasonable and did not involve welfare loss in 1957, then 1980 average fare levels, at least in a relative sense, probably were not inflated, considering the favorable price movement comparison. Thus, given the examples of the cigarette and chewing gum manufactures, a case could be made for the notion that

CAB regulation may have held airline prices below what they might have been without regulation.

TABLE 9.4

Comparative Price Movements, Airlines versus
Selected Industries, 1957-80

Industry	1957	1980	Average Annual Rate of Increase (percent)
Trunk airlines	100	208	3.3
Poultry dressing	100	168	2.3
Chewing gum	100	308	5.0
Cigarettes	100	296	4.8
Producer price index (finished consumer goods)	100	279	4.6
Consumer price index	100	293	4.8

Sources: U.S. Department of Labor, Monthly Labor Review, June 1981, pp. 96-97; Monthly Labor Review, February 1972, pp. 110-11.

With regard to relative price movements during the post-1978 period, it is important to note that the regulatory cost pass-through apparatus was still operative as was a fare flexibility capability, which afforded carriers pricing freedom within a prescribed band. These instruments enabled the airline industry to increase average fares by 36 percent between 1978 and 1980,[18] which outpaced the changes of the other indexes listed in Table 9.4 but nonetheless served to offset only partially the 57 percent rise in operating costs[19] during the two-year span, which largely resulted from the 128 percent growth in the average cost per gallon of jet fuel.[20] By 1980 this element accounted for over 30 percent of airline-operating expenses compared to less than 13 percent ten years earlier.[21] In the aftermath of the 1978-80 experience, the CAB reported that average fares, while admittedly high, were still 10-13 percent cheaper than might have occurred under pre-1978 regulation in the 200 largest markets because of the entry factor but that prices everywhere else, where entry was less influential, were 12 percent higher.[22]

Considering that the 200 largest markets accounted for 43 percent of total passenger volumes and 45 percent of revenue passenger miles in 1980,[23] the industry was apparently able to raise prices marginally beyond the amount allowable under the pre-1978 rules and before entry became a significant pricing factor. Thus the claims during 1981[24] that deregulation had already been an unqualified success in the price area may have been premature.

It may also be useful to illustrate the difference between pricing practices by a European cartel and those that developed under CAB regulation. Within the entry-blockaded intra-European system, fares have continued to be set by the participating airlines under the auspices of the International Air Transport Association (IATA). In addition, pooling agreements in which carriers never directly compete and evenly divide revenues were, and continue to be, widespread within Europe. Table 9.5 indicates the differences in unrestricted day coach fares in two domestic market types and a typical intra-Europe market of similar mileage over a three-year period. During the summer preceding enactment of the 1978 Deregulation Act, St. Louis-Dayton coach travelers were paying nearly twice the fare charged in the dense Los Angeles-San Francisco market where Pacific Southwest, by virtue of its market dominance, controlled the pricing. However, Pacific Southwest, at the time, was still a relatively small regional carrier with a single type of aircraft and offering "no-frills" service. The comparable yield in Paris-Milan exceeded that of the St. Louis-Dayton market by 119 percent. Whereas important cost disparities were obvious between former intrastaters and the interstate carriers, no such distinctions separated the larger U.S. airlines from their European counterparts, many of which were government supported and whose operations extended across both long- and short- distance segments necessitating a variety of aircraft. The European carriers were, for a long time, able to charge whatever the traffic would bear, since entry had been blocked and the predominant intra-European travelers were businessmen whose demand was apt to be price inelastic. Moreover, since charters traditionally handled vacationers, the need to attract discretionary business was never an overriding concern until the most recent period. Indeed the most striking development by the summer of 1981 was the apparent closing of the wide gap that had existed between the U.S. interstate and the intra-European fares. Also important was the relatively close increases in the two U.S. market fares in response to the sharp rise in jet fuel prices during the period. Fuel prices rose overseas too, of course, but since Europeans were paying for fuel with weak dollars (before 1981), their costs were tempered somewhat. In addition, there existed the threat of new entry, based on a campaign

TABLE 9.5

Comparative Fares, United States and Intra-Europe,
Summer 1978 and Summer 1981

Market	(A) U.S. Intrastate Los Angeles–San Francisco	(B) U.S. Interstate St. Louis–Dayton	B/A Change (percent)	(C) Intra-Europe Paris–Milan	C/B Change (percent)
Summer 1978					
Mileage	338	338		372	
Coach fare (dollars)	28	54		130	
Price/mile	8.28¢	15.98¢	93	34.95¢	119
Summer 1981					
Coach fare (dollars)	60	125		165	
Price/mile	17.75¢	36.98¢	108	44.35¢	20

Sources: Reuben Donnelly Corp., Official Airline Guides, North American and worldwide editions, August 1978 and August 1981.

by Sir Freddie Laker with the support of British Civil Aviation Authority, which created increasingly adverse publicity for the cartel system. Nevertheless, the 20 percent differential that remained in 1981 probably understated the true margin because "Super-Saver" discounts of 30-65 percent from normal economy fares were available with minimal restrictions in all domestic markets. For instance, where 14-day advance purchase and 7-day minimum length of stay prevailed in 1978, only a 7-day advance purchase with an overnight Friday stay was required during 1981. Such bargains were rare within Europe. Thus, from a welfare standpoint, the U.S. pricing system in both periods appeared to be superior to that prevalent in Europe.

The way in which the public views an industry in comparison to others may also reflect on the issue of welfare. Measures of opinion generally indicate whether the public senses that it is receiving fair value or not. Two consumer attitude studies prepared for U.S. News and World Report in 1976 and 1977 asked respondents, among other questions, to rate 31 industries on their overall job performance.[25] In both years, the airline industry ranked highest, while aluminum companies, banks, large department stores, and supermarkets were close behind. Those at the bottom of the list included automobile insurers, appliance repair services, auto dealers, railroads, health insurers, and auto manufacturers. The discount fare splurge begun in April 1977 may have contributed to the popularity of the airlines in 1977 but would not have explained their high ranking in 1976 when average airline price increases exactly matched the rise of the consumer price index.

A 1976 Harris survey of attitudes toward big business[26] was somewhat less flattering toward air transport, ranking it tenth among 24 other industries on the question of the degree of perceived competition. The presumption was that competition was a positive trait consistent with better service and lower prices than monopoly. Respondents rated the airlines as being more competitive than banking, men's clothing, and the pharmaceutical industry, among others, while less competitive than such industries as women's clothing, appliances, television manufacturing, and soft drinks.

While such surveys are superficial, they suggest, together with the rest of the discussion, that the domestic Trunk airlines, when viewed in the context of U.S. industry, may have been unduly criticized. During the deregulation debate, the industry was depicted as engaging in monopolistic practices, encouraged by government regulation, which caused welfare loss particularly as a result of pricing policy. However, while entry had indeed been impeded until the emergence of the Kahn Board and the Airline Deregulation Act of 1978, an examination of interindustry pricing activity over time implies that the CAB may have restrained rate increases that might otherwise have developed in an oligopolistic environment. In comparison with an obvious monopoly situation such as that in Western Europe, the domestic industry comes off very well. Further evidence on consumer perceptions suggests that the airlines have provided a good product at an equitable price probably more consistently and surely at least on a par with most of U.S. industry.

INNOVATION

Discussions of innovation in the literature of industrial organization center on the relationship of market structure to research and development. The acknowledged point of departure is Schumpeter's work, which stresses the need for the continuity of technological innovation, which would enable capitalism to renew itself. This hypothesis has stimulated many studies analyzing firm size as well as relative concentration in industries and their effects on innovation.

In the airline industry, the responsibility for technological change has largely been exogenous, since aircraft manufacturers have controlled the development of flight equipment, while computer companies have engineered reservations systems. Hence, innovation among the airlines has concentrated on marketing initiatives. Caves' view of the subject, in keeping with his conviction in 1961 that the larger carriers were becoming increasingly dominant, held that the less profitable smaller airlines were driven to lead in marketing innovations out of desperation.[27] Without presenting any evidence, he held that carriers with equipment problems or other shortcomings had little to lose, since market share disadvantages could become cumulative if not reversed. While it has been nearly always true that the larger carriers dominated the field in introducing new equipment, recent evidence suggests that these carriers may also lead in service and pricing innovations. A survey of the 1975 and 1976 issues of Aviation Week and Space Technology, the comprehensive industry weekly, revealed 35 identifiable instances of marketing innovations. These included United's automatic ticket printers, a cockpit camera for takeoffs by American, a one-price system travel plan by Allegheny, and the National "no-frills" fare. Of the total, 22 innovations or 63 percent were attributable to the five largest carriers—American, Delta, Eastern, Trans World, and United—with the remainder divided among the smaller Trunks, Locals, and Intrastate carriers.

The apparent higher degree of marketing innovation among the larger carriers confirms Caves' contention that the least profitable firms were more likely to pursue actions designed to improve market share. However, Caves did not envision the reversal in industry profitability in favor of the smaller carriers in the early 1960s. Since the largest carriers mainly compete against one another, another possibility is that unsatisfactory earnings by one or more of the larger carriers may have heightened rivalry. The high level of competition and profit disparity between Eastern and Delta has been well documented and that among the so-called Big Three—American, Trans World, and United—has been evident from time to time.

PROMOTION

Among oligopolists, nonprice rivalry has long been the dominant form of competition. In some instances, governmental regulation restrained price competition, while in most others the industry structure has been responsible, owing to the kinked-demand curve phenomenon. The fact that the domestic air transport industry came under the influence of both provided ample reason for its neglect of competition in fares during most of its history. Despite a flurry of pricing activity accompanying the deregulation proceedings of the 1977-80 period, rivalry historically centered almost exclusively on product or service rivalry bolstered by advertising. The problems and impact of this product competition have been analyzed already; the following pages are devoted to a discussion of the value of airline advertising.

The incentives to advertise include its potential for expanding the market, as well as the opportunity to capture business from one's rivals. While monopolists are limited to the market growth aspect, oligopolists may achieve both ends. As was shown with respect to service rivalry, escalation of advertising expenditures by competing firms causes the industry cost curve to rise. This erodes profit margins for all unless aggregate revenues increase proportionately or else some firms are able to establish a strong product identity at the expense of others. Since the late 1950s, when the airlines began to surpass railroads and buses in passenger traffic, advertising campaigns to expand the market have declined in comparison with those designed to increase market share. Perhaps the only recent example of the former type of promotion was Pan American's appeal in 1978 to ethnic Americans to visit their original homelands, but even this was directed at the expansion of market share, since Pan American flew to more foreign destinations than any other U.S. carrier. Achievement of joint profit-maximizing advertising levels is often unattainable for reasons explainable in a Prisoner's Dilemma context in which one rival outspends or outsmarts another and consequently gains a market share advantage. While pricing actions can be matched quickly, a successful advertising strategy may take longer to overcome. Hence, this type of competition remains attractive to airline managers who usually rate themselves as more clever than their rivals.

Studies have shown high profitability to be positively correlated with heavy advertising outlays between consumer-oriented industries,[28] but within an industry, other factors such as service rivalry and cost factors generally take precedence. Among the airlines, in fact, those carriers spending a smaller percentage of revenues on advertising were inclined to be most profitable. Consistently profitable carriers such as Delta and Northwest have usually ranked among the lowest in advertising expenses as a percentage of revenues, while Continental, Pan American, and Trans World, whose income records have been spotty, regularly ranked highest in terms of the advertising/sales ratio.[29] Several factors may explain this situation. First, airlines face varying degrees of competitive intensity. For instance, a carrier such as Trans World for many years obtained the smallest amount of its traffic from monopoly segments and competed against at least two rivals in many of its important transcontinental and shorter-haul business markets. Conversely, the monopoly routes of Delta and Northwest account for from one-quarter to one-third of their traffic volume, and many of their competitive routes involve only one other airline. A smaller degree of competition requires less advertising and promotional expenditures in general. Second, less profitable carriers may feel forced to outspend their more profitable rivals simply to catch up or as a counterbalance when structural factors, such as an unfavorable route system or equipment disadvantages, create an untenable competitive situation. Moreover, small carriers attempting to gain a foothold against larger airlines may have to devote disproportionate promotional expenditures to establish a perception of product differentiation even when no such distinction is present. Such a situation confronts Continental, which faces Trans World and United in the Chicago-Denver market. Another source of advertising ratio differentials may center on the national or regional character of an airline. For example, regional carriers, such as Western which mostly operates west of the Mississippi, would have no need to engage in national television advertising or promote themselves in high-cost media areas such as New York, whereas American and United would be involved in both.

Apart from these explanations of the contrast between profitability and the advertising ratio, it may also be possible that certain firms simply advertise more effectively than others. For instance, the two most consistently profitable carriers—Delta and Northwest—have steadfastly adhered to the "hard-sell" approach, mostly in newspapers, answering the basic questions of where, when, and how much. Most others have frequently engaged in image-related advertising, which is heavily dependent on costly television, such as Eastern's "wings of man" or United's "friendly skies." However, the evidence on efficiency of the "hard-sell" approach cannot be overwhelming since image-related advertising persists.

Assuming that the current airline product at the individual market level can be described as essentially homogeneous, except for departure time, the question arises concerning the social desirability of image differentiation. While much advertising may be characterized as informative regarding schedules and prices, much may be unwanted by buyers or otherwise possess little redeeming

TABLE 9.6

Ratio of Advertising Expenditures to Receipts for
15 Consumer-Related Industries in 1977
(percent)

Industry	Ratio
Tobacco manufactures	3.7
Chemicals and allied products	3.0
Amusements and recreation services	2.6
General merchandise stores	2.5
Instruments and related products	2.1
Apparel and accessory stores	2.0
Food and kindred products	1.9
Hotels	1.8
Airlines	1.7
Eating and drinking establishments	1.7
Real estate	1.6
Business services	1.0
Banks	0.8
Food stores	0.8
Motor vehicle manufacturers	0.6

Sources: Estimated from U.S. Internal Revenue Service, 1977 Corporate Income Tax Returns (preliminary), January 1981, Table 2; Air Transport Association, Air Transport 1979, p. 13.

social value. A necessary step in determining the waste implicit
in airline advertising is to examine how airline advertising expenditures compare to those in other consumer industries. Table 9.6
indicates the ratio of advertising expenditures to total receipts in
15 industries for 1977. In that year, the airline advertising spending ratio fell toward the middle range of the industries listed, implying an average level of allocation of resources to promotional
efforts. Determining the socially necessary amount of advertising
is difficult, since such a judgment must be subjectively based and,
in any case, is apt to fail to take account of the competitive pressures that may drive up advertising expenditures.

A major criticism of advertising holds that if there is full
information, such as that which theoretically exists under perfect
competition, sales promotion is unnecessary. But from a practical standpoint, while the airline product may be considered
homogeneous in certain respects, there is a continuing need to
provide information on schedules, and increasingly after 1978, on
prices where new entry caused frequent fare changes. The media
most closely associated with the latter are newspapers and radio,
which accounted for 36 percent of total U.S. advertising expenditures and around half of domestic airline advertising spending in
1979.[30] This is not to say that newspaper and radio advertising
alone may be considered socially useful, since television and
magazines may also be helpful. Scherer, who could be termed a
critic of advertising, estimated that while the "waste" component
was bound to vary by industry, only half of all promotional spending was socially useful.[31] Applying the 50 percent ratio to Trunk
carriers would mean that in 1980, $216 million may have been
wasted on socially unnecessary advertising if one accepts the
Scherer premise. This amount, which was equivalent to 0.8 percent
of total operating expenses, might have been paid out to stockholders as higher dividends, to employees as increased wages, or to
consumers in lower prices.

NOTES

1. U.S. Civil Aeronautics Board, Handbook of Airline Statistics, 1975 edition, part VI, Table 4, p. 111.
2. George Eads, The Local Service Airline Experiment
(Washington, D.C.: Brookings Institution, 1972), pp. 150-51.
3. Handbook of Airline Statistics, 1973 edition and 1975,
1977, and 1979 supplements; Economic Report of the President 1981,
Table B-65.

4. George Douglas and James Miller III, Economic Regulation of Domestic Air Transport (Washington, D.C.: Brookings Institution, 1974), p. 152.

5. Newal Taneja, The Commercial Airline Industry (Lexington, Mass.: D. C. Heath, 1976), p. 212.

6. First National City Bank, Monthly Economic Review, various issues.

7. Business Week, various March survey issues on fourth quarter profit performance.

8. New York Times, August 9, 1981, section 3.

9. U.S. Senate, Committee on the Judiciary, Subcommittee on Administrative Practices and Procedures, "Draft Report on Civil Aeronautics Board Route-Making and Route-Procedures," June 1975.

10. Reuben Donnelly Corp, Official Airline Guide, North American edition, July 1978.

11. Ibid.

12. William Jordan, Airline Regulation in America (Baltimore: Johns Hopkins University Press, 1970, pp. 17-18.

13. "United Drive Seeks Larger Share of California Commuter Market," Aviation Week and Space Technology, January 10, 1972, p. 26.

14. U.S. Civil Aeronautics Board, Air Carrier Traffic Statistics, April, May, and June 1978; and Air Carrier Financial Statistics, second quarter 1978.

15. "Airline Profits Are Taking Wing," Business Week, June 26, 1978, p. 39.

16. A. Gary Shilling and Co., "Discount Air Fares: Throwing Caution to the Winds?," February 23, 1979.

17. Bennett Moss, "Industry and Sector Price Indexes," Monthly Labor Review, August 1965, pp. 974-82.

18. Air Transport Association, Air Transport 1981, p. 11.

19. Ibid., p. 21.

20. Ibid., p. 12.

21. Ibid.

22. Aviation Week and Space Technology, July 27, 1981, p. 24.

23. U.S. Civil Aeronautics Board, Origin-Destination Survey, fourth quarter 1980, Tables 6 and 7.

24. See John R. Meyer and Clinton V. Oster Jr., eds., Airline Deregulation—The Early Experience (Boston: Auburn House, 1981).

25. U.S. News and World Report, February 20, 1978, pp. 16-18.

26. Louis Harris & Associates, "Bigness in Business: A New Look," April 1976.

27. Richard E. Caves, Air Transport and Its Regulators (Cambridge, Mass.: Harvard University Press, 1962), p. 426.

28. W. Comanor and T. Wilson, "Advertising, Market Structure and Performance," Review of Economics and Statistics November 1967, pp. 423-40; L. Weiss, "Advertising, Profits and Corporate Taxes," Review of Economics and Statistics, November 1969, pp. 421-30.

29. Air Transport World, June 1980, pp. 40-45.

30. U.S. Department of Commerce, Statistical Abstract 1980, p. 597; and Air Transport World, June 1980, p. 43.

31. F. M. Scherer, Industrial Market Structure and Economic Performance (Chicago: Rand McNally, 1970), pp. 405-6.

10

SUMMARY AND CONCLUSIONS

The preceding pages have described airline industry behavior and its determinants in the context of historical development. For the carriers, conduct has been shaped both by the industry's inherent structure and by the long imposition of government regulation and, while the former probably constituted the dominant influence, government intervention alternatively reinforced or deflected trends dictated by structure. The official barriers to entry for most of this industry's history, for example, reduced the number of active competitors, which encouraged greater oligopolistic interdependence. At the same time, the evidence suggests that the CAB held prices below levels that might otherwise have been charged, given the tight industry structure. Despite the regulatory intrusions and the high level of firm concentration, however, quality of service remained satisfactory owing mostly to the persistence of active competition in nonprice areas throughout recent years. This was attributable to financial and market share imbalances among the competitors, which CAB partly reinforced by awarding routes to existing carriers in need of strengthening or simply to promote competition. By the late 1970s, price and product rivalry were encouraged when the CAB facilitated new entry by the nontraditional carriers. What emerged through the most recent period was an industry buffeted by competitive pressures, constrained prices, and a relatively heavy burden of input costs. The following summarizes the major points of the book.

STRUCTURAL FACTORS

With respect to concentration, the number of firms was found to be irrelevant to the intensity of rivalry within individual markets. The analysis failed to support the theoretical notion that competition within a two-carrier market will necessarily be less vigorous than that within a four-carrier market. The key determinant of the level of rivalry appears to involve the presence or absence of a carrier behaving as a maverick because of new entrant status, operating cost disparity, or small market share.

Characteristics of demand, including perceptions of price elasticity, sensitivity to the business cycle, the mix of passenger traffic, and questions of industry maturity principally influence market conduct and determine how the industry tailors its product. A review of the literature on airline price elasticity not only convinces one of the irrelevance of a single overall elasticity measure but of the futility of attempts at its determination. This is because the response of passenger traffic to price changes appears to be contingent on type of traffic, direction of price movement, and economic conditions, among other factors. Moreover, isolating price from income and quality variables has proven exceedingly difficult. Business passengers are likely to be less sensitive to price than leisure travelers owing to the more discretionary nature of travel by the latter group, while it is also probably true that fare increases, especially in an inflationary climate, will generally meet less resistance and that price reductions will prove more generative of traffic in an expanding economy than in a contracting one. The fact that the airlines have consistently pushed for fare increases during periods of insufficient demand and rising costs indicates that they have believed that business traffic in particular was price inelastic, and because they usually hurried to introduce vacation-oriented discount fares to boost sluggish demand, the carriers apparently were also convinced that demand for leisure travel tended to be price elastic. While accurate elasticity measures continue to prove elusive, the persistence of these behavioral patterns with respect to price lends more credibility to the carriers' notions of elasticity than to more theoretical explanations.

An analysis of turning points of airline traffic demand indicated that traffic peaked slightly later and reached a trough earlier than the economy at large during four business cycles. Nevertheless, the recovery phases for the airlines appeared so weak as to give the impression of a longer lasting recession, since recent economic cycles have had a V-shape reflecting a relatively deep slide followed by a rapid recovery. The slightly later start for the airline recession was attributed to a delayed employment cutback in white-collar occupations, whose members are more likely than blue-collar workers to be air travelers, while the earlier trough may also result from a smaller impact from the recession within the professional employment ranks and the return of business travel prior to general economic recovery. The sluggishness of demand

for two to three quarters subsequent to the recession trough may
be due to a lag in general employment growth among groups more
likely to contain discretionary travelers. The significance of the
slow rebuilding of traffic volumes is that airline managers have
felt compelled to introduce the price discounts mentioned above
during such periods.

Changes in the types of travelers have also affected the way
in which carriers marketed their product. For instance, structurally related increases in the proportion of vacationers as opposed to businessmen and the growth of travel agent sales have
significantly altered airline promotional practices over the years.
Also in the context of demand, the industry's maturity relates to
the possibility of a dramatic slowdown in traffic growth in the fore-
seeable future. As growth rates have decelerated in the past,
questions have arisen about what might happen to market conduct
in a climate of stagnant demand. Under conditions of sluggish demand, the only way for firms to build revenue, assuming constant
prices, is to gain market share at the expense of their rivals.
Hence, in the future in such an environment one might anticipate
"cut-throat" product and price competition. Here the evidence
suggests that in the past the slowing of growth was as much due to
the weight of numbers as to any economic factor, so that demographic and income trends, as well as increasing vacation time,
appear to favor adequate traffic expansion in the future, given a
relatively normal external environment.

The section on airline expenses explored questions of economies of scale, the extent of management's discretion in the determination of unit costs, and the issue of fixed and variable costs.
It was noted that optimum carrier size had decreased over time
but that airline size and average costs appear to be unrelated.
With respect to individual carrier unit costs, management policy
as opposed to structural factors was found to play a pivotal role.
Cross-sectional multiple regression analysis of 1980 data showed
that the single important explanatory variable was the percentage
of cargo in the total volume of passengers and cargo transported.
A high proportion of cargo business apparently meant lower unit
costs because this type of traffic is cheaper to handle than passengers. Conscious decisions to pursue cargo business and to operate
a higher proportion of wide-body aircraft that could carry more
cargo were management prerogatives and not dictated by structural
factors or regulation, although longer distance airlines were better able to participate in that side of the business.

Higher or lower unit costs involved obvious profit ramifications for individual carriers. On the matter of fixed and variable
costs, airlines had long claimed that fixed expenses dominated the

cost structure, which meant that little could be done to trim costs when demand turned sluggish. In reality, the rationale for maintaining prior schedules in such a climate appeared to be a fear that unilateral cutbacks would not be matched by the competition, thus exposing the "guinea-pig" carrier to market share losses. Not only were air carriers found to be not unduly capital intensive relative to other industries, but cost flexibility was routinely noted during times of adversity involving strikes and rapid increases in fuel prices. Moreover, the original argument was increasingly discredited as regulatory control on entry and exit was reduced during the late 1970s when carriers sought to rationalize their haphazardly developed route structures in the search for more efficient resource allocation.

Although barriers to entry to the airline industry were significantly reduced under the Airline Deregulation Act of 1978, until that point, the various impediments had been substantial. Product differentiation was not important, but prohibitive barriers based on CAB exclusion policies, economies of scale, and absolute costs presented formidable obstacles to new Trunk-like undertakings. This is not to say that limited entry was similarly inhibited. In point of fact, only the long CAB ban on new carrier participation in interstate markets prevented widespread entry of the many smaller, specialized airlines with limited objectives, which subsequently established a presence in the wake of changed regulatory policy after 1978.

The review of input markets examined the changing relationship of buyers and sellers with respect to capital equipment and the significance of labor market differentials, union strength, and salary levels. Whereas one or several carriers generally teamed up with a manufacturer to design and allocate production and delivery of a new aircraft model during the 1950s and 1960s, the manufacturers were unable to count on such sponsorship after that time due to reduced profitability and fears among the airlines of overexpansion. As a consequence, the carriers were probably able to obtain better financial terms than in earlier years because the manufacturers, whose capital requirements for any new commercial aircraft development had become prohibitive, had to secure substantial orders to successfully launch production. Paradoxically, while the number of air carriers remained practically the same over a 40-year period, the size of the airframe manufacturing industry became considerably smaller; nevertheless the greater concentration of the latter apparently failed to provide a source of market power in its dealings with the airlines.

With regard to labor input, the airlines decidedly lost in their interaction with the unions. The industry is nearly wholly unionized

while not overly strike-prone relative to other industries, but airline salaries were pushed upward by a "whipsawing" negotiating
technique of the unions based on the well-grounded fears of debili-
tating strikes. When productivity gains were rapid, especially
during the introduction of jet aircraft, the high wage structure could
be tolerated, but not when such improvements ended by the early
1970s. At that point, escalating fuel prices added to the carriers'
burden and necessitated frequent fare increases to protect faltering
profit margins. Only those airlines that courted strikes, like
Northwest and National, or else successfully prevented wide-scale
unionization like Delta, achieved decided advantages in countering
high labor input costs.

AIRLINE CONDUCT AND PERFORMANCE

Until recent times, carrier rivalry was almost always played
out in the area of product. This phenomenon was the result of
structural forces and the CAB's concern over potentially destructive
price competition. However, a dramatic shift in regulatory trends,
formalized by the Airline Deregulation Act of 1978, toward the encouragement of free market behavior, resulted in active price
rivalry by the late 1970s. The new fare competition mainly took
the form of price/service quality options in which inferior or superior services were accorded varying rates. In addition, prices
on individual segments were shaped by competitive criteria instead
of being set on a cost by distance formula as had been the case. For
roughly 40 years, the CAB had prevented these developments, but
once entry was made freer, new carriers in markets often heralded
their arrival by offering unique discounts or else existing operators
acted similarly in an attempt to forestall entry.

During most of the industry's history, airline price policy
was consistent with the oligopolistic model of administered rate
setting. A regression analysis of the cyclical nature of airline
prices confirmed an inverse relationship to the business cycle.
This indicated that airline managers, with their ingrained notion of
price inelasticity, routinely sought and received rate increases
during times of sluggish or declining demand, but felt no such com-
pulsion during times of strong traffic growth unless cost rises were
unusually large.

The product competition that dominated rivalry until very recently was essentially based on a drive for product differentiation.
Earlier forms of rivalry emphasizing new equipment purchases had
a decidedly greater impact on market share determination owing to
the time lag in matching the successful introduction of a new type of

aircraft. Where a change in meal service, for instance, might be duplicated in a matter of days, ordering and placing into service a competitive aircraft to overcome an equipment disadvantage took months or years. Until perhaps 1970 when an acute situation of overcapacity arose, equipment and scheduling competition were typical. If one carrier could offer more flights than its rivals, there existed a strong possibility that it might obtain an even greater traffic share, referred to as the S-curve phenomenon. In such a climate, however, each carrier was loath to permit a rival the potential of an S-curve advantage; thus scheduling equilibrium was often obtained only after a costly war over capacity. When fuel prices increased drastically after 1973, scheduling rivalry declined sharply in favor of less effective, more easily matched "frills" competition until price rivalry became dominant.

Rivalry in capacity remained active in markets where the new wide-bodied aircraft confronted older narrow-bodied types. Carriers operating the inferior equipment had no choice except to greatly increase frequency of service to blunt the advantages in comfort offered in the newer, spacious aircraft. An analysis of the two such instances involving American and Braniff over a three-year period indicated that the greater number of flights was apparently favored in the marketplace and led to an advantage for the narrow-bodied operator, in this case Braniff.

An investigation of the competitive patterns among different sets of rivals was also performed with misleading results. The intensity of rivalry among the main north-south carriers—Delta, Eastern, and National—was measured against that of the three principal east-west airlines—American, Trans World, and United. On the basis of relative load factor and greater carrier imbalances, the former group displayed an apparently higher degree of competition, but a concurrent survey indicated greater profitability for the same group, which suggested that greater interdependence did not guarantee a higher rate of return on investment.

As to performance in a welfare context, the domestic airline industry appeared to fare well in terms of pricing and quality of service. While interstate rates probably were held down to some extent by commission review, they nevertheless were considerably lower than intra-European price levels, which were similarly subject to regulation. Moreover, since the CAB mostly disdained product intervention while allowing piecemeal entry, carrier rivalry flourished in the area of quality of service where the European system encouraged pooling arrangements along strict cartel lines. Surveys of U.S. public opinion also found that domestic airline performance compared favorably with that offered by other consumer industries.

Critics of the domestic airlines, while conceding the industry's low level of profitability, nevertheless thought that welfare conditions as well as profits could be improved by the removal of regulation, and cited the intrastate examples where lower fares were being offered by certain profitably-run carriers. It was claimed that the ending of the regulatory barriers to entry and exit would result in reduced prices and would force existing airlines to become more cost efficient once survival was at stake. The Civil Aeronautics Board, like many other regulatory agencies, had long been regarded as protective of the industry. The initial results heartened the proponents of deregulation as price discounting and profitability flourished in 1978 and most of 1979. By the end of 1979, however, service reductions to small cities made easier by the exit provisions of the 1978 Act and spurred by new fuel price increases and sluggish demand had already aroused misgivings in the minds of some earlier political supporters of deregulation. Moreover, energy conservationists fretted about the apparent wastefulness in encouraging a larger number of carriers in markets where a sufficient amount may have already existed.

CAVES' CONTRIBUTION

Many of the observations made in this volume have simply corroborated insights offered by Caves nearly 20 years ago. In fact, his earlier descriptions and perceptions of conduct were so accurate that one could practically read his volume as an account of recent industry behavior, at least through 1975, without realizing that Air Transport and Its Regulators chronicled events only through 1961. For instance, Caves discounted seller concentration as an important factor in market conduct, pointing instead to the presence or absence of a maverick carrier as the key determinant. Regarding demand, Caves recognized the difficulty of segregating measures of price elasticity, and he similarly offered subjective explanations. On the subject of costs, Caves noted a decline in optimum size, that carrier size and average costs were unrelated, and that the industry's claim of a high fixed cost burden was exaggerated. Structural barriers to entry were thought to be only moderate and Caves correctly hypothesized that the type of entry that would occur if regulatory obstacles were removed would involve the smaller, specialized carriers with limited objectives.

However, Caves' study had its limitations. In his review of input markets, he devoted much attention to the capital-rationing process and erroneously concluded that the large carriers of his day would either devour the smaller carriers or otherwise force them out of existence. This theme was reiterated with regard to product competition. Concerning such competition, Caves argued that sheer size afforded overwhelming advantages in market share competition. It may be true that the industry will ultimately be composed of fewer firms, but the financial edge since the mid-1960s has lain with the smaller Trunk carriers, which have long been more profitable than the so-called Big Four—American, Eastern, Trans World, and United—of Caves' time. What happened just at the moment of Caves' review was a reversal in profitability as a result of which the former group, having received a greater share of new route awards, and possibly possessing better management, began to regularly surpass the giants in earnings.

Caves also did not anticipate the heightened sensitivity of air transport demand to the business cycle, the price reductions that accompanied the productivity gains of the 1960s, the rise in fuel prices, or the improved carrier-bargaining position in the new aircraft market.

While acknowledging a justification for government regulation through the earlier industry stages of development and refusing to impute base motives to the subsequent administration of regulation because of the vague guidelines of the enabling legislation, Caves nonetheless concluded that the industry should have been at least partially deregulated by 1961. His main quarrel was with the control of entry and exit, which raised the cost of air transportation by protecting inefficient carriers and encouraging wasteful service rivalry and, through an arbitrary system of route awards, created unrationalized route structures which required firms to own too many different types of aircraft. This was also the principal charge leveled at the regulatory system during the 1975-78 deregulation debates. Initially, however, the impact of Caves' statement barely caused a ripple beyond academic circles. Conditions were somewhat different 15 years later when inflation raged and the regulatory agencies came under political fire as protectors of inefficiency. In retrospect, probably even die-hard opponents of deregulation would have preferred its earlier implementation, since in the 1960s the industry was more financially secure, fuel was cheap, recessions were absent, and productivity gains from the new jet aircraft were impressive.

WHAT LIES AHEAD?

Any discussion of the airline industry future must center around the condition of market entry. More than any other factor, it was the liberalization of the rules governing entry, shortly before the passage of the 1978 Airline Deregulation Act made it official, that altered the industry structure, invigorated price competition, and forced the incumbent carriers to reevaluate their modus operandi. Under regulation from 1938 through the mid-1970s when route certificates were awarded by CAB's fiat, the number of firms was frozen and price competition was virtually dormant. Product rivalry was the lone avenue for competition, since the CAB hesitated to interfere in that area.

While the domestic deregulation experiment has already brought radical changes to the industry, the process is apparently far from complete. Before the August 1981 strike by the Professional Air Traffic Controllers (PATCO) forced a reduction of flights at major airports, a virtual explosion of new carrier formation was imminent. The activities of the fledgling airlines up to that point were detailed in Chapter 4. It may well be that the dynamic elements introduced by deregulation or the tendency toward destructive competition due to the low marginal cost associated with carrying extra traffic will cause permanent instability. However, this would run counter to the experience of most U.S. industry, which has never been subject to regulation and the California experience where airline entry went unregulated for 19 years. To be sure, substantial differences exist between even a large state and a country not to mention the problem of disparate historical reference points. Nevertheless, California was large enough to contain both business and vacation routes, while the free entry condition was operative during a sufficiently long period to permit a full trial for market forces.

The California experience has been the subject of frequent study, but the most detailed work was performed by Jordan in 1970.[1] He confined his analysis to the 1946-65 period, at which time the state regulatory statutes differed substantially from those governing the interstate network. During this period, both the California Public Utilities Commission and CAB regulated price, but whereas entry and exit were strictly controlled by the latter, such control was absent in California. Under the freer entry conditions, 16 carriers attempted operations within California, 15 of which failed.[2] The service cessations were all due to natural business causes, namely insolvency, the outright sale of assets, or the redeployment of assets to other uses. Entry primarily took place during periods when equipment surpluses existed, such as in the aftermath of World War II and during the early 1960s, when the national carriers were discarding propeller aircraft for jets. With the high failure rate, the number of active carriers never exceeded 7 at any one time. By contrast, the CAB permitted entry of the Local service carriers after World War II, but only after 1966 were these carriers allowed to compete directly with the "grandfather" Trunks. In the controlled national market, the number of Trunk and Local carriers ranged from a low of 21 in 1946 to a high of 35 in 1950. Thereafter, the number declined, but mergers rather than failures were responsible for the decrease. While no Trunk or Local service airline had officially declared bankruptcy through 1981, the Board, under the so-called "failing business doctrine," approved consolidations despite Section 408(b) of the Federal Aviation Act, which required that the Board not endorse mergers that restrained competition.[3] The 1961 United-Capital and 1972 Delta-Northeast mergers represented clear examples of consolidations approved in order to rescue failing firms even though, in the former case, the joined carriers had competed vigorously with one another.

While acknowledging that the California and national markets were dissimilar, Jordan devised a number of techniques on which rough estimates of the shape of the national market could be based, given the California experience.[4] His first device involved determining the average number of airports served by the intrastate airports and then dividing the total amount of interstate airports by that average. This assumed that carriers of intrastate size could compete effectively nationally. During the 1946-65 period, for instance, the average intrastate carrier served four airports and by dividing that number into the interstate airports served in an average year, Jordan estimated that there were 236 carriers that could presumably have been supported nationwide, or eight times the number that were actually in operation during most of the period.[5] A similar method took the average intrastate route miles operated by each carrier and divided it into the comparable interstate figure. The estimate of potential interstate airlines derived via the latter method came to 195 carriers or seven times the actual operating total.[6] The major drawback with the extrapolation technique is in the great size difference between the two carrier groups. For instance, while the average interstate carrier served around 30 airports, less than 40 airports existed in the entire state of California during the period under consideration. Thus the derived nationwide airline totals assumed an interstate system dominated by small regional-type carriers. Nevertheless, Jordan's analysis strongly implied that a free entry system would result in many more operating carriers than under the regulated arrangement and that the additional carriers would most probably be relatively small, given the large absolute cost requirements for Trunk-sized operations. Further, the high failure rate experienced by the California airlines suggested that new carriers might avoid those high-risk situations where the strongly entrenched carriers would try to undercut an attempt at entry.

The success of Southwest Airlines, an intrastater in Texas, which competed against interstate carriers during the 1970s, also contained implications for the interstate network. In the Texas case, however, the experience gained was not with regard to a free versus controlled entry situation, since the Texas Aeronautics Commission operated similarly to the CAB, but in the type of market situation that small but aggressive carriers could apparently exploit. In essence, the key to the carrier's advantage lay in its ability to achieve a quasi-monopoly in a segment—Dallas-Houston—by being allowed to provide exclusive service in both cities' older but more conveniently located airports, while its two interstate rivals were compelled to serve the market from newly built but relatively inconvenient airports. While the quasi-monopoly situation for Southwest in that market was probably unique, the fact remains that, because of cost considerations, carriers tend to concentrate operations at only one airport in multiple-airport metropolitan areas. Nevertheless, since many other large metropolitan areas operate more than one facility, opportunities similar to the Texas case were plentiful, and new entry at Chicago-Midway and New York-Newark in fact had successfully been accomplished during 1980 and 1981.

During 1981 the industry began to assume the dimensions projected by Jordan in terms of sheer numbers. The active carriers large enough to be included in the CAB's Air Carrier Traffic Statistics for March 1981 reached 72, whereas only 36 were reported at the end of 1978. Moreover, the classifications had changed to Majors, Nationals, and Large and Medium Regionals, whereas Trunks, Locals, and others had sufficed earlier. After three years of liberalized entry, the large carriers found themselves in the unenviable position of fending off competitive intrusions from each other and, more troublesome, from the regional carriers, most of whom boasted operating efficiencies that enabled them to offer sharply discounted fares. With declining traffic volumes after 1979 owing to a sluggish economy and higher aggregate prices from fuel cost pressures, two Trunks (Braniff and Pan American) hovered near insolvency, while several (American, Eastern, Trans World, and United) were struggling, and one other (Western) was a takeover target of regional airlines. The remaining Trunk (Continental) was acquired by Texas International, after a bitter battle, in October 1981. In fact only the balance sheets of Delta and Northwest, among the Trunks, appeared strong enough to withstand any contingency through the early 1980s. Thus the developing trend toward an industry structure based on a few large, full-service carriers and many smaller, regional airlines mostly offering spartan, point-to-point service seemed inevitable at the start of the 1980s.

A complete replacement of the less-efficient larger airlines by the cheaper operators was conceivable, based on developments through 1981, but unlikely. While an important barrier to entry had disappeared with the cessation of the route franchise system, a hint of future impediments developed in 1980, when federal intervention was required for New York Air to gain gate space at Washington (National) and New York (LaGuardia). The PATCO strike in 1981 also pointed out the problem of congestion, as 22 airports were forced to decrease flights by up to 50 percent. Other sources of potential limitations on existing facilities sure to occur over time involve flight curfews and airport noise reduction measures.

Another factor working to break the speed of the regional carrier advance was the realization on the part of management at the larger airlines of the need to become more competitive by negotiating work-rule improvements in labor contracts and employing fewer workers. The first major breakthrough in the work-rule area was achieved by United with its pilots during August 1981, where cockpit hours were increased and two pilot crews were established for future types of aircraft. At the same time that concessions were granted to the larger carriers, the airline unions were strenuously at work trying to organize the newer carriers. These developments would serve to narrow cost and productivity differences.

Finally, the love affair that had existed between the financial community and the young operators since deregulation had yet to be tested because only a few commuters had gone bankrupt through late 1981. (Golden Gate, a large commuter, suspended operations in August, followed a little later by Swift, Apollo, and Air Nebraska.) Once the inevitable failures among more notable carriers did occur, however, enthusiasm would surely abate, and seed money for new enterprises and additional capital for existing firms would become tighter. The California experience of 1946-65 suggested a high failure rate for new entrants, while the favorable satellite airport situations appeared less propitious by 1981. Indeed successful specialized carriers like Southwest and Midway came under attack not only from the larger Trunks but from upstarts in their own backyards. For instance, Southwest felt increasing competition from American within Texas and Muse Air in the Dallas (Love)-Houston (Hobby) segment, while in Chicago, Midway's fares were matched by United and Trans World to most destinations, and Air Chicago was scheduled for a fall 1981 start-up at Midway Airport before the PATCO strike forced a delay. [7] Air Chicago had not planned to compete directly with Midway at first, but would try to preempt Midway in places that the latter had slated for future penetration. Additionally, Peoples Express and New York Air encountered heavy price and service resistance from older incumbents in the Northeast corridor and even competed against each other on the Washington (National)-Newark market. [8]

Once the pace of entry subsides, as the above suggests it will, one can envision an industry comprised of specialized carriers blanketing the short-trip regional markets and a handful of very large airlines handling the bulk of the intermediate and long-haul business. In this mode, air transport would resemble the securities industry, with its few giant all-purpose firms and many regional and cut-rate operators. The securities industry had lost official protection when fixed commission rates were banned on "May Day" 1975. The beer industry also comes to mind with its two dominant firms—Anheuser-Busch and Miller—and about 30 local and regional brewers. [9]

In the new environment, assuming a slowdown or even a breakdown in the current ascendency of the regional carriers for whatever reason, inefficiency would not be tolerated for very long, since other carriers would sense the weakness and invade these markets. American's large-scale buildup at its Dallas hub during 1981, while sure to hurt Southwest, was primarily aimed at speeding the demise of Braniff, whose financial health had wilted badly after a giddy expansion in the wake of deregulation. It was also no accident that Delta chose to enter the New York-Dallas market, which American and Braniff had long shared, at the same time. The elimination of weak carriers would forestall undue aggressiveness on the part of a regional operator with larger aspirations, for instance, since dislodging an entrenched, financially secure adversary could prove costly. This is not to say that competitive forays into new city pairs by large or small carriers would end but only that a generally reduced level of such activity should ensue over time. Additionally, incentives for small carriers to retain a limited operation were abundant. For example, such an airline needs only a single, small type of aircraft, which might be obtained used; food service may be unnecessary due to the short flight duration, ticketing and passenger handling is simplified if interlining is avoided, aircraft crews are smaller, and overnight expenses can be avoided. None of these advantages can easily accrue to larger carriers. However, the latter type might still be willing to mount an attack on the specialized operators through cross-subsidization from other profitable centers or by organizing their own regional subsidiaries in the way that Texas International formed nonunion New York Air, but such measures would tempt trouble from the parent company unions and perhaps attract antitrust scrutiny.

Concerning the issue of deregulation itself, the subject will no doubt yield reams of books, articles, and dissertations as the post-1978 period lengthens. To date, proponents of deregulation have been mildly defensive about service gaps that have appeared in certain small and intermediate communities and the sharp price increases that occurred across most of the domestic system, which seemed excessive even in light of the fuel price run-up after 1978. The old-line carriers, meanwhile, have accepted the new rules, some more enthusiastically than others, and have designed strategies for achieving viability. The industry generally acknowledges that, short of war or some other situation requiring strict rationing of resources, no return to the classic CAB style of control is possible. At the same time, however, a major point concerning regulation that tends to be overlooked, especially by academicians, is that the air transport system will always be subject to some physical, technical, or environmental constraints based on limited airport facilities, crowded airspace, uncertain fuel supplies, anticompetitive foreign practices, etc. Thus, while pricing and marketing rivalry may remain free in the new environment, supply will frequently come under regulation although the exercise of it will likely appear at the local level. It is likely then that once the post-deregulation "shake-out" period passes and calmer conditions prevail again, traditional oligopolistic interdependence should again become pervasive among the remaining firms.

NOTES

1. William Jordan, Airline Regulation in America (Baltimore: Johns Hopkins University Press, 1970).
2. Ibid., pp. 17-19.
3. Nawal Taneja, The Commercial Airline Industry (Lexington, Mass.: D. C. Heath, 1976), p. 246.
4. Jordan, Airline Regulation, pp. 24-33.
5. Ibid.
6. Ibid.
7. Business Week, June 15, 1981, pp. 78-92.
8. Ibid.
9. Business Week, September 29, 1980, p. 120.

BIBLIOGRAPHY

Books

Bain, Joe S. Barriers to New Competition. Cambridge, Mass.:
Harvard University Press, 1956.

Baran, Paul A., and Sweezy, Paul M. Monopoly Capitalism. New
York: Monthly Review Press, 1966.

Burkhardt, Robert. The Civil Aeronautics Board. Dulles Airport,
Va.: Green Hills, 1974.

Caves, Richard E. Air Transport and Its Regulators. Cambridge,
Mass.: Harvard University Press, 1962.

Cherington, Paul. Airline Price Policy. Boston: Harvard Business School, 1958.

Corbett, David. Politics and the Airlines. London: George Allen
& Unwin, 1965.

Douglas, George W., and Miller, James C. III, 80 Economic Regulation of Domestic Air Transport: Theory and Policy. Washington, D.C.: Brookings Institution, 1974.

Eads, George. The Local Service Airline Experiment. Washington, D.C.: Brookings Institution, 1972.

Freudenthal, Elsbeth E. The Aviation Business from Kitty Hawk to
Wall Street. New York: McGraw-Hill, 1940.

Friedman, Milton. Capitalism and Freedom. Chicago: University
of Chicago Press, 1962.

Fruhan, William. The Fight for Competitive Advantage: A Study
of the U.S. Domestic Trunk Carriers. Boston: Harvard Business School, 1972.

Gellhorn, Walter. Individual Freedom and Government Restraints.
Baton Rouge: Louisiana State University Press, 1956.

Gordon, Robert J. "Airline Costs and Managerial Efficiency." In Transportation Economics. New York: Columbia University Press for the National Bureau of Economic Research, 1965.

Gray, Horace. "Air Transportation." In The Structure of American Industry, edited by Walter Adams. New York: Macmillan, 1954.

Hamilton, Waldon H. Price and Price Policies. New York: McGraw-Hill, 1938.

Hayek, Friedrich A. The Road to Serfdom. Chicago: University of Chicago Press, 1944.

Jordan, William. Airline Regulation in America. Baltimore: Johns Hopkins University Press, 1970.

Kahn, Alfred E. The Economics of Regulation: Principles and Institutions. New York: John Wiley, 1971. 2 vols.

Kane, Robert, and Vose, Allan. Air Transportation. Dubuque, Iowa: Kendall/Hunt, 1971.

Kolko, Gabriel. The Triumph of Conservatism. New York: Free Press of Glencoe, 1962.

Meyer, John R., and Oster, Clinton V., eds. Airline Deregulation: The Early Experience. Boston: Auburn House, 1981.

Nicholson, Joseph. Air Transportation Management. New York: John Wiley, 1951.

Puffer, Claude. Air Transportation. Philadelphia: Blakeston, 1941.

Richmond, Samuel. Regulation and Competition in Air Transportation. New York: Columbia University Press, 1962.

Scherer, F. M. Industrial Market Structure and Economic Performance. Chicago: Rand McNally, 1970.

Schwartz, Bernard. The Professor and the Commission. New York: Alfred Knopf, 1959.

Sorrell, Lewis M. Prospects and Problems in Aviation, edited by Leverett S. Lyon. Chicago: Lincoln Printing, 1945.

Straszheim, Mahlon. The International Airline Industry. Washington, D.C.: Brookings Institution, 1969.

Taneja, Nawal. The Commercial Airline Industry. Lexington, Mass.: D. C. Heath, 1976.

Wolfe, Thomas. Air Transportation. New York: McGraw-Hill, 1950.

Journal Articles

Archibald, G. C. "Profit-Maximizing and Non-Price Competition." Economica 31 (February 1964):13-22.

Averch, Harvey, and Johnson, Leland L. "Behavior of the Firm Under Regulation Constraint." American Economic Review 52 (December 1962):1052-69.

Caves, Richard E. "The Kennedy Subcommittee's Civil Aeronautics Board Practices and Procedures." Bell Journal of Economics 7 (Autumn 1976):733-35.

Comanor, W., and Wilson, T. "Advertising, Market Structure and Performance." Review of Economics and Statistics 40 (November 1967):423-40.

Crane, John B. "The Economics of Air Transportation." Harvard Business Review 23 (Summer 1944):495-509.

Demory, Willard L. "Deregulation, The Adjustment Process." Journal of Air Law and Commerce 41 (Autumn 1975):873-86.

Devany, A. S. "The Effect of Price and Entry Regulation on Airline Output, Capacity, and Efficiency." Bell Journal of Economics 6 (Spring 1975):327-45.

Douglas, George W., and Miller, James C. III. "Quality Competition, Industry Equilibrium, and Efficiency in the Price-Constrained Airline Market." American Economic Review 64 (September 1974):650-68.

Eads, George. "Airline Capacity Limitation Controls: Public Vice or Public Virtue?" American Economic Review Papers and Proceedings 64 (May 1974):365-71.

Eads, George, Nerlove, M., and Raduchel, W. "A Long-Run Cost Function for the Local Service Airline Industry." Review of Economics and Statistics 51 (August 1969):259-70.

Gellman, Aaron. "The Regulation of Competition in United States Domestic Air Transportation: A Judicial Survey and Analysis." Journal of Air Law and Commerce 25 (Spring 1956):152-65.

Gorrell, Edgar. "The Civil Aeronautics Act of 1938 and Democratic Government." Journal of Air Law 9 (October 1938):700-10.

Jordan, William A. "Airline Capacity Agreements—Correcting a Regulatory Imperfection." Journal of Air Law and Commerce 39 (Spring 1973):190-203.

Keeler, Theodore E. "Airline Regulation and Market Performance." Bell Journal of Economics 3 (Autumn 1972):399-424.

Koontz, Harold D. "Economic and Managerial Factors Underlying Subsidy Needs of Domestic Trunk Line Air Carriers." Journal of Air Law and Commerce 18 (Spring 1951):127-56.

LaMond, Annette. "An Evaluation of Intrastate Airline Regulation in California." Bell Journal of Economics 7 (Autumn 1976): 641-57.

Levine, Michael E. "Alternatives to Regulation: Competition in Air Transportation and the Aviation Act of 1975." Journal of Air Law and Commerce 41 (Autumn 1975):703-26.

Loevinger, Lee. "Regulation and Competition as Alternatives." Antitrust Bulletin 11 (January-April 1969):104-8.

Moss, Bennett. "Industry and Sector Price Indexes." Monthly Labor Review (August 1975):974-82.

Nelson, James R. "The Role of Competition in the Regulated Industries." Antitrust Bulletin 11 (January-April 1962):7-21.

Panzar, J. C. "Equilibrium and Welfare in Unregulated Airline Markets." American Economic Review 69 (May 1979):92-95.

Pustay, M. W. "The Transatlantic Airline Market: Exploring the Myths of Excessive, Unfair, and Predatory Competition." Quarterly Review of Economics and Business 19 (Summer 1979):47-63.

Raduchel, W. "A Long-Run Cost Function for the Local Service Airline Industry." Review of Economics and Statistics 51 (August 1969):259-70.

Reid, Samuel, and Mohrfield, James. Airline Size, Profitability, Mergers, and Regulation." Journal of Air Law and Commerce 39 (Spring 1973):167-78.

Schmalensee, Richard. "Comparative Static Properties of Regulated Airline Oligopolies." Bell Journal of Economics 8 (Autumn 1977):565-76.

Stigler, George. "Price and Non-Price Competition." Journal of Political Economy 76 (January-February 1968):149-60.

Stigler, George, and Friedland, Claire. "What Can Regulators Regulate? The Case of Electricity." Journal of Law and Economics 5 (1962):1-16.

Taffe, Edward. "Trends in Airline Passenger Traffic: A Graphic Case Study." Annals of the Association of American Geographers 49 (December 1959):395-408.

Verleger, Philip K., Jr. "Models of the Demand for Air Transportation." Bell Journal of Economics and Management Science 3 (Autumn 1972):437-57.

Weiss, Leonard W. "Advertising, Profits and Corporate Taxes." Review of Economics and Statistics 52 (November 1969):421-30.

Wellisz, Stanislaw H. "Regulation of Natural Gas Pipeline Companies: An Economic Analysis." Journal of Political Economy 71 (February 1963):30-43.

White, Lawrence J. "Quality Variation When Prices Are Regulated." Bell Journal of Economics 3 (Autumn 1972):425-36.

Yance, Joseph V. "Nonprice Competition in Jet Aircraft Capacity." Journal of Industrial Economics 21 (November 1972):55-71.

Newspapers and Magazines

"Airline Capacity Limitations." Aviation Week and Space Technology, August 12, 1974, p. 9.

"Airline Profits Are Taking Wing." Business Week, June 26, 1978, p. 39.

"Airlines: The Lounge War." Newsweek, July 2, 1973, p. 61.

Bulban, Erwin. "Third Airline Joins Cut-Rate Fight Between Braniff and Southwest." Aviation Week and Space Technology, February 26, 1973.

Burkhardt, Robert. "Browne's Board." Airline Management, August 1972.

Byrne, Harlan, and Kelliher, Eileen. "Huge Jetliner Order Cost United Airlines Months of Hard Work." Wall Street Journal, September 25, 1978.

"Capacity Pact Approved." Aviation Week and Space Technology, July 14, 1975, p. 23.

Chew, R. Z. "15 Shops Flock to Fill Pan Am's Slot." Advertising Age, May 29, 1973.

"Commuter Airline Turns First Profit." Aviation Week and Space Technology, August 6, 1973, p. 30.

Cook, R. H. "Fare Case Unaffected by Jet Surcharge." Aviation Week, February 2, 1959.

"Delta Joins the New York-Florida Scramble." Business Week, July 29, 1972, pp. 40-42.

Doty, Laurence. "American Fare Bid Draws Fire." Aviation Week and Space Technology, February 21, 1977.

_____. "CAB Chairman Browne Plans to Resign." Aviation Week and Space Technology, November 20, 1972.

"Eased Charter Rules Worry the Skeds." Business Week, September 20, 1976, pp. 34-35.

Feldman, Joan. "Is CAB Over-Managing the Airline Industry?" Air Transport World, December 6, 1973.

Gregory, William H. "CAB Economic Policies Shifting." Aviation Week and Space Techology, February 17, 1975.

_____. "Industry Appraises American's Marketing." Aviation Week and Space Technology, September 2, 1974.

Griffiths, David. "CAB Sets Broad Changes in Domestic Fare Rules." Aviation Week and Space Technology, July 17, 1978.

_____. "First Class Fare Reductions Filed." Aviation Week and Space Technology, April 24, 1978.

Henderson, Danna K. "World Airline Ad Spending Rises 9.5% to $659.5 Million in 1978." Air Transport World, July 1979.

Karr, Albert. "Carter Signs Airline Deregulation Law; CAB Will Grant Routes More Generously." Wall Street Journal, October 25, 1978.

_____. "CAB Is an Enthusiastic Backer of Moves to Trim Airline Service, Increase Fares." Wall Street Journal, August 13, 1974.

Lindsey, Robert. "CAB Seeks a Role in Flight Schedules." New York Times, December 6, 1973.

Loving, Rush, Jr. "How the Airlines Will Cope with Deregulation." Fortune, November 20, 1978.

McSurely, Alexander. "Management Key to Martin Money." Aviation Week, January 14, 1952.

Montgomery, Jim. "Eastern Airlines Fires New Salvos in Attempt to Slow Delta's Gains." Wall Street Journal, April 12, 1978.

Murphy, C., and Wise, T. "The Problem of Howard Hughes." Fortune, January 1959.

O'Lone, Richard. "American, Delta Order 767's." Aviation Week and Space Technology, November 20, 1978.

Passell, Peter, and Ross, Leonard. "The CAB Pilots the Planes." New York Times Magazine, August 12, 1973.

"Permanent Authority Urged for Three More Supplementals." Aviation Week and Space Technology, December 26, 1966, p. 33.

Samuelson, Robert. "CAB Is Not a Taxi." Airline Pilot, August 1973.

Schneider, Charles E. "CAB Moratorium on Route Cases Easing." Aviation Week and Space Technology, October 20, 1975.

_____. "Capacity Pact Blocked by Court." Aviation Week and Space Technology, April 28, 1975.

_____. "Tampering Charged in CAB Investigation." Aviation Week and Space Technology, March 31, 1975.

_____. CAB to Review Capacity Pact Decision." Aviation Week and Space Technology, November 25, 1974.

_____. "CAB Liquor War Role Studied." Aviation Week and Space Technology, November 11, 1974.

Serling, Robert J. "Boeing Goes for Broke." Airline Executive, February 1978.

"Timm Resigns, Hits White House Staff." Aviation Week and Space Technology, December 15, 1975, p. 28.

"Upstarts in the Sky." Business Week, June 15, 1981, pp. 78-92.

Watkins, Harold. "TWA Asks for Surcharge, Higher Tariffs for Peak Season." Aviation Week and Space Technology, March 23, 1970.

"What Ails American Airlines?" Business Week, May 12, 1973, pp. 134-36.

"Why Northwest Airlines Is No. 1 in Profits." Business Week, February 16, 1976, p. 78.

General References

Air Transport. Annual yearbook. Air Transport Association of America. Washington, D.C.

Air Transport World. Monthly industry magazine. Stamford, Conn.: Reinhold Publishing Co.

Airline Executive. Monthly industry magazine. Washington, D.C.: Airline Publishing Group, Inc.

Aviation Daily. Daily industry newsletter. Washington, D.C.:
Ziff-Davis Publishing Co.

Aviation Week and Space Technology. Weekly airline and aerospace
magazine. New York: McGraw-Hill Publishing Co.

Commerce Clearing House. Aviation law reports. Chicago, Ill.

Commuter Airline Annual Report. Commuter Airline Association
of America, Washington, D.C.

Monthly Economic Review. Citibank, New York, N.Y.

Moody's Transportation Manual. Moody's Investors Service, New
York, N.Y.

Official Airline Guide. Monthly catalogue of schedules and rates.
The Reuben H. Donnelly Corp., Oak Brook, Ill.

World Air Transport Statistics. International Air Transport Association, Geneva, Switzerland.

Reports

A. Gary Shilling & Company. Discount Air Fares: Throwing Caution to the Winds? New York, February 23, 1979.

Allegheny Airlines. Justification in Support of Simple-Saver Fares.
May 1977.

Boeing Company. Flight Equipment Age: U.S. Domestic Trunks
and Pan American. Seattle, June 1976.

The Conference Board. Roadmaps of Industry, no. 1799. New
York, January 1977.

Eastern Airlines. Brief to Civil Aeronautics Board. Docket
21866-9. May 22, 1972.

Gallup Organization. The Frequency of Flying Among the General
Public. Princeton, N.J., 1970-81.

_____. A Study of the U.S. Air Traveler Conducted for American
Express. Princeton, N.J., 1975.

General Electric Corp., Aircraft Engine Group. Aircraft Operating Indices. Cincinnati, various issues.

Louis Harris & Associates. Bigness in Business: A New Look. New York, April 1976.

Maldutis, Julius. Salomon Brothers, Stock Research Department. The Airlines—More Monopoly Power. December 1978.

_____. Salomon Brothers, Stock Research Department. Airline Industry Monopoly Power Revisited. March 1978.

Midway Airlines. Prospectus for Regional Air Service. Chicago, September 1976.

Opinion Research Corporation. Determinants of Airline Selection. Princeton, N.J., 1969.

PSA, Inc. Annual Reports. Various issues.

Southwest Airlines. Annual Reports. Various issues.

Trans World Airlines. 1977 Marketing Plan. New York.

Transcontinental and Western Air, Inc. Additional North-South California Services. 4 CAB 373, 375 (1943).

United Research, Inc. Federal Regulation of the Domestic Air Transport Industry. Cambridge, Mass., 1958.

Government Publications and Documents

California, State of. Constitution. Public Utilities Code and Related Constitutional Provisions. Sacramento, 1965.

U.S. Civil Aeronautics Board. Annual Report to Congress. 1938-80.

_____. Air Carrier Financial Statistics. 1946-81.

_____. Air Carrier Traffic Statistics. 1940-81.

_____. Capacity Reductions Agreements Case. Docket 22908. Initial Decision of C. Robert Seaver, November 18, 1974.

_____. Competition Among Domestic Air Carriers. 1959-65.

_____. Domestic Passenger Fare Investigation. 1976.

_____. Form 41 Reports. Various reports.

_____. General Passenger Fare Investigation. Docket 8008. 1960.

_____. Handbook of Airline Statistics. 1961 and 1973.

_____. Improved Authority to Wichita Case. Docket 28848. 1978.

_____. New York-Florida Case. 24 CAB 94. 1956.

_____. New York-San Francisco Nonstop Service Case. 29 CAB 811. 1959.

_____. Official Board Orders. Various orders.

_____. Origin-Destination Survey. 1959-80.

_____. Report on Airline Service, Fares, Traffic, Load Factors and Market Shares. July 1979.

_____. Service to Harlingen Case. Docket 28068. 1975.

_____. Supplements to Handbook of Airline Statistics. 1975, 1977, and 1979.

U.S. Congress. Senate. Committee on Governmental Affairs. Interlocking Directorates Among the Major U.S. Corporations. 95th Cong., 2d sess., 1978.

_____. Committee on the Judiciary, Subcommittee on Administrative Practices. Draft Report on Civil Aeronautics Route-Making and Route Procedures. 93d Cong., 1st sess., 1975.

U.S. Department of Commerce. Bureau of the Census. Current Population Reports. Series P-25 (February 1975).

_____. Bureau of Economic Analysis. Business Conditions Digest. Various issues.

_____. Bureau of Economic Analysis. Economic Indicators. Various issues.

_____. Bureau of Economic Analysis. The National Income and Product Accounts of the United States. 1929-65.

_____. Bureau of Economic Analysis. Statistical Abstract. 1981.

_____. Bureau of Economic Analysis. Survey of Current Business. Various issues.

U.S. Department of Labor, Bureau of Labor Statistics. Handbook of Labor Statistics. Washington, D.C., 1980.

U.S. Department of Transportation, Air Transportation Policy Staff. An Analysis of the Intrastate and Carrier Regulation Forum. Washington, D.C., January 1976.

U.S. Government, Executive Branch. Economic Report of the President. Washington, D.C., 1981.

Unpublished Material

American Airlines. "Domestic Operating Statistics." Various reports.

Bartlett, Hale. "The Demand for Passenger Air Transportation 1947-62." Ph.D. dissertation, University of Chicago, 1962.

Crandall, R. L., senior vice-president, American Airlines. Remarks to Management Meeting. May 1978.

Dorman, Gary J. "Airline Competition: A Theoretical and Empirical Analysis." Ph.D. dissertation, University of California, Berkeley, 1976.

McMillen, James E. "The Effect of Scale in the Airline Industry." M.S. thesis, MIT, 1971.

Miller, James C. "Scheduling and Airline Efficiency." Ph.D. dissertation, Virginia, 1969.

Mize, Jan Lee. "An Econometric Analysis of the Demand for Airline Passenger Transportation—Domestic Routes." Ph.D. dissertation, Georgia State, 1968.

Oswald, Donald. "Pricing for Reduction of Domestic Airline Excess Capacity." Ph.D. dissertation, Washington State University, 1977.

Pan American World Airways, Fleet Planning Department. "Aircraft Inventory and Orders of Selected Airlines." New York, November 1978.

Panzar, John C. "Regulation, Service Quality, and Market Performance: A Model of Airline Rivalry." Ph.D. dissertation, Stanford University, 1974.

Renaud, Gilles. "Competition in Air Transportation: An Econometric Approach." M.S. thesis, MIT, 1970.

Trans World Airlines. "Continuous On-Board Surveys." Various surveys.

United Airlines. "Operating Statistics." Various reports.

Verleger, Philip K. "A Point-to-Point Model of the Demand for Air Transportation." Ph.D. dissertation, MIT, 1971.

INDEX

absolute size requirements, 53

advertising, 160-63

Airbus Industrie, 66, 67, 73, 125

Air California, 5, 10, 52, 57, 135

Air Chicago, 60, 178

aircraft: development, 10, 64-67, 73, 170; ownership, 42; role in competition, 26, 53, 96, 104, 106, 123-30

Air Florida, 5, 12, 52, 55, 57, 113, 135

Airline Deregulation Act of 1978, 145; and earlier laws, 82-83; dorman authority, 8, 82; exit rules, 88; new entry, 51, 88, 91; provisions, 79-81

airline industry: debt, 14, expenses, 35-36, 40; passenger traits, 24-25; prices, 153-58; profitability, 73-74, 123, 145-50; wage rates, 69, 71-72

airline investment, 46, 55, 72-73

Air Transport Association, 66, 98

Air Wisconsin, 4

"A-J-W" effect, 78

American Airlines, 2, 6, 7, 13, 54, 66-67, 70, 73-74, 114, 123-30, 131-32, 133, 134-39, 177-79

Aspen Airlines, 4

Averch, Harvey, 78

Bain, Joe S., 52

Bankers Trust Company, 14

Baran, Paul, 79

Boeing Company, 64-66, 67, 125-26

Borman, Frank, 66

Braniff Airlines, 2, 6, 10, 14, 47, 56-57, 73, 111, 123-30, 135, 177, 179

British Civil Aviation Authority, 158

Browne, Secor, 94, 98

business cycle: Impact on air travel, 27-30, 168-69; impact on price, 114-19

cabotage, 60

California intrastate experience, 57, 109-10, 151, 175-76

California Public Utilities Commission, 109-10, 175

capacity-limiting agreements, 13, 23, 97-98, 137

Capital Airlines, 26, 66, 73, 104-5, 124

capital investment, 46

Capitol Airlines, 13, 58, 134

Caves, Richard E., 7, 22, 40, 47, 53, 54, 63, 80, 92, 104, 105, 106, 115-16, 135-36, 159-60, 173-74

Chase Manhattan Bank, 14

Chemical Bank, 14

Cherington, Paul, 18, 116

Civil Aeronautics Act of 1938 (McCarran-Lea Act), 64; "grandfather" clause, 87; provisions, 79-80, 82

ABOUT THE AUTHOR

PAUL S. BIEDERMAN has been involved in various airline planning activities at Trans World Airlines for 12 years. As manager of the forecasting group since 1976, he has had to closely monitor air transport industry reaction to general economic developments and particularly the changes wrought by deregulation. Prior to his airline industry experience, he spent two years on the corporate economics staff at the International Business Machines Corporation where the emphasis was on macroeconomic analysis. He also spent three years as assistant to the Chief Economist at the Conference Board, a nonprofit business research organization. Among his published material while at the Board, he edited the Economic Almanac 1967-1968, New York: Macmillan.

Dr. Biederman received his Bachelor of Arts and Master of Arts degrees in Economics from Rutgers University and a Doctor of Philosophy degree in Economics from the Graduate Faculty, New School for Social Research in New York City where he currently resides.